# START THE FIRE keep it burning and Claim the Blessing

BY DR. LEE ROBERSON

University Publishers
P. O. Box 3571
Chattanooga, Tennessee 37404

## DEDICATION

This great volume of dynamic messages on the subject of missions is lovingly dedicated to those choice servants of God who have given their lives and talents to the winning of the lost around the world.

# START THE FIRE



COVER DESIGN BY STEVE HUNZIKER

ALL SCRIPTURE QUOTATIONS ARE TAKEN FROM
THE AUTHORIZED KING JAMES VERSION

ISBN 0-931117-04-6

# CONTENTS

Chapter Page

## Part Three
## Claim The Blessings

# Foreword

A little lady in Huntington, West Virginia, always writes interesting magnificent letters. She writes about the ordinary things of life, but to her they are not ordinary! She ends every sentence with an exclamation point. I counted fifty-five exclamation points in one letter.

To this dear friend, life is exciting! (I've got the habit, too.) She has no money, but she has faith. She has no family, but she has friends. She has no beautiful, earthly home, but she has the promise of a mansion in glory.

Life should be exciting for every one of us! When Christ came in, we became members of the family of God. God is our Father. We can pray to Him. We can bring every need to Him. He knows all about us — our weaknesses and our strengths.

Every worthwhile Christian has a fire burning in his soul! When Christ entered his life, a holy blaze was ignited.

The Christian wants others to hear the gospel. He is concerned for lost people at home and to the ends of the earth. Yes, he has a burden for souls.

NOW KEEP THAT FIRE BURNING! Don't let the world, the flesh, and the devil dampen your ardor.

Keep within your heart a compassionate concern for a lost and dying world. That's what Paul had. Read Romans 9:1-3:

> *"I say the truth in Christ, I lie not, my conscience also bearing me witness in the Holy Ghost,*
>
> *That I have great heaviness and continual sorrow in my heart. For I could wish that myself were accursed from Christ for my brethren, my kinsmen according to the flesh:"*

Start the fire — keep it burning — claim the blessing! The command of our Lord has been given: *"Go ye into all the world, and preach the gospel to every creature."*

Obedience to His command brings His blessings upon us!

# Part One
# Start The Fire

# 1
# Light Your Candle

*"Then spake Jesus again unto them, saying, I am the light of the world: he that followeth me shall not walk in darkness, but shall have the light of life."*

—John 8:12

A few days ago I read this magnificent story.

Hugh Latimer, with Bishop Ridley, was burned at the stake during the reign of Bloody Mary in England. They delivered themselves to the executioner, and when the fire was lit, these prophetic words were uttered: "Play the man, Master Ridley," said Latimer, as he stood in the flames. "We shall this day light such a candle by God's grace as I trust shall never be put out." The burning took place at Oxford.

The story is told of Hugh Latimer, that he saw a New Testament written in Latin — he purchased this New Testament, and his eyes chanced to fall upon one sentence, and with that sentence, the light of day broke upon his soul. The sentence was: *"This is a faithful saying, and worthy of all acceptation, that Christ Jesus came into the world to save sinners; of whom I am chief"* (I Timothy 1:15). It was a great day for Latimer.

He appeared before royalty — "It is worthy of all acceptation" — "it is worthy — Your Majesty! For this proclamation craves on patronage. It is worthy — Your Excellency; my lords, ladies, gentlemen, all: for the Gospel asks no favors." Hugh Latimer stood before kings and courtiers and declared the faithful saying. Never once did he forget the dignity and the challenge of this message. It was faithful! It was worthy in its own right of the acceptance of the lordliest; and Latimer staked his life upon it to the very last!

This is the message dedicated to the business of "shining for Christ." This Bible says, *"Let your light so shine before men, that they may see your good works, and glorify your Father which is in heaven"* (Matthew 5:16).

First, to shine for Christ, we must know Him as Saviour. Here is the great essential for shining! Just being good is not enough. Just knowing about the Bible is not enough. We must know Him, the Saviour.

Jesus said: *". . . Ye must be born again"* (John 3:7). Then in a very particular way He said: *"He that believeth on him is not condemned: but he that believeth not is condemned already, because he hath not believed in the name of the only begotten Son of God"* (John 3:18).

Now, permit me to give three simple truths.

## THE ADMONITION OF THE BIBLE IS TO SHINE — TO GIVE LIGHT

Jesus said, *"Let your light so shine."*

GIVE THOUGHT TO THE DARKNESS OF THIS WORLD. We are now living in the night time of world history. The darkness is about us. There is no spot where Satan's power is not felt.

If we read the papers, we see the news of sin in every place.

If we walk the streets, we see the evidences of evil, rebellion, and wickedness.

If we enter the world of politics, we find sin on every hand. Sin is everywhere — in business, in social life, and church life.

Some years ago, I paid a visit to a certain church organization in another state. Only men reside in the Abbey of Gethsemane. They enter this ecclesiastical order to give the rest of their days to living and working in that one location.

Many times during the day they have a call to prayer. They go through the form of prayers. They recite their rituals. Early in the evening they retire to their small rooms. At daybreak, they come together for prayer and worship. The day is spent in work and silence.

But have they ruled out sin? Is Satan kept outside the gates? Not on your life. Satan invades even such a cloistered establishment as this. Darkness of the world is found in that place as in all others.

The Bible says that we are to shine in the darkness of this world.

SECOND, GIVE THOUGHT TO THE DESTITUTION OF THIS WORLD. By the word destitution, I am referring to the wreckage of society, as it is today.

Many people run to the world and seek help — the world cannot help you! This is a world of sin and emptiness. This is a world that is headed for the judgment of God.

THIRD, THINK OF THE DECEPTION OF THE WORLD. Yes, the world tries to deceive you and turn you away from Christ. The world tries to make you think that all is well; but your own heart testifies to the fact that evil surrounds you.

The magic tricks of Satan are always at evidence. We read in II Corinthians 2:11 — *"Lest Satan should get an advantage of us: for we are not ignorant of his devices."* The Devil is ever working to deceive you and turn you aside.

But in the midst of darkness, destitution, and deception, we are to shine!

FIRST, KNOW THAT CHRIST IS YOUR SAVIOUR.

SECOND, KEEP YOURSELF IN TOUCH WITH HIM DAILY. Show forth his grace and mercy to a lost and dying world.

But you say, "Shining for Jesus is costly." Yes, it is. Shining for the Saviour may mean suffering. To shine for Christ may mean financial loss. To shine for Christ may mean the surrender of your popularity. To stand for your convictions may mean loss and pain.

But say what you may, the Bible still says, *"Let your light so shine."*

We must shine consistently and permanently. It is tragic that some people shine brightly for Christ for a while, and then they permit something to come between them and the Lord. They are not the light of the world which God intended them to be.

A blind man walked down the street one night with a lighted lantern in his hand. Someone said to him, "Why do you carry a lighted lantern? You can't see. It doesn't do you any good." "Oh, yes it does," he said. "It keeps other people from stumbling over me."

Christians are to so live that no one will stumble over them. The light must shine forth from our lives. It isn't necessary that we boast and brag about our goodness. It is simply necessary that we know Christ as Saviour, and that we walk in His steps and thereby we shine for Jesus.

Miss Blanche Groves was for many years a faithful missionary in China. One day in Soochow, she stood on the curb of the street and watched three men being led to execution by the Japanese. One of them recognized her, broke away from his captor and ran up to her. He cried out, "Thank you for telling me about Jesus. I'm not afraid to die now. I will die at sunset, but I will spend the night with Jesus." This one was faithful unto death. He was shining "as the light of the world."

## AVOID EVERYTHING THAT DIMS YOUR SHINING

*"Abstain from all appearance of evil."*

—I Thessalonians 5:22

FIRST, AVOID EVERYTHING THAT IS QUESTIONABLE. The Christian's life must be open — not shady. If there is a question mark upon something, then the chances are that that thing is wrong.

SECOND, AVOID EVERYTHING THAT ROBS HIM OF GLORY. It seems like a rather small thing for Demas to turn away from the Apostle Paul. It was not a small matter to the apostle. He knew that the quitting spirit of Demas was robbing God of the glory that belonged to Him. Not only so, Demas brought shame upon the cause of Christ.

THIRD, AVOID EVERYTHING THAT KEEPS OTHERS FROM SEEING CHRIST IN YOU. This is the goal of your life — to be Christlike!

A few days ago, I was trying to think just what it means to get people to live the consecrated life. I thought of the importance of Bible study; and yet, I do recall that some professing Christians have spent many years in Bible study and still have turned away from the side of our Saviour.

I know some churches that call themselves Bible churches — that is, they give emphasis to the Word of God in every way. And yet, at the same time these people are too tired to have a Sunday evening service, and too indifferent to have a prayer meeting on Wednesday night. These great Bible believers come to church only once per week.

Is it prayer that makes one a shining Christian? Surely prayer is essential to all Christian growth. We must pray. We need to pray. We cannot live without prayer. And yet, sometimes prayer becomes just a form, and if we are not careful, prayer will be meaningless.

And then I thought of tragic happenings. Is this the key to shining? Does it take something tragic to bring a person out of his indifference and bring him to the Saviour? For a number of years I thought that this was so. In the years of my ministry, I have watched people live indifferently for a while. Then because of the sudden death of a loved one, or perhaps a tragic accident, they have turned back to God. I have watched them come forward in the church, rededicate their lives, and for a number of months live a consecrated, devoted, shining life. And then, all of a sudden I lost track of them. They failed to be in church. They were not in the place of service. They had turned away. And so I must say that it is not the matter of tragic happenings.

What does it take then to bring a person to consecration and dedicated shining for Christ? I think that I can name some things that it surely takes.

FIRST, WE MUST SEE CHRIST. We see and know this beloved One. Jesus Christ must mean everything to us. He is more than just the words of a song. He is our Saviour, our Companion, our Helper, and our Guide. I do not think that there is such a thing as consecration, unless there is a definite vision of Jesus.

SECOND, I BELIEVE THAT WE MUST SEE THE AWFULNESS OF SINFUL FLESH. We must see the weakness of our own bodies. We must see the corruptness of our minds. Furthermore, we must understand that accepting Jesus Christ as Saviour does not remove us from the touch of Satan. The danger of carnality is always before us.

THIRD, I BELIEVE THAT WE MUST SEE THE GREATNESS OF SALVATION. The wonder of being saved must never escape us. The miracle of His touch upon our hearts to redeem us and bring us unto Himself must never be lost. The experience of coming to know Christ as Saviour must ever be real.

FOURTH, I BELIEVE THAT CONSECRATION MEANS SEEING A LOST WORLD. This will kill the selfishness of the average life. The true seeing of a lost and dying world will make generous Christians. We must remember that the man without Christ is lost. *"The soul that sinneth, it shall die."* (Ezekiel 18:4). It is our business to warn the wicked of his way. If we fail to do so, then the blood of others will be upon us.

FIFTH, I BELIEVE THAT CONSECRATION WILL COME BY REMEMBERING THAT ONE DAY WE SHALL STAND BEFORE THE LORD JESUS CHRIST. It seems that this is what Paul was trying to get over to the Christians in Rome. He said "*. . . for we shall all stand before the judgment seat of Christ*" (Romans 14:12). Now, if I can remember this, it will surely transform my life. it will cause me to be cautious in life and deed.

Yes, avoid everything that dims your shining.

## THE PRESENCE OF GOD IS WITH THE SHINING CHRISTIAN

Dedication, obedience, and shining will mean His presence, for He said, "*. . .lo, I am with you alway, even unto the end of the world. Amen*" (Matthew 28:20).

FIRST, HIS PRESENCE GIVES COURAGE. Hugh Latimer stood in the flames and displayed the courage that God had given him. He said to his fellow sufferer, "We shall this day light such a candle by God's grace as I trust shall never be put out."

It is courage that is so sorely needed in our present day society. We do not need the foolhardiness of the marching mobs, but we need the courage that comes from the presence of God. The Lord said to Joshua: *"Only be thou strong and very courageous . . ."* (Joshua 1:7).

SECOND, HIS PRESENCE GIVES THE PRIVILEGE OF PRAYER. If I know Christ as my Saviour and walk with Him, then I have the privilege of coming before Him and praying. Remember, when I walk with the Lord, I can know that my prayers will receive His Divine answers.

This is the promise that Jesus gave to His disciples and to us: *"And whatsoever ye shall ask in my name, that will I do, that the Father may be glorified in the Son. If ye shall ask anything in my name, I will do it* " (John 14:13,14).

A recent issue of the *Reader's Digest* had an article entitled "Try Talking To Yourself." The author of this article, Mr. William D. Ellis, spent much time in establishing his belief that it will do all of us good to spend time in talking with ourselves day by day. Mr. Ellis advocates that we get aside and talk for minutes or hours with ourselves day by day. Let me recommend something ten thousand times better: get aside and talk with God. There is nothing that will so lift the shadows from your heart as a time of prayer. When the burdens of life are heavy, and you feel that you cannot go on, this is the time to seek His face and to make your needs known unto Him.

There are days and nights when the burdens and the worries of this world crowd in upon me. But these things last only so long as it takes me to come to the place of prayer.

THIRD, HIS PRESENCE GIVES PEACE. To all of us the Lord is saying, *"Peace I leave with you, my peace I give unto you: not as the world giveth, give I unto you. Let not your heart be troubled, neither let it be afraid"* (John 14:27). I need the serenity and the calmness that God can give to His believing children.

FOURTH, HIS PRESENCE GIVES WITNESSING POWER. We are commanded to go with the Gospel of our Lord Jesus; but woe be unto us if we go without His power.

Every child of God should desire the fullness of the Holy Spirit. We have the Holy Spirit as our indwelling Guest. But does the Holy Spirit have us?

Men are lost and dying without Jesus Christ. We must go

with the power of God upon us. We must go with a radiant testimony for our Saviour upon our lips. And as we go, we must remember that His presence will give the witnessing power.

As I mentioned a moment ago, Jesus commanded us to go into all the world and preach the Gospel. He gave His promise that He would be with us, even unto "the end of the world." He does not promise to be with us, as we walk the ways of sin and worldliness. But He does promise to be with us as we do His will and carry out His command. Dr. G. Campbell Morgan was preaching from this text: "*. . .Lo, I am with you*" (Matthew 28:20). He called this a promise. A woman came up to him later and said, "that is not a promise. It is a fact." That is true. Jesus did not say, *"I will be with you."* But, *"I am with you."*

You have often heard me speak of David Livingstone and of his experiences in Africa. You will recall that when he received an honorary degree from Glasgow University he calmed a rebellious crowd by saying, "My favorite verse is this: *'lo, I am with you alway, even unto the end of the world. Amen'*" (Matthew 28:20). But you see, there was a time when David Livingstone was in great danger in Africa. By the flickering candlelight, he read the words, *"Lo, I am with you."* Then he said, "That settles it. These are the words of the gentleman of sacred honor. I will trust Him and not be afraid."

Let us give ourselves to the great task of witnessing; knowing that this is the work that He has committed unto us.

Years ago, it was harvest time in the great wheat fields of the West. Hundreds of men came to work the fields which covered thousands of acres. One day a group of children were playing in the field. They came in at nightfall, but a little three year old boy was missing. His mother was frantic. Her boy was somewhere out in the vast fields, subject to all the dangers of the elements.

When the harvesters came in, they set out to find the boy. All night they searched in vain. Finally, one of the men said, "I know that we are all tired, but let's try one more thing. Let's join hands and walk across the fields and search every foot of ground."

So they joined hands and started out. In a few hours time, someone shouted, "Here he is." And in a little crevice, overgrown by grain, they found the dead body of the little boy. They took the little body and put it in his mother's arms and said, "We did our best. We don't know what else we could have done. We did our best."

And the brokenhearted mother said, "I am not blaming you. I know that you did your best. But oh, why didn't you think of joining hands together before you did?"

Yes, this is our need, to join hands in doing the task that God has given unto us.

Christ said, "*. . .I am the light of the world. . .*" (John 8:12). We are to go everywhere, showing forth Jesus Christ. We are to shine that they may see and know that we belong to the Saviour.

Has something been dimming your light? Perhaps God is speaking now, urging you to come for the rededication of your life.

Perhaps you have never accepted Jesus Christ as Saviour. This is the time to repent and believe and be saved. Salvation is fully and completely in Him. You cannot shine until first you know Jesus Christ, the light.

# 2
# Immediately

*"And straightway they forsook their nets, and followed him"*

— (Mark 1:18).

The key word of the Gospel of Mark is "straightway," or "immediately." In the first chapter the two words *straightway,* and *immediately* occur eight times. The Spirit of God is evidently emphasizing how quickly things were done, and the completeness with which they were done.

There were times when Jesus told His disciples to wait. At His ascension, he said, *"And, behold, I send the promise of my Father upon you: but tarry ye in the city of Jerusalem, until ye be endued with power from on high"* (Luke 24:49). It was necessary that the disciples have spiritual power before going out in the work of Christ. This is a good lesson for all of us. We need to be filled with the Spirit, surrendered unto God before endeavoring to do Christian service. Still we must remember that this filling of the Spirit waits only for the willingness of the believer and his surrender in the dispensation.

The Word of God puts emphasis on doing things at once — straightway, immediately.

## THE WORD TEACHES THE NEED OF IMMEDIATE ACCEPTANCE OF CHRIST

*"(For he saith, I have heard thee in a time accepted, and in the day of salvation have I succoured thee: behold, now is the accepted time; behold, now is the day of salvation.)"* — II Corinthians 6:2

That eternal place of separation, suffering and torment will be full of those who procrastinated.

The opportunity to be saved was presented to Felix when Paul preached before him, but Felix said, ". . .*Go thy way for this time; when I have a convenient season, I will call for thee*" (Acts 24:25). We have no evidence that this man Felix ever turned to the Saviour. He should have accepted Him immediately, but he did not.

King Agrippa also made a fatal mistake when he put off Christ. Under the persuasive preaching of Paul, he said, ". . .*Almost thou persuadest me to be a Christian*" (Acts 26:28). History gives no evidence that Agrippa ever turned to Christ. He has long since discovered that "almost persuaded" is altogether lost.

Pilate also had an opportunity to be saved. He stood face to face with Christ. He heard the Saviour speak. He confessed that he could find no fault in Him, and yet he did not accept Jesus. Instead, he washed his hands of the matter and sought to take a "middle of the road" position. In so doing, he rejected Christ and lost his soul.

In dealing with lost people, there are two words I have heard more than anything else. They are "not now." These words have been spoken more often than criticism of churches, preachers, and Christian people. These words have been spoken more than the words, "I am too great a sinner." They have been spoken more than "I do not understand the way of salvation." For many do understand the way of salvation. They know that God is able to save unto the uttermost, but Satan causes them to procrastinate.

Friend, there is danger, death, and eternal destruction in delay. God is calling for your immediate acceptance of Christ. The Holy Spirit is convicting your heart of your need of the

Saviour. Accept Him now.

**THE WORD TEACHES IMMEDIATE CONFESSION.**

> *"That if thou shalt confess with thy mouth the Lord Jesus, and shalt believe in thine heart that God hath raised him from the dead, thou shalt be saved. For with the heart man believeth unto righteousness; and with the mouth confession is made unto salvation"*
> (Romans 10:9, 10).

Jesus said, *"Whosoever therefore shall confess me before men, him will I confess also before my Father which is in heaven. But whosoever will deny me before men, him will I also deny before my Father which is in heaven"* (Matthew 10:32-33).

After acceptance of Christ, there must be confession of the Saviour. This confession should be made openly. There are some who through fear want to make their confession in secret. This is not God's way.

Nicodemus and Joseph of Arimathea sought to be secret disciples for fear of the Jews. After the death of Christ, they came out more boldly, and even requested His body and tenderly put it away in Joseph's new tomb.

It is regrettable that they did not take an open stand for Jesus during His earthly ministry. Their secret discipleship leaves much to be desired, and opens the way for criticism of their profession.

Let us not be ashamed of Christ, and let us not be afraid of man. If you are a believer in Christ, then stand foursquare for Him, without fear or favor.

**THE WORD OF GOD CALLS FOR IMMEDIATE OBEDIENCE IN BAPTISM**

Salvation is by grace, through faith in Christ. "*. . .the gift of*

*God is eternal life through Jesus Christ our Lord"* (Romans 6:23). The Word does not teach that baptism is essential to salvation.

The Word does teach that as followers of Christ, we should follow Him in baptism. This act of obedience should come immediately after your conversion.

In the book of the Acts, three thousand were saved on the day of Pentecost and they were baptized. In Acts 8, the Ethiopian eunuch was led to Christ by Philip, and the same hour was baptized. In Acts 9, after the conversion of Paul, he followed Christ in baptism. In Acts 10, Cornelius and his household heard the message of Jesus, received the Saviour, and followed Christ in baptism. In Acts 16, Lydia, a prominent woman and her household, came to Christ and they were baptized. In the same chapter, the jailor in Philippi, hearing the way of salvation, believed on Jesus and followed Christ in baptism – he and all his straightway, that is, the same night.

Our church is following the example of the New Testament Christian when we invite people to be baptized immediately after they are converted. This is the way of the Lord. Having a probationary period is not scriptural. Demanding many promises from new converts before baptism is not according to the New Testament. Allowing a pastor or board of deacons to decide the fitness of a candidate for baptism is likewise unscriptural.

God calls for immediate obedience, and this we should give wholeheartedly.

## THE WORD CALLS FOR IMMEDIATE SERVICE

Too often new converts will say, "I do not want a job in the church right now. I want to observe things for a while." Or some will say, "I want to spend more time in study before I try to do anything." To study is commendable, but the Word of

God calls for immediate service on the part of those who come to Jesus.

For example, when Andrew found Christ, he went out at once and found his brother Simon, and brought him to Jesus. When Philip was saved, he found Nathanael and brought him to Christ.

When the woman at the well heard the words of Jesus, and believed, she went out and told others, and they came and heard Him, and believed.

When Saul of Tarsus was saved, "*. . .straightway he preached Christ in the synagogues, that he is the Son of God*" (Acts 9:20). The people were amazed that this enemy of Christians should so quickly change, and become an exponent of the Christian faith.

Here is our example: We are saved to serve. The time to begin is now. The place to begin is where you are. The person to bring to Jesus is the nearest and dearest to you.

The Christian who delays entering into service quite often never begins at all.

J. Hudson Taylor tells of a Chinese pastor, who upon meeting a young convert, asked him if it was true that he had known the Lord three months. He replied, "Yes, it is blessedly true."

The pastor continued, "And how many have you won to Jesus?"

"Oh," said the convert, "I am only a learner. I did not possess a complete New Testament until yesterday."

"Do you use candles in your home?"

"Yes," was the answer.

"Do you expect the candle to begin to shine when it is burned halfway down?" questioned the pastor.

"No, as soon as it is lit."

The young convert saw the lesson, and went to work. Within six months several of his neighbors and others were saved.

If you are a child of God, the Lord has chosen you to be a soul winner. It is not a matter of your choice—He has already made the choice for you—it is ours to obey or disobey. Let us immediately obey Him, and enter into service.

# 3
# The Greatest Task Given To Man

*"The sower soweth the word."*

—Mark 4:14

Somewhere I read that we don't remember years as much as we remember "giant hours." I agree with this.

It was a giant hour when I accepted Christ as my Saviour. I could never forget many particulars of that momentous occasion when I received the Lord Jesus.

It was a giant hour when God called me to preach. This happened in the old Cedar Creek Baptist Church near Louisville, Kentucky.

It was a giant hour when I preached my first sermon — many years ago. I will never forget the little church on the edge of Jefferstown, Kentucky. I preached on Mark 4, the passage that I read to you a moment ago. I had my sermon typed on green typing paper. The church was small, the building was crowded.

It was a giant hour when I was ordained at the Virginia Av enue Church in Louisville, Kentucky.

It was a giant hour when I baptized my first person at the Prescott Memorial Baptist Church in Memphis, Tennessee.

History has a way of recording giant hours. It was a giant hour when Patrick Henry said, "Give me liberty or give me death."

It was a giant hour when Abraham Lincoln gave the Gettysburg Address.

It was a giant hour when General Douglas MacArthur said, "Old soldiers never die; they just fade away."

The Bible records many giant hours. It was certainly a giant hour for Elijah on Mt. Carmel. Think of the amazement which came over the people as they saw the fire come down from heaven and consume the altar, the wood and the sacrifice.

It was a giant hour for Daniel in the lions' den. The story is given in a plain, matter of fact way in the Word of God, but for staunch Daniel it was a giant hour.

It was surely a giant hour when Saul of Tarsus was stopped on the road to Damascus, when a voice spoke out of heaven and said, *". . .Saul, Saul, why persecutest thou me"* (Acts 9:4)? Saul gave his answer that day; Christ came into his heart.

But of all my giant hours (I invite you to think of the great hours in your life), I think that one of the greatest was when God called me to preach — I was commanded to go out and sow the Word.

The parable given in Mark 4 is well known to every Bible lover. It tells us of the sower going out to sow. Some seed fell by the wayside and the fowls of the air came and devoured it up. Some fell on stony ground. It sprang up, but it did not last. Some fell among thorns and the thorns choked it. It yielded no fruit. And other fell on good ground and did yield fruit that sprang up and increased and brought forth some thirty, some sixty, and some an hundred.

Jesus gave the interpretation of this parable when he pictured Himself as the sower of the Word, and when He also identified all others who give out the Word as sowers of the Word.

Now, let us give some thought to this matter of proclaiming

the Word.

### IN SOWING THE WORD, WE FOLLOW HIM.

Our Christ was the Sower — "*. . .a sower went forth to sow*" (Matthew 13:3).

We cannot follow Christ in all ways — why? The limitations of the flesh. He was the incarnate Son of God. he was perfect, sinless, and holy. We are weak, finite, and carnal.

But, we can follow Him in some ways. For example, we can follow our Saviour in baptism. Every convert should rejoice to obey the Lord in believer's baptism. Our Saviour was baptized and we can follow His example.

We can also follow Him in sowing the Word. The Bible is our most valuable, visible possession. We must not hesitate to sow this Word everywhere.

A few years ago the British sovereign was presented with a copy of the Bible. The words used in making the presentation were as follows: "To keep your Majesty ever mindful of the law and gospel of God, as the rule for the whole life and government of Christian princes, we present you with this Book, the most valuable thing that this world affords. Here is wisdom. This is the royal law. These are the lively oracles of God."

The Bible has great value because it provides us with a picture of our Heavenly Father. We may gain some knowledge of God as we look into the beauty of the heavens, or as we gaze upon the flowers and trees of this earth, but our greatest picture of God is found in His Word.

The Bible also has great value because it gives us our only dependable picture of man. It tells us that man is a sinner and that as a sinner, he needs salvation. "*For all have sinned, and come short of the glory of God*" (Romans 3:23).

The Bible is valuable also because it gives us a picture of the world in which we live. We are made to see the sinfulness of men. We are made to see man's lost condition in every part of the world. The Bible commands us to go and to give this message and sow the Word, that sinners might be saved.

## IN SOWING THE WORD, WE MINISTER TO THE DEEPEST NEEDS OF MAN

Poor men need this Book! They must have this comfort and this solid help.

In a very unique way the Bible ministers to all people. The Bible speaks to the young. Let no young person turn away from the Book of Proverbs. Solomon declares this to every youth, *"Trust in the LORD with all thine heart; and lean not unto thine own understanding. In all thy ways acknowledge him, and he shall direct thy paths"* (Proverbs 3:5,6).

This Book ministers to the aged. Just as the baby Jesus brought joy to the heart of Simeon, so will Christ the Saviour bring joy to the hearts of all who are of advanced age. Yes, just as Christ brought joy to Anna, the prophetess, so will Christ bring joy to all who have come to advanced years. Notice what Paul says to the aged:

> "That the aged men be sober, grave, temperate, sound in faith, in charity, in patience
>
> "The aged women likewise, that they be in behaviour as becometh holiness, not false accusers, not given to much wine, teachers of good things;
>
> "That they may teach the young women to be sober, to love their husbands, to love their children."
>
> — Titus 2:2-4

The Bible ministers to the sorrowing. We shall not take the space in this chapter to recite for you from John 14 and I

Corinthians 15, plus scores of other precious portions which have been used to comfort those who are in deep sorrow. Nothing in this world can bring peace to the troubled heart like the Word of God.

But remember, the Bible ministers also to the successful. I have only to turn to the book of James and find adequate admonitions for all who may be financially successful. Hear him as he speaks:

> *"Go to now, ye rich men, weep and howl for your miseries that shall come upon you.*
>
> *"Your riches are corrupted, and your garments are moth-eaten.*
>
> *"Your gold and silver is cankered; and the rust of them shall be a witness against you, and shall eat your flesh as it were fire. Ye have heaped treasure together for the last days."*
>
> —James 5:1-3

We find James continuing in his words to the successful that they look for the coming of the Lord Jesus Christ.

This Bible ministers to the lost. The deepest need of man is salvation; therefore, we must sow the Word, preach it, teach it, give the message, for through this message men will learn of Christ and will come to salvation. Through this Word, satisfaction can be given to the individual heart.

The Bible must be burned into hearts. This is the only way. Hearts must be branded by the message of God's Word.

Quite often people ask me what do I consider the greatest worth of Camp Joy. I have a quick answer — memorizing of the Word of God. The young people go to our camp and hear the Bible from the first day that they reach there to the last day. They memorize many verses. These verses are stamped upon their minds and upon their hearts. These verses will help them throughout a solid life-time, to live for God and be true to His commands.

**IN SOWING THE WORD, WE OBEY HIS COMMAND.**

> *"Go ye therefore, and teach all nations, baptizing them in the name of the Father, and of the Son, and of the Holy Ghost:*
>
> *"Teaching them to observe all things whatsoever I have commanded you: and, lo, I am with you alway, even unto the end of the world. Amen."*
>
> — Matthew 28:19,20

The great commission has been given and we must obey. We must sow the Word to men through the world. We must not be selfish and think only of the people in our neighborhood, but we must think of men and women and children on every part of the globe. We must obey His command!

Deacon Stephen obeyed the command of our Saviour. His great message to the Israelites is give to us in Acts 7. He stood his ground, he preached the Word, he delivered the message to them. They killed him, but he obeyed the command of Christ.

Deacon Philip obeyed the command also. His story is given to us in Acts 8. The Holy Spirit pulled him out of a successful revival and sent him out in the desert country where he joined himself to a man of Ethiopia, and delivered the message of Christ.

In Acts 9 we find that Saul of Tarsus obeyed the command of our Saviour. After his salvation we read the words, *"And straightway he preached Christ in the synagogues, that he is the Son of God"* (Acts 9:20).

In Acts 10, Simon Peter obeyed the command of Christ.

After a vision had been given to him, he went from Joppa to the household of Cornelius, and preached the message, and many souls were saved. The text for Simon Peter's message was this: *"To him give all the prophets witness, that through his name whosoever believeth in him shall receive remission of sins"* (Acts 10:43).

## IN SOWING THE WORD, WE TOUCH HEAVEN

Sowing the Word is a spiritual task. Other works are earthly, temporal, fleeting, but this is spiritual and lasting.

Sowing the Word is a heavenly task, for by giving the message of Christ, we are getting people ready for eternity and heaven.

In sowing the Word, we are telling of Jesus, our Saviour, who is now at the right hand of God. When we preach the message of Christ, we tell of His coming into this world, His life, His death, His resurrection. Then we tell also of His coming again.

In my life one of the giant experiences which I have had was my last conversation with Mrs. C. B. Miller. She had been sent to the West End Baptist Hospital of Birmingham because of illness. I talked to her after five o'clock one afternoon. In the course of the conversation she said, "Son, I want you to preach my funeral sermon. I will be gone before ten o'clock tonight. I do not want my husband to have any part in the service, or any of his friends, but I want you to give the message. You believe in the second coming of Christ. I want you to stand and tell the people of Christ, the Saviour, and of His return to this earth." I gave my promise to Mrs. Miller. That evening before nine o'clock she went out to be with God.

The Bible tells us of the way to heaven. It is so clear, so plain, that everyone can understand. Sometime ago I talked to a pastor about coming to his church for a meeting. He instructed me on how to reach the church, but from his instructions it is a wonder that I could have found the church at all. His church was located in a large city, and I would have had real difficulty in getting there from the instructions which he gave to me on the telephone. But, when his assistant sent a map and marked the church on the map, I knew that I would have no difficulty. I could then see the streets, the highways, the various number of city markings until the location of the church was clear to me.

So it is with the Word of God. Many may confuse you, but listen to this Book. Jesus said, *". . .I am the way, the truth, and the life: no man cometh unto the Father, but by me"* (John 14:6).

The way is clear. You need not be confused. You need not be lost. You can be saved by simple faith in the Son of God.

> *"Neither is there salvation in any other: for there is none other name under heaven given among men, whereby we must be saved."*
>
> —Acts 4:12

This can be a giant hour for you. Right now you can do that which you will never forget. Accept Jesus as your Saviour. Let Christ come into your heart. Make Him the King of your life. Let this be for you a giant hour.

# 4
# Seventy Went Out

*"After these things the Lord appointed other seventy also, and sent them two and two before his face into ever city and place, whither he himself would come."*

—Luke 10:1

The Bible has a plan and program for the work of every individual and every church. If we follow His plan, success will be given. If we refuse His plan, we fail. There may be a measure of success in man-made ways, but eventually failure will result.

For many years our church conducted a venture of faith. We sought fo follow the Bible way in evangelism, missions, personal soul winning, and finances. When we kept closely to the Bible plan, success resulted. Where we adhered closely to the Word of God, there was no venture at all. It was merely an acceptance of God's promises.

In the days ahead, we intend to read even more carefully the Word of God, and proceed on its teachings as the Holy Spirit gives us light.

Before us is an account not mentioned in the other Gospels. Seventy men (we believe they were all men) were selected by Jesus to go before His face. They were advanced evangelists, preparing the way for Christ.

The outline of the story is simple, but instructive.

## THE SEVENTY APPOINTED

*"After these things the Lord appointed other seventy also . . . ."*

—Luke 10:1

The sending of the seventy was something new in the method of Jesus. It was a planned intensive campaign. It was a carefully organized movement to visit a great many of places. To this end our Lord directed seventy men and sent them out two by two. This means that there were thirty-five teams touching many needy places.

The Lord gives us instruction in soul winning, when he sent out the men, two by two. This has ever been the Bible way. Paul and Barnabas went forth on the first missionary journey. Later Paul associated himself with Silas, and then Paul and Timothy. When Barnabas separated from the Apostle Paul, he took with him John Mark as his companion in the work of Christ.

There are many reasons why it is good for soul winning to be done by teams. Dr. R. A. Neighbor suggests five advantages:

> FIRST, TEAM WORK ASSURES POWER IN PRAYER. Christ has said, "*. . .if two of you shall agree on earth as touching any thing that they shall ask, it shall be done for them of my Father which is in heaven*" (Matt. 18:19). Again He said, "*For where two or three are gathered together in my name, there am I in the midst of them*" (Matt. 18:20).
>
> SECOND, TEAM WORK ASSURES MUTUAL ENCOURAGEMENT. One can hold up the hands of another, even as Aaron and Hur held up the hands of Moses. There come times when one might become fainthearted. The touch of a hand, and the cheer of a voice of comradeship presses the disheartened on to victory.
>
> THIRD, TEAM WORK CARRIES WITH IT THE SHARING

OF RESPONSIBILITY. There are problems which are too great for one to bear. Moses felt this when he said unto the Lord, *"I am not able to bear all this people alone. . ."* (Numbers 11:14). One may be able to discern what the other fails to see. Where one lacks, the other may supply.

FOURTH, TEAM WORK ADDS FORCE TO TESTIMONY. In the mouth of two or three witnesses every word is established. In giving testimony to Christ, that testimony is augmented and its weight greatly strengthened when a second party stands hard by the first.

FIFTH, TEAM WORK MAKES POSSIBLE THE ACCOMPLISHMENT OF A LARGER WORK. What one cannot do, two can do. Where one lacks the other can supply. All gifts never belong to one person. To one is given the spirit of wisdom, to another the spirit of knowledge; to one is given faith, to another is given prophecy.

Our Lord had good reason for sending out the people two by two, and we do well to follow His example.

It is worthy to note that these teams were sent out into neglected and needy Berea. They were sent with these words, *". . . The harvest truly is plenteous, but the labourers are few; Pray ye therefore the Lord of the harvest, that he will send forth labourers into his harvest"* (Matt. 9:37-38).

Three times Jesus used this figure of speech. The first time was doubtless when he was in Samaria. he said, *"Say not ye, There are yet four months, and then cometh the harvest? Behold, I say unto you, Lift up your eyes, and look on the fields; for they are white already to harvest"* (John 4:35).

If the disciples had been investigating Samaria as a field of work, they would have doubtless used entirely different words from our Lord. They might have said, "The country needs the Gospel, but it's a hard field. There must be much work done before we can hope to reap any harvest. Much preparation must be made." But Jesus said, "*. . .Lift up your eyes, and look on the fields; for they are white already to harvest*" (John 4:35).

The second time Christ used this picture of the harvest was in Galilee. We read in Matthew 9:35-38 that Jesus looked upon the multitudes and he was moved with compassion because they fainted and were scattered abroad as sheep having no shepherd. Then He said, "*. . .The harvest truly is plenteous, but the labourers are few; Pray ye therefore the Lord of the harvest, that he will send forth labourers into his harvest*" (Matt. 9:37-38).

The third time the Lord used this figure of the harvest is in the Scripture before us. He looked upon neglected Berea and he said that this was their harvest field. Two commands were given to the seventy. One was to pray and the other was to go. They were to pray for additional laborers for the harvest. They were to go by His authority and command.

Now, notice these words: "*Go your ways: behold, I send you forth as lambs among wolves*" (Luke 10:3). The emphasis should be placed upon the "I." Christ sent them forth. This formed the basis for their entrance into villages and towns.

As you go visiting and witnessing for Christ, remember you are doing it at the command of the Saviour. If people resent this, then keep in mind that they resent the Lord. It is not you they are fighting — it is Christ.

## THE SEVENTY INSTRUCTED

Christ gave to the seventy a seven-fold instruction:

FIRST, HE TOLD THEM TO GO, AND AS THEY WENT, TO PRAY. They were instructed to pray for laborers for the harvest field. This is always the need. There are many who will volunteer, but not many who will labor. There are plenty of overseers, but not many laborers. There are plenty who want to enter the ministry, but not many who want to work.

It should be the constant prayer of every church that God should raise up laborers to enter the field of harvest.

SECOND, THEY WERE TO GO AS LAMBS AMONG WOLVES. A lamb is gentle. A Christian is to be gentle. The lamb is protected by the shepherd. We are protected by Christ, the good Shepherd. Therefore, we need not fear. Though all the world be against us, the Lord will watch over us. Someone has said, "Christ did not send forth the seventy as *rams*, to fight their way by the power of their heads, but as *lambs*, entirely under the protection of the ever-watchful Shepherd. And as such, they represent heart-life more than head-life."

The wolves represent the world in which we live, antagonistic to Christ and the Gospel. The Lord never portrays the way of service as an easy way. Though the Apostle Paul was filled with the Spirit and walking in the will of God, he had great adversities. He suffered in every way that a servant of Christ could suffer. But he counted it all joy for the glory of God.

THIRD GO AS POOR MEN. *"Carry neither purse, nor scrip, nor shoes. . ."* (Luke 10:4). Those who go out for Christ are not to seek to impress the world with their riches. They are not to desire money for their services.

As poor men, they are to labor uncomplainingly. They are to remain in the same house where they are placed. They are to eat what is set before them.

FOURTH, HE SAID, GO IN HASTE. *". . .SALUTE NO MAN BY*

*THE WAY"* (Luke 10:4). Salutations in the East take much time. No such waste of time was to be permitted. They were not to be discourteous, but they were to be as men with a special task.

FIFTH, GO WITH THE MESSAGE OF PEACE. *"And into whatsoever house ye enter, first say, Peace be to this house"* (Luke 10:5). It is always a message of peace that we carry to those who know not Christ. If they will receive the message of Christ, the peace of God will fill and flood their souls.

SIXTH, GO TO DO GOOD. *"And heal the sick that are therein, and say unto them, The kingdom of God is come nigh unto you"* (Luke 10:9). The Christian servant is always intent on doing good and not harm. We are to bring the message of peace, pray for the sick, and seek to help all men to know their need of Christ.

SEVENTH, CHRIST INSTRUCTED THE SEVENTY TO LEAVE A CITY IF THAT CITY WOULD NOT RECEIVE HIS MESSAGE. *"But into whatsoever city ye enter, and they receive you not, go your ways out into the streets of the same, and say, Even the very dust of your city, which cleaveth on us, we do wipe off against you: notwithstanding, be ye sure of this, that the kingdom of God is come nigh unto you"* (Luke 10:10-11).

And again, our Lord said, *"He that heareth you heareth me; and he that despiseth you despiseth me; and he that despiseth me despiseth him that sent me"* (Luke 10:16).

Those who go in the name of Christ need not be offended when men refuse the message. It is against Christ and against God who sent Christ into the world.

It seems that some people have decided to go to Hell. This is their choice. Such people often violently refuse the testimony of Christians. This is their privilege, but may we not be discouraged by their actions.

## THE SEVENTY RETURNED

*"And the seventy returned again with joy, saying, Lord, even the devils are subject unto us through thy name."* —*Luke 10:17*

It is the duty of the Christian to rejoice. We are dishonoring our Christ when we are sad and mournful. God is not dead! Christ is not in the tomb! God lives, Christ is at His right hand, and we have a right to rejoice.

It is a joy to serve Christ. The seventy discovered this. God grant that everyone of you may know this tremendous joy. What we do for the world passes away. What we do for Christ abides forever.

The greatest joy that can come to anyone is to have part in leading a precious soul unto salvation. In this work we see Satan defeated and the power of God working.

Christ said to the seventy, *". . .I beheld Satan as lightning fall from heaven"* (Luke 10:18). In other words, He saw the devil falling from his pinnacle and coming to his ultimate destruction and defeat because of the witness of the servants of Christ.

Jesus said, *"Behold, I give unto you power to tread on serpents and scorpions, and over all the power of the enemy; and nothing shall by any means hurt you"* (Luke 10:19). Christian servant, observe these words, *". . .nothing shall by any means hurt you"* (Luke 10:19).

Let it be our joy to serve Him without fear of man. Let us depend on His power and see demons defeated, souls saved, and lives transformed.

And finally, the seventy are told of the greatness of salvation. *"Notwithstanding in this rejoice not, that the spirits are subject unto you; but rather rejoice, because your names are written in heaven"* (Luke 19:20). To me this is one of the great verses of the Bible. We are not to rejoice in our personal successes, but we are to rejoice that we belong to the family of God, and our names are written down in the Book of life.

The joy of salvation cannot be measured. Through Christ the sin debt is gone.

"Jesus paid it all, All to Him I owe;
Sin had left a crimson stain
He washed it white as snow."

The story is told of a poor man who had an awful debt. He was a good workman, but every day his work became poorer until finally he could do almost nothing. And the owner noticed this condition and spoke to the foreman about it. The foreman said, "He cannot work, for he is worried about his obligations. His eyes are often filled with tears. His hand is trembly. He will not be able to work until the debt is paid." The owner said, "Go and tell him that I have paid his debt." The message was delivered. From the moment that the workman heard the good news, his hands trembled no more, his eyes were not dimmed with tears. He worked happily and skillfully. Joy filled his heart.

FIRST, THROUGH CHRIST OUR SIN DEBT HAS BEEN PAID. We are free from conaemnation. We are now the heirs of God and joint heirs with Jesus Christ.

SECOND, WE CAN REJOICE IN THAT GOD IS OUR PRESENT HELP. "*God is our refuge and strength, a very present help in trouble. Therefore will not we fear, though the earth be removed, and though the mountains be carried into the midst of the sea*" (Psalm 46:1-2).

LAST, THROUGH CHRIST HEAVEN IS OUR PROSPECT. The joy of salvation will not fade away. Worldly joy is like fireworks. They burn for a moment and then disappear. Worldly joy is like lightning that flashes for a few seconds, and then is gone. The joy of heaven is like the bright light of the sun, shining beautifully and steadily.

Let every Christian rejoice today that your name is written in heaven. Let us not stop with our rejoicing. Let us be concerned for those whose names have not been written down. May we press to them with the message of our Christ. We have been appointed by the Master. The Bible gives us instructions. We must give an account of ourselves to Him.

# 5
# Finding Others

*"Philip findeth Nathanael, and saith unto him, We have found him, of whom Moses in the law, and the prophets, did write, Jesus of Nazareth, the son of Joseph."*

—John 1:45

This is a message about Christ and men. No more interesting and important subject could be given to us. The Saviour and His dealings with men from a subject that never grows old.

Jesus saw what men could become by His grace. I am reminded of the story which tells of the artist who had a studio on the second floor of a downtown building. From his window he could see the speeding traffic and rushing multitudes. Every morning a beggar would appear and seek alms from passers-by. His clothes were tattered, torn, and dirty. His beard was grown and his hair disheveled. With beseeching eyes and a pleading voice he would beg for coins. The artist would stand by the window morning after morning and sketch the beggar as he solicited on the sidewalk in front of the studio.

One day the artist opened his window, attracted the attention of the beggar and invited him to come up to the studio. When he came in, the artist showed him his canvas and the beautiful sketch on it.

The beggar asked, "Who is it?"

The artist said, "This is you."

"Me!" cried the astonished beggar. "Me!"

"Yes," said the artist, "that is what I see in you."

The beggar looked at the master and said, "If that's the kind of man you see in me, that's the kind of man I'm going to be."

The Lord Jesus saw in men what they could become. He saw beyond their self-righteousness, their hypocrisy, their undesirable characteristics. He saw what salvation could do for them.

Now, with the Word of God before us, let us see the story of one who found another and brought him to Jesus.

## THE ACTION OF PHILIP

> *"The day following Jesus would go forth into Galilee, and findeth Philip, and saith unto him, Follow me.*
>
> *"Now Philip was of Bethsaida, the city of Andrew and Peter.*
>
> *"Philip findeth Nathanael, and saith unto him, We have him, of whom Moses in the law, and the prophets, did write, Jesus of Nazareth, the son of Joseph."*
>
> —John 1:43-45

Here is an interesting story. It shows us how the Lord Jesus went after the lost sheep. He found Philip and brought him unto Himself and said, *"Follow me."*

In every case it is the Lord Jesus who looks out for the sinners. He may use us or He may seek for the sinner alone, but it is always Christ. If we engage in soul winning, it is because of our Master and of His command to us.

It is interesting to note that Philip came from Bethsaida, the city of Andrew and Peter. It was Andrew who brought his brother, Simon Peter, to the Lord Jesus Christ. Now out of the same city comes another to the Lord.

*"Philip findeth Nathanael. . ."* In these words we see the action of one who was found by the Lord. Here is a new believer who has partaken of the spirit of Christ. The compassion of the Saviour for the lost now fills his heart. he reaches out unto the perishing. It is impossible for him to remain silent.

Oh, that such might be true of every one of us. After we come to the Lord Jesus Christ there should be within us a constant pull to tell the story of Jesus to others. Now, in this story I find three simple things.

FIRST, PHILIP FOUND NATHANAEL. Finding sinners is important. What better place fo find them than with those we know; our families, our loved ones, our neighbors, our friends. To find them means to recognize their need. It means to go after them with all of our hearts and to seek their salvation. To find them means to recognize their need and not to overlook it. There is a danger that we will go on and on and fail to manifest even the slightest interest in those who are lost and dying.

How often I visit a home and talk to a wife who has never spoken once to her husband about the Lord Jesus. She may be a professing Christian and very definite in her testimony, but she has failed to tell her loved one about the Lord. Philip found Nathanael. Let this be an example that we might take unto ourselves.

SECOND, PHILIP TOLD NATHANAEL. He said to him, *". . .We have him, of whom Moses in the law, and the prophets, did write, Jesus of Nazareth, the son of Joseph."* Telling others is not an intricate or difficult matter. It is simply the simple matter of telling people about the Saviour who has come into our hearts. The best of soul winners are the ones who begin to tell others about Jesus when they are saved.

They must not wait, they cannot wait! The best evidence that a person is saved is found in his urgency to tell the story of Jesus. We might well doubt the salvation of the person who is saved and lets no one know about it.

THIRD, PHILIP MAINTAINED HIS PATIENCE. He gave the message to Nathanael, but Nathanael seemed to have some honest doubt. We have no reason to believe that he was trying to evade the issue or offer some hypocritical quibble. Rather he was voicing a genuine difficulty. In the face of this Philip maintained patience and we find no expression of impatience or anger.

Now, let this action of Philip stir you to the place where you will want to tell others about Jesus Christ.

**THE REACTION OF NATHANAEL**

> *"And Nathanael said unto him, can there any good thing come out of Nazareth? Philip saith unto him, Come and see."*
>
> —John 1:46

Although Jesus was born in Bethlehem, He was brought up in Nazareth. Nazareth was an insignificant and perhaps an almost unhappy place from which to come. To Nathanael it was a matter of believing that the greatest of all prophets could come from such an unlikely place. Like Nicodemus, he was disposed to ask, "*. . .How can these things be*" (John 3:9)?

Nathanael was honest in his doubts.

We must conclude that all questions put to us are asked in a carping spirit. There are some people who have real difficulties and when they suggest them, we should endeavor to have the right answers from the Word of God. We cannot err if we present Jesus Christ and His way. Nathanael was a good man. Jesus said of him that he was "*. . .an Israelite indeed, in* *whom is no guile"* (John 1:47)! His heart was ready to receive the Word of God, but he still had his doubts and these doubts had to be settled.

See this man Nathanael as honest, open minded, and desiring to know. This will bring us to our third point.

## THE RESPONSE OF PHILIP

"...Philip saith unto him, Come and see."

Philip, a young disciple, had the best answer. He invited Nathanael to come and see Jesus.

We must follow this pattern — we too must invite people to the Lord Jesus. No one can find fault with Him; however, they can find fault with many things. They can find fault with the church, the officers, and the members, but they cannot find fault with our Lord. We make mistakes, but Christ made none. People must be brought face to face with the Lord Jesus. Unless we can do this, they will remain in their sins, lost and undone.

I have a stock way that I talk to sinners, especially to ones who seem to be shrugging their shoulders and going on their ways, ignoring the Christ. Quite often I will say, "Do you hate God?" The answer is always, "No." I have never had a man, woman, or young person to say, "Yes, I hate God." Not one.

Next I say, "Do you hate Jesus Christ?"

"Why, no."

Then I give this statement, "My friend, if you don't hate God, if you do not hate Jesus, then why do you reject the Saviour and refuse His love?"

I have never had a person to give an answer to this question. I have had some to stop and think and to receive Christ as Saviour.

The sinner must remember this: The Bible says, *"He that is not with me is against me. . ."* (Matthew 12:30). If a man is not for Christ, he is against Him. It takes a very hard-hearted person to accept the fact that he is against Christ.

We must get people to Jesus, not to ourselves — not to our organizations — but to Jesus.

Some way we must erase the mystic clouds of doubt from their eyes and bring them face to face with the Son of God. They must come and see. unless they can see Christ, then all is lost.

So you wonder if Christ can save your soul? Then, my friend, come and see. So you wonder if He can give you peace and joy? Come and see. Do you wonder if the Saviour satisfies the deepest longings of your heart? Then come and see. We present the Lord Jesus to you, and we urge you to receive Him as Saviour.

## THE REGENERATION OF NATHANAEL

> *"Jesus saw Nathanael coming to him, and saith of him, Behold and Israelite indeed, in whom is no guile!*
>
> *"Nathanael saith unto him, Whence knowest thou me? Jesus answered and said unto him, Before that Philip called thee, when thou wast under the fig tree, I saw thee.*
>
> *"Nathanael answered and saith unto him, Rabbi, thou art the Son of God; thou art the King of Israel."*
>
> — John 1:47-49

The Lord Jesus manifested Himself to this honest seeker as the gracious and merciful heart-searcher. He said, "*. . .Before that Philip called thee. . .I saw thee.*" It was then that Christ was from heaven. Nazareth faded out of the picture His doubts were dissolved. He received Christ as his own personal Saviour.

The confession that he made was fearless and full. He saw Christ as the Son of God, mighty to save. He saw the Lord as the King of Israel and gave to Him entire submission. He confessed Him plainly and let all know that he had received Christ of God.

Do you want to be saved? Then this is the way:

> *"That if thou shalt confess with thy mouth the Lord Jesus, and shalt believe in thine heart that God hath raised him from the dead, thou shalt be saved.*
>
> *"For with the heart man believeth unto righteousness; and with the mouth confession is made unto salvation."*
>
> —Romans 10:9,10

There is but one way for a person to be saved and that is by faith in the Son of God. The church cannot save you. Ordinances of the church cannot bring salvation. Salvation is wholly and completely in the Son of God.

> *"But as many as received him to them gave he power to become the sons of God, even to them that believe on his name."*
>
> —John 1:12

Now, see the regeneration of Nathanael. He accepted Christ. He confessed Him. He was fearless in taking his stand for Him before others.

Let me lay upon your hearts that you come to the Lord Jesus in the same way. Come and see the Christ who is pictured in this Word of God. Do not turn away and ask for further revelations. Do not waste your time in looking to people, but look to Christ. Come and see Him.

Some day you might be tempted to say, *"If I had only known the truth about this matter. . ."* My friend, I am seeking to give you the truth about it. Salvation is in Christ Jesus, the Son of God. Receive Him now as your personal Saviour.

We have often read the story of when Jesus was born in Bethlehem. Many sermons and poems have been written about the Saviour who was born in the stable because there was no room for Him in the inn. Please note if they had known what we know now, there would have been room for Jesus. If they had known that one day the name of this little Child, for whom they had no room, would be the greatest among all the names the world has ever known, or ever will know; if they had known that the story of His birth and His life and the meaning of His death would one day be the theme of a Book whose circulation would many times outstrip that of any other book coming from the pen of man, they would have opened their doors and made room for Him.

If they had known that in that day millions of the earth's people would one day proudly acknowledge themselves to be His followers; if they had known that one day churches would be built throughout the entire world for the worship of the Son of God; if they had known the world's greatest statesmen, greatest philosophers, the greatest poets, the greatest scholars would one day bow in humble reverence at His feet; if they had known that the world's greatest masterpieces of painting and sculpture, its greatest oratorios and orations would all be about Jesus; this Christ who was born in the stable — if they had simply known, yes, if they had known, how quickly and gladly they would have made room for him.

And you, my friend, will you make room for Jesus now if I can impress upon your heart that the only source of joy and peace and security must come from Him?

Philip found Nathanael and brought him to Jesus. May we have the joy of bringing you to the Saviour today?

# 6
# The Mighty Ordination

*"And he saith unto them, Follow me, and I will make you fishers of men. And they straightway left their nets, and followed him."*

— Matthew 4:19,20

My public ordination at the hands of men was a very important function for me.

I was ordained on the official vote of a local church — The Virginia Avenue Baptist Church of Louisville, Kentucky. The examining council and the service were arranged by the pastor, Rev. L. W. Benedict. The council was composed of pastors in the city and some professors from the seminary.

The ordination sermon was delivered by Rev. J. N. Binford, the man who baptized me, and the man who counseled me when I was called to preach. The hands of men were placed on my head.

Yes, this service was important to me, but I remind myself that I was called of God and ordained of God before the council was ever assembled. Some men have felt the heavenly ordination so keenly that they never asked for ordination of men. Such was the case of Moody and Spurgeon.

But I am speaking now of a mighty ordination — an ordination that takes in the masses — an ordination that encompasses all Christians.

All Christians have been ordained for God's work. To every one of us the Lord is saying "*. . .as my Father hath sent me, even so send I you*" (John 20:21).

This is the truth that we must grasp. The preacher, the teacher, the missionary, the businessman, the housewife, the young person; yea, all Christians have been ordained of God.

Now some appear to be ignorant of this ordination. Perhaps some of you are in this state. You may be saying, "I never knew this. I never thought of it like that."

Some Christians seem to know this and indifferently disregard it.

Some Christians give spasmodic obedience unto Christ. They seem conscious for a time of this ordination, and then turn away from it.

Yes, some Christians deliberately turn away from Him and from His call.

But, he calls — He ordains! He places His hands upon us. He says to every Christian, "I have a task for you."

This is the thought to inspire us when discouragement comes.

This is the thought to strengthen me and steady me when temptation comes against me.

This is the thought to keep me firm when the world is changing.

This is the thought that sends me on when critical opposition is leveled against me.

Now notice our going is a "going with Him," rather than a "going for Him." Jesus said, "*. . .lo, I am with you. . .*" (Matthew 28:20).

The fact of the presence of God with us is well established by the Word of God.

For example, when Moses was called of God for a certain task, the Lord said, "*. . .I will be with thy mouth, and teach thee what thou shalt say*" (Exodus 4:12). When God laid His hand upon Joshua, He said to this dedicated soldier: "*. . .as I* *was with Moses, so I will be with thee: I will not fail thee, nor forsake thee"* (Joshua 1:5).

Here is a truth that everyone must grasp. The missionary must see it. The missionary is a sent one, but he is accompanied by the Lord. Here is the truth for the pastor — the pastor has been called of God, but he must remember that he is not alone. Christ is with him.

Here is the truth for every Christian! If you are a child of God, then He has promised to be with you and will guide you, and will strengthen you and will bless you day by day.

His hands are upon you — His ordaining hands. This is the mighty ordination that I want to impress upon your hearts and your minds for this evening.

Now consider this outline:

**WE HAVE BEEN ORDAINED TO SERVE**

> Jesus said, "*. . .as my Father hath sent me, even so send I you.*"
>
> — John 20:21

As Christ came to serve, so are we called to serve. Let us notice these familiar verses found in Mark 10:43-45:

> *"But so shall it not be among you: but whosoever will be great among you, shall be your minister: and whosoever of you will be the chiefest, shall be servant of all. For even the Son of man came not to be ministered unto, but to minister, and to give his life a ransom for many."*

Let this challenging thought lay hold upon you. Awaken to its meaning. Grasp its importance.

To serve Christ is an honor! We are servants, not bosses — we are servants, not dictators.

FIRST, WE REMIND OURSELVES THAT SERVANTS TAKE OR-

DERS. He commands and we obey. Have you been obeying Christ?

SECOND, GOOD SERVANTS ALWAYS OBEY. I have been observing through these years that certain kinds of Christians seem to excel. I have noticed that it is not always the matter of talents that causes them to excel. It is certainly not personality that makes them to be excellent servants. There is one thing that is apparent on the part of every outstanding Christian, and that is a willingness to obey the Saviour.

THIRD, SERVANTS OCCUPY A NEARNESS TO THEIR MASTER. It should ever be our desire to live just as close to the Lord as we can. This means that we must sit at His feet as His servants. There must be a willingness to be submissive to His will. We must listen to His words and be ready to give obedience to His commands.

Give thought to your life — what you are doing — what you are saying — how you are obeying Him. Are you using wisely the time which is given to you? Is your life centered upon service for Him?

On our radio station, WDYN-FM, I heard a most interesting story. I think that I can recount it to you. It was the story of a man — perhaps forty-five years of age — who was seated at a table and was considering the bills that were pressing in upon him. He was somewhat distressed by the fact that he was short of money, but he did not have enough to pay all of his bills. In the midst of his contemplation, his young son came running to him, jumped up into his lap and said, "Daddy, this is your birthday, and I have come to wish you a happy birthday." Then the boy said, "Daddy, I am going to kiss you one time for every year of your life. I will kiss you forty-five times." The boy began. Then the father somewhat harshly pushed his boy away and said, "I am too busy. Come back another time. I must consider these bills. I have no time for this." Brokenhearted, the lad turned and walked away. It was apparent that the action of his father had greatly hurt his little heart.

Later in the day the father called the boy to him and said, "Now son, you can finish what you started this morning. I am ready now for you to kiss me and wish me a happy birthday." But this time the boy was not of the mind to do so; and instead of coming to his father and kissing him, he walked away very serious in attitude and apparently troubled in heart.

Two months went by and the boy was out swimming. In the course of his recreation, he was drowned. The precious little son of the mother and father was gone from them. The funeral service was conducted. When it was all over the father had only one pitiful cry: "Oh, if I could call my boy back and let him kiss me and tell me that he loves me, and let me tell him how much I love him." But you see, it was too late. The boy was gone.

Let that story speak to your hearts. We have been ordained of God to serve. Remember, servants take orders. Servants obey. Servants occupy a nearness to their Master. Enter now into close fellowship with Him and rejoice in service.

**YOU HAVE BEEN ORDAINED TO FAITHFUL SERVICE**

> *"His lord said unto him, Well done, thou good and faithful servant: thou hast been faithful over a few things, I will make thee ruler over many things: enter thou into the joy of thy lord."*
>
> — Matthew 25:21
>
> *"Moreover it is required in stewards, that a man be found faithful."*
>
> — I Corinthians 4:2

> *". . .Be thou faithful unto death, and I will give thee a crown of life."*
>
> — Revelation 2:10b

Yes, you have been ordained to faithful service — in season and out of season — in youth and in age — in rain or in shine.

So many people are unfaithful. This takes in the majority of professing Christians. When I speak to the new members of our church, I usually say that according to the percentages throughout the nation, seventy-five percent of those who make professions of faith and join churches will soon disappear from the scene of action.

Unfaithfulness troubled our Lord. When men turned away from Jesus Christ, He said to the twelve, *"Will ye also go away?"* It is plainly evident that the blessed Son of God was disturbed because of unfaithfulness.

Unfaithfulness troubled the Apostle Paul. When John turned away from Paul and Barnabas on the first missionary journey, this disturbed the great apostle. When Demas forsook him and returned to Thessalonica, it troubled Paul.

Unfaithfulness troubles God's sincere people today. We should so live that we are troubled by the half-hearted, the indifferent, by the lukewarm.

For some years I asked the Lord to take away from me the deep troubling of my soul, when I notice the unfaithfulness of people. But somehow, after many years, He has never taken it away. I am still troubled by the unfaithfulness of deacons, or Sunday School teachers, or officers, or ushers, or choir members, or orchestra members. When services are over, I am still conscious of the absence of certain people from places of leadership or from their usual places in the service of Christ. It is my belief that faithful Christians should be troubled by unfaithfulness. We should pray that God would make us what we should be, and we should pray for others to come up to the Bible standard.

Unfaithfulness hinders His work. Unfaithfulness to the services of the church will hinder the services of the church. Unfaithfulness to the work of the Sunday School will hinder the Sunday School. Unfaithfulness to the task of soul winning will hinder soul winning.

What is the greatest hindrance to the work of God? It is unfaithfulness. God grant that we might be what He would have us to be.

## YOU HAVE BEEN ORDAINED TO PRODUCTIVE SERVICE

> *"He that goeth forth and weepeth, bearing precious seed, shall doubtless come again with rejoicing, bringing his sheaves with him."*
>
> —Psalm 126:6
>
> *"The fruit of the righteous is a tree of life; and he that winneth souls is wise."*
>
> —Proverbs 11:30
>
> *"A true witness delivereth souls: but a deceitful witness speaketh lies."*
>
> —Proverbs 14:25

Results can be obtained if we are faithful in our living and in our witnessing.

Every life must produce! The lowliest and the most despised life — yes, all must produce in the service of the Lord Jesus.

We can be productive in the winning of souls if we are diligent.

There is nothing in this world that gives as much joy to the

Christian as the winning of another to Christ. I am still rejoicing over that which happened in the service in a distant city. I felt impressed to speak to a husband and wife at the rear of the church building. After some conversation, they came to the front and knelt at the altar. The pastor and his wife came and talked with them and dealt with them. In a few moments tears were flowing. They arose to their feet rejoicing. I was made so happy by the fact that I had had a small part in getting them to come to the front.

But I did not rejoice but a few moments, until I noticed a dear mother of some years rise to her feet—she too had been praying at the altar—and she saw by her side her son and her daughter-in-law. She had been kneeling in prayer and asking God to save them. As she prayed, I felt impressed to speak to them, and I brought them to the front. That evening they were saved. This couple was saved from a life of sin. Their sins greatly burdened the heart of the mother, and she was praying for their salvation.

You have been ordained to productive service! Be sure that you are getting results in the work that you are doing for our Saviour.

## YOU HAVE BEEN ORDAINED TO THE SERVICE NEAREST HIS HEART

Witnessing for the Lord Jesus Christ is the work nearest to our Saviour.

Proclaiming the message of Christ and sharing the good news is the work that will bring the greatest reward.

> *"For God so loved the world, that he gave his only begotten Son, that whosoever believeth in him should not perish, but have everlasting life."*
>
> —John 3:16

> *"But God commendeth his love toward us, in that, while we were yet sinners, Christ died for us."*
> —Romans 5:8

The work nearest to His heart is the work of witnessing and of winning.

This Bible says that, "*. . .we are labourers together with God: ye are God's husbandry, ye are God's building*" (I Corinthians 3:9).

This mighty ordination has come upon every Christian, and you have been ordained to do that service which is nearest to the heart of the eternal God.

FIRST, WE ARE TO TELL MEN OF GOD'S LOVE. This should not be hard. Sometimes we hesitate to speak of the love of God.

SECOND, WE ARE TO POINT MEN TO THE CROSS. The cross is the sealing evidence of the love of God. Men must see the blood of the Lord Jesus Christ, and must know that Christ died for sinners. The heart of the Word of God is encompassed in the words, "*. . .Christ died for our sins according to the scriptures*" (I Corinthians 15:3).

THIRD, WE ARE TO WARN MEN OF HELL. They must see that they are lost and condemned without the Saviour.

We must understand that we will have bloody hands, if we do not warn the wicked in his way.

> *"So thou, O son of man, I have set thee a watchman unto the house of Israel; therefore thou shalt hear the word at my mouth, and warn them from me."*
>
> *"When I say unto the wicked, O wicked man, thou shalt surely die; if thou dost not speak to warn the wicked from his way, that wicked man shall die in his iniquity; but his blood will I require at thine hand."*
> —Ezekiel 33:7,8

Can you see that this is the service which is nearest to the heart of God?

Now, we come to a question like this: "Am I serving God?" Or a question like this: "What am I doing for Him?" or this question: "Am I pointing others to Christ?"

The other day I read this heartbreaking story which gives a picture of love — love that we need to have for others.

The phone rang in a fashionable suburban home. "Hi, Mom. I am coming home." It was a serviceman in San Diego, who had just returned from the Korean War. The mother was wild with joy that her boy was alive.

"I am bringing a buddy with me," the boy said. "He got hurt bad. He only has one eye, one arm, and one leg. He has no home, and I would like for him to stay and live with us."

"Sure, Son," the mother said. He can stay with us for a while."

"Mom, you don't understand. I want him to always live with us."

"Well, okay," the mother relented. "We will try him a whole year."

"But mom, I want him to be with us always. He is in bad shape."

The mother was impatient. "Son, you are too emotional about this. You have been in the war. The boy will be a drag on you."

Suddenly, the boy hung up.

The next day the parents received a shocking telegram from the Navy. The night before their son had leaped to his death from the twelfth floor of a San Diego hotel.

And when the boy's body was shipped home, the parents found he had one eye, one arm, and one leg.

God grant us compassion for a lost and dying world. We

have been ordained to service for Him and to the service which is nearest to His Heart. We have been ordained to be witnesses and winners of souls. We must not fail Him. We must do our best to bring others to the Saviour.

# 7
# Beaten Paths Are For Beaten Men!

*"So they, being sent forth by the Holy Ghost. . ."*
—Acts 13:4

I recall so well the old highway that went up Monteagle Mountain. It was a twisting uncertain affair. it was like "W Road" only worse. The Greyhound buses had to stop and back up in order to make some of the turns up to the top of the mountain. The old highway followed the line of least resistance, but not so, the new highway. The mountain side was blasted away. The curves of the old road disappeared. Some lives are like the old highway — crooked and devious. They follow the line of least resistance.

I have often looked at the map of Palestine and noted the twisting and turning of the Jordan River. The distance is not great between the Sea of Galilee and the Dead Sea, but the Jordan River twists and turns again and again carrying the waters from the Sea of Galilee into the salty depths of the Dead Sea.

Many are like the old highway going up Monteagle Mountain and many are like the Jordan River. They prefer the old roads. They do not like the strenuous effort of a new way.

The Apostle Paul could have sat down in Antioch for the rest of his life. He could have refused God's leading and the Holy Spirit's pressure upon his heart. Yes, he could have done so, but he would have been out of the will of God. His life would have been useless and selfish.

But Paul obeyed his God. He took the unbeaten path as the Holy Spirit directed. He lived a useful life — a life that will tell for eternity.

When the Holy Spirit issued a call to Saul of Tarsus, he at once "struck out" for new areas. He became a missionary, a church builder, a pastor, a counselor to youth, an evangelist.

Paul was not a beaten man — he was alive, vibrant, endued with power from on high.

The world is filled with beaten men. BEATEN MEN WHO DOUBT GOD. They doubt God's ability to miracles. They doubt God's ability to supply their needs.

BEATEN MEN BLAME OTHERS. It is a common thing for a man to try to blame someone else for his failure. This has ever been true. The Bible records instances of this, and we see it happen in the present day. A man will say, "I never had a chance." Or he might say, "Folks have always been against me." Or he might alibi, "I come out of a poor family."

BEATEN MEN REFUSE OPPORTUNITIES. All around us are the golden opportunities for serving Christ and serving others, but so many do not take these opportunities. They stand back and do nothing!

BEATEN MEN EMPHASIZE THEIR WEAKNESS INSTEAD OF GOD'S STRENGTH. The promise of power and of strength is given unto us by our Lord. He said, "*. . .All power is given unto me in heaven and in earth. Go ye therefore. . . .*" (Matthew 28:18,19). He tells us, "*But ye shall receive power, after that the Holy Ghost is come upon you. . . .*" (Acts 1:8). There is sufficient strength for every man. There is adequate power for living and for witnessing. But many are beaten and refuse to take the way of victory.

Let us take a few moments of time and study the matter of

what the Christian has.

**THE CHRISTIAN HAS A GUIDE.**

> *"Howbeit when he, the Spirit of truth, is come, he will guide you into all truth. . . ."*
>
> —John 16:13

When we receive the Lord Jesus Christ as Saviour, the Holy Spirit comes in to abide in our hearts. Jesus said, *"And I will pray the Father, and he shall give you another Comforter, that he may abide with you for ever"* (John 14:16).

Now, it is for us to recognize Him. He is the indwelling guest. He is the One given unto us to guide us.

We must be sensitive to Him. We must recognize His leadership.

A few days ago in a magazine coming out of Canada, I saw some statements about the Holy Spirit and missions. It seemed quite shocking. Here is one of them, "Eighty percent of all mission work today is being done without the Holy Spirit." The magazine went on to say, "This shocking charge could be more comfortably dismissed were it not an echo of the growing concern expressed by perceptive Christian leaders everywhere."

I am afraid this magazine is quite true in its evaluation of conditions today; and when we say that the Holy Spirit is ignored in mission work, we must recognize that He is ignored also in the work of our local churches. We do not wait upon Him as we should. We resort to committees and drives and programs inside the local church, and we do not wait upon God to direct us by the Holy Spirit.

We must confess that we need the Holy Spirit today. We need Him personally, and we need Him in our churches. The forces of evil are fighting against the powerless churches of today. God's people are bowing resignedly to the onslaught of the devil.

Someone said, "We have banked more on prestige than prayer. We have organized more than we have agonized. We have allowed ritual to obscure reality. We have thought more of conferences than of consecration. In short, we have displaced the Holy Spirit and it is high time that we recognized the cause of our spiritual stringency."

The Christian should be led by the Holy spirit. A devout Christian woman was once asked how she knew the voice of the Spirit. She answered, "How do you know your husband's step and your child's cry from the step and cry of others? I cannot tell you how I know the voice of the Spirit, but it is as real to me as the voice of any other person I know."

I think the lady is right. We can know the voice of the Holy Spirit, and He will lead us if we bow before Him.

We have a beautiful story given to us in Acts 8. It tells about Philip preaching in the desert country and leading a man to the Lord Jesus. But you see, the Bible says very plainly that Philip was Spirit-led. He did not hesitate to leave a going revival in Samaria and launch out into the desert land. He knew his Bible; therefore, he did not hesitate to talk about religion with this dignitary from Ethiopia. He knew personal work, and his message was Jesus. He got results, for the man of Ethiopia received Christ as Saviour and Philip went on his way quietly.

I repeat, we must be led by the Holy Spirit. As He leads us, we will sometimes find ourselves going into unbeaten paths.

And then, of course, to work successfully, we must be endued with the Spirit. Paul told the people in Ephesus, *"And be not drunk with wine, wherein is excess; but be filled with the Spirit"* (Ephesians 5:18). It was written of the early Christians in Jerusalem, *". . .and they were all filled with the Holy Ghost, and they spake the Word of God with boldness"* (Acts 4:31).

We need the filling of the Holy Spirit. Nothing will so take the place of this. If we are to work successfully, then we must be clothed with God's power. Without His power, there will be a great deal of Christian work carried on with noise, advertising, and sensationalism, but without power. But when the Holy Spirit endues us, then He will use all of our abilities, our training, our personality, yea, all things, for the glory of God. When we read the book of the Acts, we are reading the record of Christians who were empowered by the Holy Spirit.

The world of today needs men who are following the leadership of the Spirit of God. In Genesis 41:38, we find the most interesting thought. It reads as follows: *"And Pharaoh said unto his servants, Can we find such a one as this is, a man in whom the Spirit of God is?"*

The Pharaoh was referring to Joseph, and he called him "a man in whom the Spirit of God is." If there is one thing we need in this day, in the leadership of our nation, as well as in the leadership of all things, it is a man of this sort.

Yes, the Christian has a guide — the Holy Spirit.

## A PIONEERING SPIRIT

Your salvation gives you this and yet you may not respond to it. When you become a child of God, you become a "new creature" in Christ Jesus.

As we study the Bible, we see that this is written in big letters in all parts of it. In the book of the Acts, when men were regenerated by the Spirit of God, they became new creatures and launched out into work in new areas.

But not only in the New Testament, but we find also throughout the entire Word when men were dominated by the Lord, they walked into new fields. For example:

Noah listened to God. He defied the world and built the ark. Abraham, a great man of faith, walked with God into new places.

God's promises are always on the ascending scale. He said to Abraham, "*. . . Get thee out of thy country, and from thy kindred, and from thy father's house, unto a land that I will shew thee*" (Genesis 12:1). He told him that He would make of him a great nation and make his children to be as the sands of the sea.

But we must not forget something, all of this came to Abraham only because he obeyed his God. There was about this man who believed in God a pioneering spirit. He was not afraid to walk by faith. He followed God into new territories. He built his altars unto God and prayed and sought God's guidance.

Moses was another who had a pioneering spirit. What a story of this man who spent forty years in Egypt, forty years in the desert country, and at eighty years, God called him to be a pioneer. If you read the story carefully, you will notice that Moses pleaded for exemption on the basis that he could not speak, but notice he did not plead for exemption on the matter of his age. He pioneered for God!

Joshua was another who pioneered for God. When Moses died, Joshua came into his place. He was ready to take over. On a marble tablet in Westminster Abbey which bears the portraits of John and Charles Wesley, is this inscription: "God buries the workers but carries on the work." So it is that God always carries on His work. Joshua came into the leadership of the nation. He had a small, ragged, weary army, but he was sent of God to conquer Canaan land. Canaan was a land of fortified cities, war-like inhabitants and unlimited supplies.

Joshua divided the land into twelve divisions for the twelve tribes. He believed God and God honored his faith. He had the spirit of a pioneer.

When we come to the New Testament, we find the same pioneering spirit on the part of Simon Peter. When Jesus saved Simon, he said, "*. . . Thou art Simon the son of Jona: thou shalt be called Cephas, which is by interpretation, A stone*" (John 1:42). He saw what Simon Peter would become.

It is said that Michelangelo would stand before rough blocks of marble and describe to the onlookers the marvelous statues he saw in fancy. Then, he would set to work and carve out of the rough marble the figures he had envisioned. So it was, that Jesus looked upon Simon Peter and saw the rock he would become. He saw how this rough, unlettered man could become one of the great leaders of the early church. Simon Peter, headstrong, impulsive, and opinionated, would become a great preacher of the Gospel of Christ.

The Apostle Peter was a pioneer. He followed the leadership of the Lord and hence we find him going and preaching to the Gentiles. He did not hesitate to obey the Spirit of God, even though he knew that it would bring him into conflict with others. He pioneered!

We would need to say much about Paul and his pioneering spirit.

John Kelman said, "Paul is one of the titanic figures of the past. He is the master empire builder of the kingdom of God in the world. Such a man's conversion is a tremendous affair."

Arthur P. Stanley said, "That event changed the fortunes of mankind,"

Edwin Lee said, "It ranks by the side of the call of Abraham, and the reformation of the sixteenth century."

Philip Schaff said, "The conversion of such a man and with such results is one of the strongest proofs of the resurrection." When Saul of Tarsus saw Jesus Christ, the Son of God, and received Him as Saviour, he became a new creature and his life became a pioneering life — the old beaten paths were gone. He was ready now to walk in a new way.

It has been well said, "If a man once gets a good look at Jesus Christ, he will never be the same again."

We could mention many others to illustrate this second point, but I think I have given enough to let you see that the pioneering, adventuring spirit has been given unto all of us when we put our faith in Jesus Christ, the Son of God.

## A DEFINITE CALL

We are discussing what the Christian has — First, he has a Guide — the Holy Spirit. Second, he has a pioneering spirit, for God has led him into a new way. Third, there is a definite call to the child of God.

FIRST, THERE IS A CALL TO STAND AGAINST THE WORLD. It will do you good to see this. For if you fail to understand it, you will be constantly tossed about by every conflict and emotion of the day. Here is what John had to say:

> *"Love not the world, neither the things that are in the world. If any man love the world, the love of the Father is not in him."* — I John 2:15

The Apostle Paul expressed himself quite forcibly on the matter of the world when he said, *"Put on the whole armour of God, that ye may be able to stand against the wiles of the devil"* (Ephesians 6:11).

We find this challenging call coming to us out of II Corinthians 6.

> *"Wherefore come out from among them, and be ye separate, saith the Lord, and touch not the unclean thing; and I will receive you,*
> *"And will be a Father unto you, and ye shall be my sons and daughters, saith the Lord Almighty."* — II Corinthians 6:17,18

Here is a definite call to stand against the world. I give you my promise that if you stand against the world, you will have to have the pioneering spirit and depend upon the Holy Spirit.

SECOND, WE HAVE A DEFINITE CALL TO PROCLAIM CHRIST. We are to be concerned about a lost and dying world. Someone made the comment, "Modern Christians sleep too well at night." This person is simply expressing the thought that we are not as concerned as we ought to be.

The Apostle Paul was *"pressed in the Spirit"* (Acts 18:5).

Paul had great *"heaviness and continual sorrow"* (Romans 9:2).

It is our business to proclaim Christ. We must do so in the fullness of the Holy Spirit. We must do so for the glory of God.

We must give the message unto everyone. We must proclaim the Gospel to the high and the low, to the rich and the poor.

A pastor said to me a few days ago, that his church was unable to minister to the poorer classes of people. He said, "We have built our church with the upper classes, and my people do not work too well with the poor ones."

Such a pastor needs to study the Lord Jesus Christ and His work. What a poor prospect was the woman of Samaria, and yet Jesus took much time to deal with this one and to point her unto salvation. Her character was disreputable. Her tongue was loose. She was of a despised race. But Jesus Christ did not count her as a hopeless one. Hearing His message, she received Him as Saviour. And the scriptures tell us that she went everywhere telling people about Christ.

Fairbairn remarked: "It is strange that Christ should often speak His most remarkable words to the least remarkable persons."

Christ was concerned about all sinners, and we must be concerned. We must see the needs of others and give ourselves to the task of pointing them to Jesus Christ, the Saviour of the world.

In the east end of London, workmen were digging a deep trench for the installation of a sewer. Suddenly the shoring gave way and tons of earth fell upon several of the laborers burying them alive. Instantly volunteers set feverishly to extricate the unfortunate men while a great crowd gathered to watch. Standing with the crowd was a man with his hands in his pockets, only casually interested. Soon an acquaintance rushed up to him and said, "Bill, your brother is down there." Off came the bystander's coat, and in a moment he too was hard at work to save the entombed men. I think that story has its own interpretation to your hearts. It is our business to give the Gospel, proclaim the message, and point people to the Saviour. We must not fail.

A few years ago I heard Bill Bright, head of the Campus Crusades of America, relate a very strange and interesting story. He said that he sat at a table and had lunch with a man in Nazareth in Galilee. He talked to the man about his need of Christ, but he said, "I thought within myself that I would wait until after the meal to press for a decision." But suddenly as he talked to the man he saw deep conviction upon his face. Then the man bowed his head and accepted Christ as his Saviour. He offered a prayer thanking God for the salvation which he had in Jesus Christ.

As they sat there at the table, the man of Nazareth said a very strange thing to Bill Bright. He said, "Oh, sir, send someone to Nazareth to tell them of Jesus."

Imagine that! It was in Nazareth where Jesus had lived. He spent his boyhood and young manhood in that town, and yet, here was a man who had just been saved begging that someone come to Nazareth and tell the story of Jesus.

The call of God has been given to us, and we must not fail. We are to be "His witnesses." Are you witnessing for the Saviour? Are you telling people about His power to redeem and transform? This is God's call to all of us.

# 8
# The Great Commission

*"And Jesus came and spake unto them, saying, all power is given unto me in heaven and in earth.*
*"Go ye therefore...."*

—Matthew 28:18-19b

In this chapter I want us to study the Great Commission of our Saviour. Let's notice seven important features of the Great Commission.

## THE PERSON WHO GAVE IT

It was Jesus who met with His disciples in the appointed place before his ascension.

It was Christ, who spake not as the scribes and Pharisees, but, as one with authority. Not only did He speak as one with authority, but He had authority. He spoke as God's Son. The weight of heaven was behind his words.

Also, we must remember that this one who gave the great commission was Christ who conquered death. Death and the grave could not hold Him. He came forth according to His promise on the third day. As He commanded His disciples to go and preach the Gospel, he stood before them with the nail prints in His hands and feet, and with the scars on His brow.

It is amazing that the Scripture tells us that some doubted. It is but another proof of the sinfulness of man. Just as some doubt Him, so do some disobey Him, and refuse to carry out the commission.

## THE PLAN OF IT

> *"Go ye therefore, and teach all nations, baptizing them in the name of the Father, and of the Son, and of the Holy Ghost:*
>
> *"Teaching them to observe all things whatsoever I have commanded you. . ."*
>
> — Matthew 28:19,20

Mark gives it in this way, "*. . .Go ye into all the world, and preach the gospel to every creature*" (Mark 16:15).

The plan of the great commission is exceedingly simple. It is for Christ's followers to take the Gospel to every nation and every creature. After they have heard the Gospel and believed, then they are to baptized in the name of the Father, Son, and Holy Spirit, and then they are to be taught the things that Christ had given to His early disciples.

It is tragic that this simple plan has so often been set aside for some involved program which is not authorized in the Word of God. Consequently, the spread of the Gospel has been hindered. The evangelization of nations has been hurt and souls have been lost.

It is the purpose of our church to accept the plan as given by the Saviour, and send forth missionaries to the ends of the earth, and to give our obedience to Christ in carrying out His express orders.

## THE PERSONS TO WHOM IT WAS GIVEN

Jesus spoke these words to his disciples. They were saved men, chosen men, and commissioned men.

The command is no less to us. We who are saved are called to be God's ambassadors, His co-workers, witnesses of His power and missionaries to the nations.

To each Christian Christ is saying, "*. . .as my Father hath* *sent me, even so send I you"* (John 20:21). There is a part for every Christian to play in the carrying out of His commission. Some can go, others can give, all can pray.

The commission is not given just to those who feel God's call to go to some heathen country. The commission is to all of God's children.

## THE PRICE OF IT

There is a price to be paid, if we are to obey.

Going means leaving. For our dear friends who have gone to the Belgian Congo, Africa, it meant leaving the friends and loved ones they had here, and going to a distant land.

Because of the price, only a few people go as missionaries. It has been said that out of every one hundred young people who publicly declare they have been called of God to foreign mission service, only one goes to the field and stays with the work. The others drop by the wayside somewhere.

There is a price to be paid. It was indicated by the Saviour when He said, *"If any man come to me, and hate not his father, and mother, and wife, and children, and brethren, and sisters, yea, and his own life also, he cannot be my disciple. And whosoever doth not bear his cross, and come after me, cannot be my disciple"* (Luke 14:26,27).

To obey the command of Christ means forsaking your own plans, turning from selfish pleasures, and dedication to the greatest of all works. How few are willing to pay the price.

## THE POWER BEHIND IT

Christ said, *". . .All power is given unto me in heaven and in earth"* (Matthew 28:18). The power of the risen Saviour is back of the commission and those who obey it.

If we do mission work and soul winning, we must remember that the power of Almighty God is back of this work.

Christ demonstrated His power by His life, His mighty miracles, His victory over death and the grave, His resurrection and ascension. It is this power which is ours as we go for Him.

## THE PROMISE WITH IT

*". . .and, lo, I am with you alway, even unto the end of the world. . ."*

— Matthew 28:20

The promise of Christ is, *". . .I will never leave thee, nor forsake thee"* (Hebrews 13:5)

All mission work is bound to fail, and all missionaries will soon cease unless there is a consciousness of His divine presence.

It is as man feels God's presence with him that he is able to stand and go forward. Noah stood against the multitude of his day because of the consciousness of God's presence. Elijah stood against the prophets of Baal and the sinful people because he knew that God was with him. Daniel did not falter and fail in his allegiance to God because he felt the Lord's presence.

As we go and obey, He goes with us. It must be noted that this promise is for those who obey His commission.

## THE PURPOSE OF IT

We cannot discuss the great commission without remembering that God's divine purpose is to bring people unto Himself. Man is a free moral agent. He has the power of choice. God will not force his will, but the purpose of the great commission is to give all men an opportunity to be saved.

During these days the Lord is taking out a people for His name. From every kindred, race, and nation, men and women are receiving Christ. God is saving all who will hear and believe.

Some day, it may be soon, Christ is coming. The redeemed will meet Him in the air. The Chinese, the Japanese, the Germans, the Jews, the white, the black, from all nations. The living will be changed, and caught up into His presence.

What a glorious hour that will be when God's people from every nation will be brought into the presence of the Saviour. Perhaps a song will be announced. There will be no need to sing, "Come ye, sinners, poor and needy, weak and wounded, sick and sore; Jesus, ready stands to save you, Full of pity, love and power."

"He is able, He is able, He is willing, Doubt no more."

No, that song will not be in order, for all who stand there will be saved.

The great song, "Just as I am, without one plea; But that thy blood was shed for me, And that thou bidd'st me come to thee, O Lamb of God, I come, I come," will also be out of order in that assembly.

These redeemed hosts, washed in the blood of the Lamb, led to the Saviour, by preachers, teachers, and missionaries — these saved multitudes, brought to Christ by consecrated soul winners, will be able to sing only a song of praise to the Lamb of God. Perhaps it will be:

> "All hail the power of Jesus' name,
> Let angels prostrate fall,
> Bring forth the royal diadem,
> And crown Him Lord of all.
> Bring forth the royal diadem,
> And crown Him Lord of all!"

# 9

# To Every Creature

*"And he said unto them, Go ye into all the world, and preach the gospel to every creature."*

—Mark 16:15

The plan for giving the Gospel to every creature came from our Saviour. It did not originate in a sinful world. It is not a Satanic plan. It is not a conspiracy of evil powers to cause us to dissipate our talents and possessions. It is a plan given by the Lord Himself.

It is a plan straight from the Heart of God.

It is a plan given by the heavenly Father when sin first came into this world of ours. When man was still groggy from the effects of sin, God gave the promise of salvation. In this promise we have a part; first, in our salvation, and second, in the telling of the good news.

It is the plan of God to save man from the tragic woe of an eternal hell; a hell replete with the ultimate in punishment and extending for the ultimate in time.

It is a plan for making sinful men and women into the children of God. In plain and simple words this is given to us in the Scriptures.

*"But as many as received him, to them gave he power to become the sons of God, even to them that believe on his name."*

—John 1:12

There are three things that I want us to see as we think of

the "*. . .gospel to every creature.*"

## THE CHARGE

Jesus said, "*. . .Go ye into all the world, and preach the gospel to every creature.*" There are some things that need to be repeated often.

We rejoice to repeat the message of salvation and those of us who are saved, rejoice to hear it again and again.

We rejoice to speak of the second coming and the events related to the coming of our Saviour.

We rejoice to think of the blessedness of our possessions in Christ, both now and forever.

We should also rejoice to repeat the command given by our Lord to get the Gospel to the ends of the earth. Let every child of God remember that Jesus said these words, "*. . .Go ye into all the world, and preach the gospel to every creature.*"

This command was given by our Lord Himself. The Son of God spoke these words, the One who cannot lie. Jesus said, "*. . .Go ye. . .*" and Jesus never wasted words. No useless expressions ever came from his lips. He said, "*. . .Go. . .*"

Again, we must remember that this was His parting command to His disciples. We are reminded again of the importance of last words. How often we have treasured in our hearts some last word given by a friend or loved one. Perhaps that one is on the other side in the presence of God, but the word still remains with us.

So it was that Jesus, when he was ready to ascend into glory, said to His disciples, "*Go ye therefore, and teach all nations. . .*" The most important thing He said last. It is so easy for Christians to pick up certain remarks made by the Saviour and to emphasize them. Is this wrong? No, for everything that Jesus said was important. But there is a special importance to the last words of our Saviour, when he gave this parting command — a command which is given to us likewise.

This command relates itself to the age in which we are living; the age which began with our Saviour and will continue until He comes. Let there be no cessation on our part in the carrying out of His word in the preaching of the Gospel.

Again, the command is just as binding upon us as it was upon the first Christians. There are some who try to escape the responsibility of these words when Jesus said, "*. . .and ye shall be witnesses unto me both in Jerusalem, and in all Judaea, and in Samaria, and unto the uttermost part of the earth*" (Acts 1:8).

There are some who feel that Jesus was speaking to a particular crowd and that he does not mean us. My friends, when you read the entire account of our Saviour's ascension, and of His words before going back to the Father, you are made to see that the responsibility for getting the Gospel to every creature is upon us.

Let us see what the Apostle Paul had to say about this matter:

> *"To wit, that God was in Christ, reconciling the world unto himself, not imputing their trespasses unto them; and hath committed unto us the word of reconciliation."*
>
> — II Corinthians 5:19

And again we find the Apostle Paul saying to the church in Rome,

> *"For whosoever shall call upon the name of the Lord shall be saved.*
>
> *"How than shall they call on him in whom they have not believed? and how shall they believe in him of whom they have not heard? and how shall they hear without a preacher?*

*"And how shall they preach, except they be sent? as it is written, How beautiful are the feet of them that preach the gospel of peace, and bring glad tidings of good things!*

*"But they have not all obeyed the gospel. For Esaias saith, Lord, who hath believed our report?*

*"So then faith cometh by hearing, and hearing by the word of God."*

—Romans 10:13-17

When we are born into the family of God, we must take our share of the responsibility. The Gospel must be given! The charge has been made unto us. His command must be obeyed.

## THE CARELESSNESS

How slow Christians have been to obey the command of Christ! How careless in the doing of His will! Obedience to the Lord's Word has been spasmodic. There have been ages of partial obedience and some centuries when almost nothing was done.

Back of our carelessness and indifference is fleshly sinfulness. Individuals have been beset by it. It was so in the day of the Apostle Paul. He found fault with the church when he said, *"For all see their own, not the things which are Jesus Christ's"* (Philippians 2:21).

Churches have been selfish. They have engaged in big building programs, but have omitted the weightier matters of getting out the Gospel through missions. They have been interested in promotion of social endeavors, but have failed in the great work of getting the Gospel to the dying millions.

When we read of the early church, we find no indications about buildings of equipment, but we find an indication of a great concern for others. This same concern should be ours today as we think of the dying millions.

Not only individuals, but it is sad when an entire denomination becomes selfish and fails in the great task of doing God's work.

Here is an illustration: A leader of a sizable denomination in the North came by our church a few years ago. He is a man of vision and spiritual power. He has been trying to impart this to the people of his denomination. With tears in his eyes he said, "Last year our entire denomination had only one addition." This does not mean that there was only one profession of faith in an entire year in that denomination, but it means that when the figures were tabulated of gains and losses, the denomination had gained but one person. His heart was broken. He was troubled by the selfishness, the ease and lethargy of his people.

Now let us put down three things about carelessness:

FIRST, OUR CARELESSNESS ROBS US. There is a joy, a rich joy, in obeying Christ. There is a joy in doing the will of God which this world knows nothing about. Every child of God will testify to this fact. When you have given your obedience to the Lord, there is a joy within your heart.

SECOND, OUR CARELESSNESS ROBS OTHERS. Men are robbed of hearing the glorious Gospel message of Christ because we have been careless. Around the world, people are waiting for salvation; waiting for the best gifts, but we have robbed them. We have withheld our money, our time, and our people, and the Gospel has not gone out.

Every Christian will agree that salvation is the greatest gift of all, and yet think of the people who have never heard of Jesus Christ! Think of the ones who have heard only once or twice! We have robbed these individuals of the great joy of hearing of Jesus and the salvation that He offers.

THIRD, OUR CARELESSNESS ROBS GOD OF THE GLORY WHICH BELONGS TO HIM. No one denies the fact that God is glorified by the obedience of His children, nor can we argue the fact that disobedience neither pleases God nor brings glory to His name. When we are careless in getting out the Gospel and selfish in withholding the message of Christ, then God is not glorified.

There has been a gross carelessness on the part of God's people down through the ages and that carelessness seems to have reached its peak in this selfish time in which we live. May the Spirit of God awaken our hearts that we might do the will of God.

## THE CONCERN

We speak now of the concern or the compassion of our Saviour. We speak now of that concern which we should have for the souls of men.

The command has been given to us. We, the recipients of the grace of God, have heard His voice. It has been given to us by our Lord, the one we profess to love.

The issue is plain — do we love Christ? Are we concerned about obeying Him? Do we desire to do His will? Do we care for others as Jesus cared?

Are we concerned for the multitudes which have never heard the Gospel the first time? Are we concerned for the millions who have heard only scantily, perhaps once or twice, and that in a very fragmentary fashion?

Do we recognize the shortness of time? It was Paul who said, "*. . .the time is short. . .*" (I Corinthians 7:29). In this he surely meant that time is short dispensationally. "*. . .the coming of the Lord draweth nigh*" (James 5:18). Each day brings us closer to Him and His appearing.

The time is short politically. Doors are closing in various parts of the world — in China, in India, in South America.

The time is short spiritually — for souls are passing away. The question comes again, Do we recognize the shortness of time? God grant that we may!

Will we take advantage of various methods of getting the Gospel unto others?

FIRST, BY PRAYER WE CAN GIVE THE MESSAGE TO MEN AROUND THE WORLD. We are told by the Lord to pray that laborers may be called into harvest fields.

SECOND, WE MUST SEND THE GOSPEL OUT BY OUR GIVING. Every child of God should be regular and systematic in the giving of what he has to the Lord. We should give unselfishly. We should give prayerfully that the Gospel might reach unto all men.

A little boy of eleven years was very ill and could not join the other boys and girls in play. He thought about things that children do not bother their heads about. One day when he thought that he would not be well again, he called his mother and said, "I wish you would bring the pennies that I have saved for Christmas gifts."

The pennies were brought. "Give them to some missionary," he said, "who will use them for little boys and girls who don't have a Sunday School or a nice preacher like Daddy."

The pennies were given to Rev. Franklin Pierce Lynch who was on furlough from his mission station in the Congo. Then word came that this hospital had been destroyed by a flood of the Congo River. Taking the sixty pennies, he toured the country and told the story. In this way he was able to raise enough money to rebuild the hospital and continue the work.

We must learn lessons of giving. We must give lovingly, unselfishly, and faithfully.

THIRD, WE CAN GET THE GOSPEL OUT TO OTHERS BY BEING WILLING TO GO OURSELVES. It is true that all cannot go in person, but some can go. Perhaps the Lord has been speaking to you about giving your life to this great task of missions.

Barnabas and Saul were the best men that God had in Antioch. As we read the story and study the accounts on the ancient field, we are reminded that doubtless both Barnabas and Saul were badly needed in Antioch. But God called them out to the mission fields, and they gladly went.

Now, the last question, "What do you think of missions? What part should missions play in the Christian's life?" Certainly there should be a sense of compulsion. The Gospel must be given and we must go with the message.

There should be a width of vision. Only by way of missions can the vision be enlarged. The church without a missionary vision will be a narrow church.

Missions will give to us a largeness of spiritual life. Selfishness will take over the heart of a person who is not interested in missions. The church without a missionary program will fail.

Have we heard the Macedonian call? When Paul waited upon the Spirit for leadership, there stood a man of Macedonia and prayed him, saying, "*. . .Come over into Macedonia, and help us" (Acts 16:9).*

The man from Macedonia represents all the people of the world. He wears every kind of clothing. He has all degrees of education or lack of it. Sometimes he may be a Roman or a Jew or a Frenchman or a German. He may live in India, in

Japan, in China. The man of Macedonia may be a white man, a black man, a yellow man, or a red man. The man from Macedonia speaks every language under the sun. But, there is one thing about him — he is a man who needs help. He needs Christ. We must not close our ears to the cry of this lost world for help. The men of all languages are saying, "Come over and help us!" Will you give of yourself and of your possessions that the Gospel may go to men and women around this world?

With this illustration I close:

A missionary was visiting in a home of our land. He was a missionary who had spent many years in South America. As he talked of his country, he told this story:

"I was visiting a village for the first time. I spoke to a small group of people and read from the New Testament, portions that told of the life and sacrificial death of our Lord Jesus Christ. At an appointed time, the next day, the people came again eager to hear more of this wonderful story. I read to them again, from the Scriptures, more about our Lord's Gospel of love and salvation.

"At the close of the service a man came up to me, and looking into my face earnestly asked, 'Did you know the man in the book?'"

"Tears glistened in the eyes of this grand old soldier of the cross as he said, 'Thank God, I did know the man in the book. I knew Him as my Lord and Saviour, and I was able to introduce Him to these people who had never known His love and forgiveness.'"

We are talking today about the Lord Jesus Christ. We are talking about getting the Gospel throughout the world. Now we want to give the question to you: Do you know Jesus Christ as your Saviour? Have you been saved? Are you a child of God? Settle the question at this time.

# 10
# The Call of Our Eternal God

*"Whereupon, O king Agrippa, I was not disobedient unto the heavenly vision."*

—Acts 26:29

There is no peace in any heart outside of obedience to God. The lost soul can never know abiding peace. The saved soul cannot know true peace apart from complete obedience to the Lord's commands. There is no peace to be found in money, in pleasure, or in position.

The call of God is plainly given to us in the last words of Christ spoken before His ascension.

*"Go ye therefore, and teach all nations, baptizing them in the name of the Father, and of the Son, and of the Holy Ghost: Teaching them to observe all things whatsoever I have commanded you: and, lo, I am with you alway, even unto the end of the world. Amen."*

—Matthew 28:19,20

The call of God is plain. We are to go with the Gospel. We may go in different ways, but we are to go and to give the Gospel unto men everywhere.

Yes, there will be many hindering causes.

FIRST, THERE IS THE CLAMOR OF THE WORLD. The noise of many things around us will try to take away our minds from the call of God. In my own experience, I can think back upon the days when God was definitely calling me to the work of preaching His Word and the winning of lost souls. My own heart was reaching out after a certain field of music. I thought this was the thing I should do. It was strongly upon me and was made more emphatic because of many amazing opportunities, but in spite of the clamor of the world, I determined that I would do the thing that God had called me to do.

SECOND, THERE IS AN UNWILLINGNESS OF HEART WHICH OFTEN KEEPS PEOPLE FROM DOING THE WILL OF GOD. God speaks, the person hears, but the unwillingness is still present. Satan fights and endeavors to keep the child of God from full surrender unto the Lord. Sometimes the heart becomes hard. Often it is preoccupied and life goes by because of an unwillingness of heart to release the things of the world, and to do the will of God.

Only this week I have talked with a man who said he was called of God to preach many years ago. He is now forty-nine years of age, but as yet, has not preached his first sermon. Still, he says that he knows God has called him. How sinful and terrible is unwillingness of heart!

THIRD, ABSORPTION IN MANY THINGS WILL KEEP PEOPLE FROM THE WILL OF GOD. God calls many who are so taken up with the business of making money and getting ahead in life, that they have no time for the things of God. Some are engrossed in having a good time until they feel that anything else will have to be secondary.

There are many hindering causes to hearing what God has to say to us. May we endeavor now to hear His voice, and to do His bidding.

## THE CALL TO SOME

Some people receive a call from God to give all of themselves and their time in the service of Christ. This is a call that must be heeded. It should not be treated with lightness or contempt. God's voice speaks plainly, solemnly, and earnestly. It should be ours to respond to the call of God.

FIRST, THIS CALL IS DEFINITE. It was definite to Moses. Moses tried to escape doing the thing God wanted him to do, but because of the urgency of the call, and the definiteness of it, he agreed to do the will of God.

The call of God to Joshua was definite. Try as he might, he could not get away from the call. God poured into him strength and power and overcame the hesitancy of Joshua to do the thing that God wanted him to do.

The call to Gideon was a definite call. Gideon, of parentage, could not believe that God wanted him for the special task of delivering the people of Israel, therefore, Gideon said to the Lord,

> *"...Let not thine anger be hot against me, and I will speak but this once: let me prove, I pray thee, but this once with the fleece; let it now be day only upon the fleece, and upon all the ground let there be dew."*
>
> —Judges 6:39

God gave Gideon the proof that He was calling him, and the servant of God obeyed, and went forward.

The Apostle Paul had a definite call from God. Do you not see him as he makes his way toward Damascus to persecute Christians, when Christ met him and Saul of Tarsus was cast to the ground? His conversion is an old story. It is one worth repeating. Think of it, and see that God calls in a definite way.

SECOND, THE CALL OF GOD TO SOME IS A PARTICULAR CALL. He wants you and your talents in a very definite way to serve Him.

Someone has put it in this little verse:

"Mine was the boat, but His the voice,
And His the call, yet mine the choice."

Frederick W. Robertson was a famous clergyman in England, but his desire had been to be a soldier. his family had served its country so. Young Robertson was appointed an officer of the Dragoon Guards. Proudly he donned his uniform and buckled his sword. Turning to admire himself in the mirror, suddenly something happened. He heard the call of Christ to devote himself to a higher cause. He took off his sword. He divested himself of his resplendent uniform and resumed his civilian clothes. Then he wrote his resignation. One of his biographers wittingly says that Robertson's first funeral service was his own. He buried the soldier, but Christ's servant was born.

God has a particular call for many of you. He has a task that you must do. Do not turn away from His call.

THIRD, THE CALL OF GOD IS A LOVING CALL. There is a place for the one who loves God and loves the souls of men. The love of Christ must be shed abroad in our hearts so that we will desire that they should hear the message of Christ and salvation.

When the Rev. George Pentecost had finished a discourse in the city of Edinburgh, Horatio Bonar put his hand upon his shoulder and said, "You love to preach to men, don't you?"

And Dr. Pentecost answered, "Yes."

Dr. Bonar said, "Do you love the men you preach to?"

When Jesus spoke to men, He loved them. *"But when he saw the multitudes, he was moved with compassion. . ."* (Matthew 9:36).

Your message, young friend, is the message of Christ, the Redeemer. You are sent to proclaim unto men that Jesus died for sinners. Someone had put it in this way:

"Preachers are sent, not to preach sociology, but salvation.

Not economics, but evangelism.
Not reform, but redemption.
Not culture, but conversion.
Not progress, but pardon.
Not a new social order, but the new birth.
Not revolution, but revival.
Not resuscitation, but resurrection.
Not a new organization, but a new creation.
Not democracy, but the Gospel.
Not civilization, but Christ.
We are ambassadors — not diplomatics."

The Lord may have spoken to some of you regarding a work that He wants you to do. Be sure that you give the right answer and do the thing that God is calling you to do.

## THE CALL TO MANY

There is a definite call which God gives to many men and women. It is the call to do His work in the local church and in the local field. All will not be singled out to be pastors and missionaries, but many will be called to be Sunday School teachers, youth leaders, and leaders of various enterprises in the local church.

I can never cease to thank God for a Sunday School teacher who pointed me to the Lamb of God. If it had not been for her faithfulness in proclaiming the Gospel, perhaps I would not have been saved. But because she earnestly and diligently gave the message of redeeming love, I heard and accepted Christ as my Saviour.

Someone has put the teaching business in these words:

> "I deal with the most potent, the most elusive, the most interesting thing in the world — the human

mind.

"Without me, there would be no progress. Future generations would lapse into savagery. Civilization would perish from the earth.

"Of all the professions, mine is the least paid in money, and the most richly rewarded in satisfaction.

"I am soon forgotten because what I achieve is written, not with ink or paper, but in human lives.

"I am a builder, but I do not build bridges—I build the builder of bridges.

"I am often unpopular because I must try to please so many people.

"My work is often undervalued because it is not understood."

These words may apply to the average teacher, but to the teacher of Sunday School and the teacher of religious subjects, the truth of this article can be multiplied a thousandfold. You, as a Sunday School teacher, are dealing with an eternal soul. Someone will hear of salvation and redeeming love because of your decision to give it.

The greatest happiness you can ever know will come by helping others. Determine that you will accept God's call and if it is to be a Sunday School teacher, a youth leader, or a leader in any organization or place of the church, accept it as a call from God.

"Others, Lord, yes, others,
Let this my motto be;
Help me to live for others,
That I may live for Thee."

## THE CALL TO EVERY CHRISTIAN

We began by specifying that some would be called into full time service as preachers, missionaries and Christian workers. This will not apply to everyone, but it will apply to some.

Second, I spoke to you of the call to many — the call to teach Sunday School, to lead young people, to work in the various agencies of the local church. Now, we come to consider the call to every child of God. What is this call?

FIRST, IT IS TO LIVE FOR CHRIST. Was there ever a day when there was such a need for men and women to live wholly and completely for Christ? Was there ever a day when the call was so urgent that we live without compromise for our Saviour? With the Apostle Paul, we need to say, *"For to me to live is Christ. . ."* (Philippians 1:21). Yes, and when we live for Christ, to die will be gain. Determine that from this hour on you will live for Christ, whatever the cost. Let others ridicule and others find fault, but let your heart and life be fully committed unto Him.

SECOND, THE CALL TO EVERY CHRISTIAN IS TO MANIFEST AN INTEREST IN OTHERS. We must not live for self, but we must live for those who are around us. One of the greatest evidences of your salvation will be your interest in someone else. Be concerned for the spiritual needs of those who are around you.

THIRD, THE CALL TO EVERY CHRISTIAN IS TO SPEAK TO MANY ABOUT OUR SAVIOUR. The greatest work in this world is to point hell-bound sinners to Jesus Christ. There is no task, no job, equal to this one. It is the greatest work of all.

Someone said that once only do we read that Jesus, a man of sorrows and acquainted with grief, actually rejoiced in spirit. It was not in the hour when He stood on the Mount of Transfiguration, His face shining like the sun in its strength. It was not when He rode along the streets of the capital, hearing the hosannas of the people. But it was in that hour when those seventy unnamed disciples returned from their evangelistic campaign, and reported how many had turned to Jesus and found the way of eternal life.

Is it not so that our Saviour is still rejoicing in this hour, when we bring others unto Him?

Let the call of God burn within your soul to yourself as one who needs to be busy giving out the Gospel.

Be blind to the things around you, so distracting and so disillusioning. Be blind to all things save the major business of getting out the Gospel of Jesus Christ.

Third, be blessed by the knowledge that you are doing what God has commanded you to do.

There is a definite call to every child of God. Will you take the call as it comes to you, and to the work which God has for you to do? Let your heart and life be burdened for the souls of others!

# 11
# Compel Them To Come In

> *"And the lord said unto the servant, Go out into the highways and hedges, and compel them to come in, that my house may be filled."*
>
> — Luke 14:23

The great gospel supper is now ready. God is sending out invitations. These invitations are extended by every servant of Christ, through churches, radio broadcasts, gospel tracts, gospel songs — yea, God's invitations to come to the gospel feast are now heard in all parts of the earth.

He invites men to come, for all things are now ready. Every spiritual and temporal blessing, for time and eternity, is now ready in Christ. There is no waiting period for those who will come.

He invites all classes to come, the poor, the maimed, the halt, and the blind.

He invites again and again, for yet there is room. Men are coming to the Saviour daily, but still there is room at the supper table. There is room for those who desire to partake of God's bountiful provision: Forgiveness, peace, salvation, and justification. You can thank God this morning that the door is still open. One day it will be closed. This day of grace will be over, but now the door is open to receive all who will come.

In the parable before us, a certain man made a great supper, and sent out many invitations. When the supper was ready he sent his servants to say to them that were bidden, *"Come, for all things are now ready·"* Those who had received invitations began to make excuses. One said, *"I have bought a piece of ground, and I must needs go and see it."* Another said, *"I have bought five yoke of oxen, and I must go prove them."* And another said, *"I have married a wife, and therefore, I cannot come."* When the servant came back and told the Lord these things, the master of the house became angry and sent his servant into the streets and lanes of the city to bring in the poor and the maimed, the halt, and the blind. When this was done, the servant said, *"Lord it is done as thou hast commanded, and yet there is room."* Then the lord said, *"Go out into the highways and hedges, and compel them to come in, that my house may be filled."* He had sent the servant into the streets and lanes of the city, and now he commands him to go outside the city to the highways and to the hedges along the highways and compel the people to come in.

What is the meaning of this phrase, "Compel them to come in"? It could read, "Constrain them to come in." We all know that we cannot force people to be saved. We cannot make them accept the Gospel, and partake of the bounties spread by the Lord. We cannot compel, but we can constrain or persuade men to be reconciled to God. A true disciple of Christ cannot be made by force, but by certain methods, we can help people to come to the Saviour.

How can we compel and constrain men to come to Christ?

## BY COMPASSION AND TEARS

Jesus looked upon the multitudes and had compassion. His heart was moved as He saw the people as sheep without a shepherd.

On one occasion the Master looked over the city of Jerusalem and He wept. His tears were for the people who had rejected Him, and had turned their backs upon God.

A real burden for souls will give us compassion, and will cause us to shed tears over lost sinners. Paul said, *"I say the truth in Christ, I lie not, my conscience also bearing me witness in the Holy Ghost, That I have great heaviness and continual sorrow in my heart. For I could wish that myself were accursed from Christ for my brethren, my kinsmen according to the flesh:"* (Romans 9:1-3).

I know of no better way to bring your friends and loved ones to the Saviour than to have a real compassion for them. It must be from the heart. Other hearts are moved when your heart is moved. We must not be afraid to make bare our hearts unto men, to let them know how deeply we feel the need of their salvation. We must not be afraid of showing our emotions.

## WE CAN CONSTRAIN MEN TO COME TO CHRIST BY EARNESTNESS AND ENTHUSIASM

If we worked at our daily jobs like we work at winning men to Christ, we would all starve within a few days. What a lack of earnestness and enthusiasm we find on the part of Christian workers. We cheer our favorite football team until our voices are gone, but we are afraid to show the slightest enthusiasm regarding spiritual matters. We fear that somebody might term us a fanatic; therefore, we draw into a shell, and we labor without fire and fervor.

There is nothing more wonderful to behold than the earnestness and enthusiasm of a new Christian, going after lost people. He disregards all interests. He forgets self. He will not take "No" for an answer. I have seen young Christians in our church with the fire and fervor of a new-born soul plead with lost men with the earnestness and zeal, exceeding the world's greatest evangelist. I have watched some of them in the early days when they scarcely knew one verse in the Bible, and yet they were not content for a Lord's Day to go by without bringing someone to the front, confessing Christ.

But tragedy of tragedies—I have seen the fire of soul-winning dwindle down to a mere ember. There was no longer any real enthusiasm for the task. They lost their first drive. They became professional. This is the saddest thing to behold in all Christian service. It is the thing that ruins preachers and evangelists. It is the dry rot that kills churches. 999 people out of 1,000 lose their earnestness and enthusiasm after the passing of a few weeks. Self-satisfaction sets in. A smugness possesses the soul. At first you were satisfied only when winning souls, but after a while you were satisfied if you merely taught a Sunday School class, or had a part in the Training Union.

Perhaps one person out of a thousand retains that first zeal and fervor. He is the exception, and God blesses his efforts.

The Apostle Paul never lost his first enthusiasm for soul-winning. Down to his last days, in the Roman dungeon, he was winning others to Christ. May God grant that we might recover that earnestness and enthusiasm which possessed our souls when first we found the Lord. God grant unto us the zeal of Andrew, who went after his brother, Simon Peter, and brought him at once to the Lord. Yes, we can constrain men to come to Christ if we are in dead earnest.

## WE CAN COMPEL OR CONSTRAIN MEN TO COME TO THE SAVIOUR BY PERSISTENT EFFORT

A spasmodic interest in lost souls will never impress lost men. A church that gets concerned two weeks out of the year, during a revival effort, about lost souls, and then forgets the dying, destitute condition of men for the rest of the year, will never compel anyone to come to Christ. The church that wins is the church that acts.

I received a letter from on outstanding evangelistic church in the north, and I found this motto on the bottom of the stationery: "Everlastingly at it." This church believes that persistent effort constrains men to be saved.

A few years ago I was visiting in Detroit, Michigan, and one night listened to a radio broadcast from a church, and heard this testimony. A young man was speaking: "I thank God for this church. I was lost in sin until a few weeks ago. More than a year ago the people of this church began to visit me. Every week someone would come to my door and invite me to church, and talk to me about my soul. I turned them away, and after a few visits, I became rude, but still they came on. Finally, I began to leave the house when I thought they were coming. I refused to answer the door, but still they came. Every week for a solid year someone from this church knocked on my door. They did not get angry at my rudeness. They did not give up, and finally, after an entire year, I agreed to visit the church on Sunday. I came to the church, heard the Gospel, and the Lord saved me. I am now busy for the Saviour, working as a superintendent of the young people's department. I thank God for the people who kept after me until I came under the sound of the Gospel."

That young man is a vigorous enthusiastic leader of young people. He was constrained to come to Christ because of the constant, persistent effort of others.

We, too, can constrain men to be saved by constantly keeping at it, refusing to take "No" for an answer, refusing to be discouraged, but always pressing the battle to the gates.

If we want to win souls, we must have compassion, tears, earnestness, enthusiasm, and back it up with persistent effort.

## WE CAN CONSTRAIN MEN TO COME IN TO THE GOSPEL BY FERVENT PRAYER

Our prayers must be more than merely saying, "Lord, bless and save my loved ones." We must pray and agonize for them by name. We must feel as did Samuel, that it is a sin if we fail to pray for others. The prophet said, ". . .*God forbid that I should sin against the Lord in ceasing to pray for you. . .*" (I Samuel 12:23).

Our prayers need to be offered, not only fervently, but faithfully. George Mueller, the mighty man of prayer, prayed for a group of his friends. He saw many of them saved, but some of them refused Christ. Shortly before his death, Dr. A. T. Pierson asked Mr. Mueller if he had every prayed for anything that God had not granted. Mr. Mueller told him that he had prayed sixty-two years, three months, five days, and two hours for two men to be converted, and neither of them showed any signs of that happening. Dr. Pierson said, "Do you expect God to convert them?"

Mr. Mueller replied, "Certainly. Do you suppose that God would put upon His child for sixty-two years the burden for two souls if He had no purpose of their conversion?" Shortly after Mr. Mueller died, Dr. Pierson was preaching in Bristol. He referred to this conversation and as he was leaving the building, a lady said, "One of those men was my uncle, and he was converted, and died a few weeks ago. The other man was also converted after the death of Mr. Mueller. His conversion took place in Dublin, Ireland."

Fervent and faithful prayer — this is our need. No doubt, thousands of prayers are never answered because we cease praying. It is said that a certain man spent thousands of dollars drilling for oil. He became discouraged and sold the field for a trifle. The purchaser started to drill, and in six hours, found a flowing rich oil well. The Christians lose heart in prayer just when the answer is about to be granted.

Let us pray for others — pray for them by name — pray for them daily — never give up praying for them if God has given you a burden for their souls.

## WE CAN CONSTRAIN MEN TO COME TO CHRIST BY CONSISTENT CHRISTIAN LIVING

Inconsistent living drives men away from the Saviour. Consistent living draws them to the Saviour. Paul said, "*. . .Destroy not him with thy meat, for whom Christ died*" (Romans 14:15).

The apostle's statement, *"No man lives to himself, and no man dies to himself,"* tells us of the power of influence.

We cannot expect to win souls if we are not living out Christ before them. Worldliness will hinder us in soul-winning. Lost men are alert to point out the deficiencies in the lives of Christians.

But lost people are just as alert to note the inconsistent living of loved ones and friends. They admire sincerity. They despise hypocrisy.

For many years I have been telling the story of the judge who was won to Christ after a long life of rejection. To the surprise of the pastor and people, he attended the church near home. When the invitation was given, he came to the front, and confessed his faith in Christ. The judge had been such a hard and difficult man to reach that the pastor was interested to know what it was that had touched his heart and brought him to the Saviour.

The judge said, "I'm a Christian today because of that little woman back there."

Near the rear of the church sat the judge's wife. She was bent forward with her face resting upon the back of a bench before her. She was weeping for joy.

The judge continued, "Through all of our married life, my wife has been a Christian. She attended the services Sunday morning,Sunday night,and the prayer service on Wednesday night. She never missed a revival service. Often when she would return home, I would ridicule her for going to the church. I made fun of her faith in prayer and the Bible. I did everything I could to discourage her, but she continued on.

"Perhaps the thing that disturbed me most was her prayer each evening before retiring. She would always kneel by the side of the bed. She did not pray aloud, but sometimes I could hear whispers of her prayer. I even made fun of this, but still she prayed on. I knew she was praying for me in every prayer, and it made me angry.

"A few nights ago my wife returned from a service in this church. I had already gone to bed, and pretended I was asleep. When she was ready to come to bed, she knelt and began to pray. I could hear some whispers as words escaped her lips, and then my wife began to pray and sob. She cried as though her heart would break and when I heard the prayer and the tears, I could stand it no longer. I got out of bed, and on my knees by the side of my wife, asked her to pray for me that I might be saved. She did pray for me, and God answered prayer and saved my soul. I am a Christian today because of the consistent faithful living of my wife."

Friends, that is what we mean by constraining or compelling people to come to the Lord. We cannot force anyone to be saved with the gun or the whip, but by compassion and tears, earnestness and zeal, persistent effort, and faithful prayers, and consistent Christ-like living, we can constrain men to be saved. Let us wrap around our lost loved ones the cords of love and compassion, and draw them to the Saviour.

Lost man, the feast is ready, the invitation is going out. God is calling you to come now. Come to God's banquet, partake of forgiveness, salvation, peace and eternal life.

# 12
# The Weeping Tourist

*"Serving the Lord with all humility of mind, and with many tears, and temptations, which befell me by the lying in wait of the Jews."*

—Acts 20:19

The apostle was an itinerant preacher. He traveled from place to place preaching the Word of God.

When I began my ministry many years ago, I made up my mind that I would imitate the Apostle Paul. By this I simply meant that I would not stay long in any one place. I read about how the apostle would go from town to town preaching the Gospel and establishing churches. I could see only the romance of his traveling and the excitement of new places. But it is apparent that God changed my mind and also the plan of my life. Hence, I have had these many years in one place—I rejoice in every year!

The Apostle Paul was a constant traveler. He was ever on the move. Oh, there were times when he settled down for a few months; but in the entire study of his life, we find that this man was traveling for God.

Remember, he was not traveling for pleasure. He was a tourist, but not as we think of tourists in this day. A tourist travels for pleasure. Paul traveled for a purpose! He was concerned about getting the Gospel to the ends of the earth; and to do this, he gave himself unstintingly.

I checked some of the authorities on the matter of travel. I discovered that almost four million people travel from the United States into foreign countries. We have around two million people coming from foreign countries into our nation every year. They are travelers. They are with us for just a brief time.

An issue of *Newsweek* tells us that the record number of tourists visiting Israel was made in 1968. In that year 432,000 came into the country. Another interesting thing given by *Newsweek Magazine* is that 60 percent of all the tourists were Jewish and 40 percent were Gentiles. I cannot help but think of all the millions and millions of dollars spent by the travelers in this nation and other nations.

Paul was not only a constant traveler but was a concerned traveler. In Acts 20 we learned a little about his tears. This man had a deep concern for people, and this led to the shedding of tears. A few good things could be made to happen in many of our foreign countries, if those who travel would do so with concerned hearts.

So we are thinking today about this "weeping tourist." But remember, Paul traveled for a purpose.

**WHEN PAUL TRAVELED, WHAT DID PAUL SEE?**

Our minds go back to that vigorous scene given to us in the first part of Acts 9. Paul was traveling on the road to Damascus going to that city to find men and women who professed to know Christ. There came a bright light shining from heaven down upon him and a voice spoke his name and questioned, *"Why persecutest thou me?"* Saul of Tarsus questioned, *"Who art thou, Lord? And the Lord said, I am Jesus whom thou persecutest: it is hard for thee to kick against the pricks"* (Acts 9:4,5).

And then we find the words, *"And he trembling and astonished said, Lord, what wilt thou have me to do. . ."* (Acts

9:6)? The Lord gave him instructions and told him what to do. It is my firm belief that Paul came to an acceptance of Jesus Christ on the road to Damascus. He was blind for a while and Ananias came to him and put his hands upon him that he might receive his sight.

Paul was sent out by the Lord to preach the Gospel. He did so with his eyes wide open.

FIRST, HE SAW A LOST MANKIND. We cannot forget that the Apostle Paul was himself a rabid opponent of Jesus Christ until He came face to face with the Lord. He was a leader of the multitudes that hated Christ and desired to exterminate this religion from the face of the earth.

But when Paul got saved, his eyes were opened and he saw men lost and condemned. At once he began to preach: Christ was the Son of God, and that He had the power to save and transform all who would come unto Him.

SECOND, PAUL SAW WHAT JESUS SAW. In our recent Bible-Missionary Conference we have had a number of men to read from Matthew 9 the words about the Lord Jesus Christ: *"But when he saw the multitudes, he was moved with compassion on them, because they fainted, and were scattered abroad as sheep having no shepherd"* (Matthew 9:36). Paul saw people as Jesus saw them — lost, undone, "as sheep without a shepherd."

THIRD, PAUL SAW THE SORE NEED OF MAN. Man's need is salvation. In the first chapters of the book of Romans, the apostle tells of the sinfulness of man. In vivid verses we are told of the rank, wicked sins of a lost mankind. Then the apostle points us to the remedy: salvation in Jesus Christ. Let me read you four verses:

> *"For all have sinned, and come short of the glory of God;*

*"Being justified freely by his grace through the redemption that is in Christ Jesus:*

*"Whom God hath set forth to be a propitiation through faith in his blood, to declare his righteousness for the remission of sins that are past, through the forbearance of God;*

*"To declare, I say, at this time his righteousness: that he might be just, and the justifier of him which believeth in Jesus."*

— Romans 3:23-26

FOURTH, PAUL SAW ENOUGH TO BRING TEARS. When Paul looked upon a lost mankind, he saw the trembling, weak and hopeless condition of men. This broke his heart and he wept! Paul said regarding his kinsmen, the Jews:

*"That I have great heaviness and continual sorrow in my heart.*

*"For I could wish that myself were accursed from Christ for my brethren, my kinsmen according to the flesh."*

— Romans 9:23

Paul cared! I don't suppose there is anything in this world we need more today than people who care. In a world that is careless and dirty and wicked and proud, we need men and women who care — men and women who are concerned about others, men and women who will go out of their way to win precious souls to the Saviour.

Perhaps I should add one more word about Paul the traveler and his sight. I need to say that he saw the only hope of man — Jesus Christ. It is high time that we see this also and that we declare it from every vantage point in our cities, in our states, and throughout this world. Christ is the only Saviour of lost mankind.

Now when Paul traveled around and saw lost mankind, he saw people as sheep without a shepherd. He saw the sore need of man — salvation. He saw enough to bring tears, and he saw the only hope of man — Jesus Christ.

**WHEN PAUL TRAVELED, WHAT DID PAUL DO?**

This is surely answered by the Word of God.

FIRST, HE PREACHED THE WORD. The heart of what he said is given to us in I Corinthians 15:3 —

> *"For I delivered unto you first of all that which I also received, how that Christ died for our sins according to the Scriptures."*
>
> — I Corinthians 15:3

He preached the death, burial, resurrection, and ascension of our Lord Jesus.

When Paul wrote to young Timothy, he said very plainly: *"Preach the Word; be instant in season, out of season; reprove, rebuke, exhort with all longsuffering and doctrine"* (II Timothy 4:2).

Here is the message that this lost world needs: the message of Christ the Redeemer. We must repeat and repeat: Christ died for our sins.

On one occasion when Lord Tennyson, the great poet, was on vacation in a country village, he asked an old Methodist woman, "Is there any news?"

"Well, Mr. Tennyson," she replied, "there is only piece of news that I know and that is: Christ died for sinners."

The poet responded, "That is old news and good news and new news."

SECOND, WHAT DID PAUL DO? He won souls. This was the aim of the ministry of Paul. John Wesley said to his preachers,

"You have only one business and that is the salvation of souls." We must count our ministries as failures if people are not getting saved.

You must count your Christian life as empty and selfish unless from your life some man, woman, some child is coming to Christ.

> "Must I go and empty handed?
> Must I meet my Saviour so?
> Not one soul with which to greet Him?
> Must I empty handed go?"

It is our business to press the claims of Jesus Christ upon lost sinners. They must be made to see that they are lost and undone and that only one can save them.

The daughter of General Booth, the founder of the Salvation Army, used to say to Christian workers, "My brothers, my sisters, it is your business when preaching the Gospel to shoot to kill."

I think a good word was given by a professor with regard to preaching. He said, "Don't preach above people's heads. The man who shoots above people's heads, the man who shoots above the target, does not prove that he has superior ammunition. He just proves he can't shoot."

Paul's business was the winning of souls, and this he did. Our business is to bring people to the Saviour.

THIRD, HE ENDEAVORED TO BUILD MEN INTO CHRIST LIKENESS. Let me repeat here a verse which has been one of my favorites through the years.

> *"For even hereunto were ye called:*
> *because Christ also suffered for us,*
> *leaving us an example, that ye should*
> *follow his steps."* —I Peter 2:21

The best advertising for Christ and for His work is that we show forth the Lord Jesus in our lives.

We must not fail as did Demas. Paul wrote of him, "*. . .Demas hath forsaken me, having loved this present world*" (II Timothy 4:2).

FOURTH, WHAT DID PAUL DO? He endeavored to make soulwinners of all believers. When Jesus said, "*Ye shall be witnesses unto me*" (Acts 1:8), the Saviour meant that every person is to be a witness. Some people have an idea that witnessing is just the business of preachers and missionaries but not so. Witnessing is the business of every child of God. Paul in his travels from place to place gave himself to the winning of souls and then laid upon the hearts of those who were won, the obligation to win others.

FIFTH, PAUL BUILT NEW TESTAMENT CHURCHES. The record of the churches is given to us in the New Testament. In Corinthians, in Galatians, in Ephesians, in Philippians, in Colossians, in Thessalonians, yes, here are the words given to the New Testament churches. Paul endeavored to build churches true to the Word of God. He called upon Christians to live separated from the world. He emphasized the leadership of the Holy Spirit.

And then he tried to press upon believers that they should have a zeal for souls.

I had no desire to build some sort of a new-fangled church in Highland Park. I was concerned about sticking by the Bible and building a church according to Bible standards. Yes, this meant the four things that I have given here: adherence to the Word, consecration of life, leadership by the Spirit, and a zeal for the lost. Other things are secondary. These things must be done or we fail our Lord.

## WHEN PAUL TRAVELED ON, WHAT DID PAUL LEAVE?

We have been looking at this "weeping tourist"—this man who traveled with a purpose. I believe I can answer this third question by giving three points.

FIRST, IN EVERY PLACE HE LEFT THE MESSAGE OF CHRIST. He preached the Word of God; and whether in the synagogues or on Mars Hill, he left the message of redeeming grace.

The message of salvation through Jesus Christ the Son of God was left in every place.

How I wish that we could all follow the apostle in this. I am sure that we could if we would allow the Holy Spirit to direct us. We should not be in any company of people for any period of time without leaving in their hearts the message of redeeming love through Christ Jesus. If we visit a home, we should leave behind us the message of Christ. If we visit a hospital room, we should leave the people the message of the Saviour.

SECOND, HE LEFT THE FRAGRANCE OF A BEAUTIFUL CHRISTIAN LIFE. May we not minimize this! We must so live before men that when we are out of their presence they still remember our faith in Christ, the purity of our lives, the correctness of our speech.

"Let others see Jesus in you.
Let others see Jesus in you.
Keep telling the story, be faithful and true.
Let others see Jesus in you."

It is tragic that some people live a long life and die leaving nothing to bless this world. Others live for years and at death leave only the blight of a wasted, sinful life.

Thank God for those who leave with us the remembrance of

a life lived for Christ. I do not say that this is easy, but it should be a sincere aim of every one of us.

When I say that Paul left the fragrance of a beautiful, Christian life, I am not saying that he did not suffer. I am simply saying that in his sufferings there was crushed from his life that beauty which is remembered to this day. The hatred that men had for him did nothing but bring out of his life the beauty of the transforming power of Christ. Hear him as he says, "*Of the Jews five times received I forty stripes save one. Thrice was I beaten with rods, once was I stoned, thrice I suffered shipwreck, a night and a day I have been in the deep*" (II Corinthians 11:24,25).

The thorn in the flesh which Paul called "*. . .the messenger of Satan to buffet me. . .*" (II Corinthians 12:7) was used to bring out of his life the sweet fragrance of heaven. Therefore, Paul could say, "*. . .I take pleasure in infirmities, in reproaches, in necessities, in persecutions, in distresses for Christ's sake: for when I am weak, then am I strong*" (II Corinthians 12:10).

THIRD, PAUL LEFT CONVERTS. This traveling evangelist — this weeping tourist — this man who traveled for a purpose won people to Christ and left behind him in every city converts to the Gospel of Jesus Christ. He went into cities and countries to win souls, and he won souls!

What I am saying here is not very pleasant to some of us, but I am emphasizing the fact that if you desire to win souls there is somebody that you can win. We must work at the job; we must pray for others; we must stay with the task until we see results.

I have a tendency to forget negative things, but we had a missionary who stood on this platform in one of our conferences that I have never forgotten. He said, "I have spent eight years on the mission field; but as far as I know, no one has been saved." The missionary went to justify his eight years of failure by telling about how hard people were and explaining the problems of evangelism in that particular area.

I'm sorry — that missionary could have won souls in that place! Some child could have been led to the Saviour. Some poor invalid standing on the threshold of eternity could have been brought to Christ. In eight long years there was surely some hungry soul who would have trusted the Lord Jesus.

A few days ago I read a story about "the world's strangest hotel." It told about a very beautiful building with clean white walls and skillfully carved red and black doors. It is an oriental hotel. Guests come from all over the world. This hotel is located not far from the China mainland. In the rooms of this hotel, there are 2,000 caskets. The hotel has three long halls and 108 rooms filled to capacity. Morning and evening the hotel staff burn fragrant incense to keep the guests happy while two great Alsatian dogs keep watch to prevent intruders from disturbing the "sleeping" occupants.

Most of the guests in the hotel are from the United States, but some come from Southeast Asia and some from South America. They arrive in all kinds of boxes and caskets. Quite naturally a man and woman are never given the same room unless they are husband and wife.

Two thousand bodies are occupying the rooms of this hotel, waiting for the time when they can be buried in China.

Someone said, "They are waiting for their last journey."

But my friends, their souls have already taken the last journey. They are now in heaven or in hell. John tells us, *"He that hath the Son hath life. . ."* (I John 5:12). There are doubtless some among the 2,000 who died as saved people. Their bodies will be raised at the first resurrection. They will come to stand before the great white throne judgment. This is the judgment of the lost dead.

There are only two kinds of people represented in the world's strangest hotel — the saved and the lost.

The great Apostle Paul gave his life to the proclamation of the Gospel. He traveled unceasingly. He labored uncomplainingly. He preached fervently. Paul said, *"For the wages of sin is death; but the gift of God is eternal life through Jesus Christ our Lord"* (Romans 6:23).

The people are divided today in the same way—the saved and the lost. Everything rests upon what we have done with the Lord Jesus.

If you have accepted Him already, we rejoice with you in your salvation. If you have not accepted Him, we plead with you to now repent of your sin — the sin of unbelief — and now receive Christ as your Saviour.

# 13
# The Sweetest Story Ever Told

*"For God so loved the world, that he gave his only begotten Son, that whosoever believeth in him should not perish, but have everlasting life."*

—John 3:16

For over forty years in the Highland Park Baptist Church we repeated the story of the Lord Jesus and of salvation in His name, over and over again. For over forty years we broadcast daily on Chattanooga radio stations telling the story of Christ. For over forty years we preached the message of our Saviour from the pulpit many times each week.

We have had the joy of telling to the world: "The Sweetest Story Ever Told."

The Bible is filled with the stories of men and their relationship to God.

The story of Abraham and Isaac is a story of sweetness and of love. Abraham loved his son, but obeyed God when he took him out to offer him as a sacrifice.

The stories of Moses are of unfailing interest to young and old. God's call to Moses at 80 years of age reveals the sweetness of our Lord and His patience in dealing with men.

Who can read the story of Daniel wthout detecting the sweetness of God? When the man of God was cast into the den of lions—God was present. He closed the mouths of the lions and delivered his prophet.

But of all the stories in the world, the sweetest story is that of our Lord Jesus.

He came for a purpose. He said to Pilate, "*. . . To this end was I born, and for this cause came I into the world, that I should bear witness unto the truth. . .*" (John 18:37). The purpose of our Lord's coming was to die upon a cross that sinners might be saved.

He fulfilled that purpose. He died. He arose from the dead. He ascended on high.

It is the children's song, but it has in it a touch of sweetness attached to the story of Jesus.

> "I think when I read that sweet story of old,
> When Jesus was here among men
> How He called little children as lambs to His fold,
> I should like to have been with them then.
> I wish that His hands had been placed on my head,
> That His arms had been thrown around me,
> And that I might have seen His kind look when He said,
> 'Let the little ones come unto me.'
> "Yet still to His footstool in prayer I may go
> And ask for a share in His love;
> And if I now earnestly seek below,
> I shall see Him and hear him above
> In that beautiful home He has gone to prepare
> For all who are washed and forgiven;
> And many dear children are gathering there,
> 'For of such is the kingdom of heaven."

The story of our Saviour is the story of divine truth. We have before us the message of man's sin, of God's love, and of the death of God's Son.

Here is the story of heavenly compassion. "*For God so loved the world, that he gave his only begotten Son. . .*" (John 3:16). "*But God commendeth his love toward us, in that, while we were yet sinners, Christ died for us*" (Romans 5:8).

The man who dislikes the story of Jesus, the man who sneers at this story, the man who rejects the message of our Christ — that man is lost! There is no other way for one to be saved but through the Lord Jesus Christ.

Now what must I do with this story?

FIRST, I MUST BELIEVE IT. I must receive the Christ who came into this world to die for sinners. My Bible says, "*But as many as received him, to them gave he power to become the sons of God, even to them that believe on his name*" (John 1:12).

SECOND, NOT ONLY MUST I BELIEVE THE STORY AND RECEIVE THE CHRIST, BUT I MUST LIVE MY CHRISTIAN FAITH BEFORE OTHERS. The Bible says, "*For none of us liveth to himself, and no man dieth to himself*" (Romans 14:7). We are commanded by the Word of God to live out Christ Jesus before others.

THIRD, I MUST TELL IT EVERYWHERE. We are commanded to be witnesses —"*. . .ye shall be witnesses unto me. . .*" (Acts 1:8). We have no command to be theologians or debaters. We are to be men and women who tell the story of Jesus Christ. I am to tell it to all people, the rich, the poor, the high, the low.

The Apostle Peter told the story. On the day of Pentecost he preached. He gave the message of Jesus Christ, and 3,000 souls were saved.

Stephen told the story. The hand of God was upon him. He witnessed with power and God used his witness.

Philip told the story. He preached to the people in Samaria and in the desert country, and God blessed his preaching.

Saul of Tarsus was converted, and he told the story. Over one half of the book of Acts is devoted to a recounting of the experiences which Paul had as he told the story of Jesus Christ.

John told the story — how effectively, how beautifully, and how simply.

I repeat again, this is the story that we must know if we are to be saved, and this is the story that must be ingrained into our minds and hearts if we are to serve God effectively.

This is the story that we must treasure. Of all things in this world, there is nothing so precious as the story of Jesus Christ.

Here is the story that we must tell. We must tell it to people everywhere. They must know that Christ is able to save unto the uttermost all who will come unto Him.

"I love to tell the story of unseen things above,
Of Jesus and His glory, of Jesus and His love;
I love to tell the story because I know 'tis true,
It satisfies my longings as nothing else can do.

"I love to tell the story more wonderful it seems
Than all the golden fancies of all our golden dreams;
I love to tell the story — It did so much for me,
And that is just the reason I tell it now to thee."

## THE STORY MUST BE GIVEN IN THE HOME

Emphasis is given, in the Word of God, to this matter of the Christian home. in the Old Testament there were many God-fearing homes. In the New Testament there were homes that received the Lord Jesus Christ and were dedicated unto Him. Adults must know the story of Jesus.

Children must hear the story of Jesus Christ.

Homes must be brought to the Saviour. Dr. Pat Neff, former governor of the state of Texas, once said, "Tear down the church and schools, and the homes will build them back, but tear down the homes and everything will crumble."

Parents must know Jesus Christ, and children must be brought to know Him. It is said that a child can read his parents' character before he knows the alphabet. The child is the canvas upon which the father and mother paint their own portrait. We all should pray earnestly that God will make our homes to be what they should be. We acknowledge our failures, but this is not enough. We must tackle the problems with determination that Christ might control and direct the home.

There is a touching story told about a young boy in a British boarding school, a boy whose mother had died in giving him birth. His father was employed in a remote foreign country. They had never met face to face, but all around Jimmy's room were evidences of his father's love for him: gifts galore from a distant land, letters which arrived faithfully every week, and above his bed a large portrait of his father.

His loneliness was bearable until the holidays came; as here the boys all eagerly talked about going home to see there parents, Jimmy hung his head because he had not parents whom he could visit and no home to go to.

He wrote his father, "This school is an awfully lonely place when all my friends are gone. Sometimes I wonder if I will ever see your face."

One day Jimmy went to his mail box and discovered a letter marked "Special." He tore it open.

"Dear Son, I will be arriving by steamer this Friday. I was able to get a short leave of absence. You and I will have a wonderful time together, won't we? Love, your Father."

Early Friday morning Jimmy was down at the docks. His heart beating excitedly at the realization that soon he would see his father in person. At ten o'clock the steamer pulled in and docked and the first man down the gangplank was the man Jimmy had been waiting for. They threw their arms around each other. All Jimmy could say was one word, "Father."

Before this moment the word "father" had been only a word. Now it became a reality.

I give that story to say to you that faith in our Christ must become a reality, and that mothers and fathers, and boys and girls, must be brought to know the Lord Jesus as a personal Saviour.

## THE STORY MUST BE SHOUTED TO THE WHOLE WORLD

We must not forget the missionary command of our Saviour, *"And he said unto them, Go ye into all the world, and preach the Gospel to every creature"* (Mark 16:15).

The great commission is given in the four Gospels and also in the book of the Acts. The book of the Acts is an account of the spread of the Gospel through men who obeyed the great commission of our Lord.

The sweetest story ever told must be shouted to the whole world. All men must hear for all men are lost. Self-righteous ones must hear. The wicked and the dirty must hear. The young and the old, yea, all must come to Jesus and be saved.

We must shout the story in the streets, in the jails, in the business houses, in the schools and everywhere.

There are four things that this story will do. FIRST, THIS STORY BRINGS LIFE. Jesus said, *". . .I am the way, the truth, and the life: no man cometh unto the Father but by me"*

(John 14:6). Again, Jesus said, *"And I give unto them eternal life; and they shall never perish, neither shall any man pluck them out of my hand"* (John 10:28).

SECOND, THIS STORY BRINGS LAUGHTER. Often we find the command that we are to "rejoice." One of the commands given by the Apostle Paul to the Thessalonians was this: *"Rejoice evermore"* (I Thessalonians 5:16).

THIRD, THIS STORY BRINGS LOOSING. We are loosed from our sins. We are loosed from the old way of life and set free to serve Christ. *"If the Son therefore shall make you free, ye shall be free indeed"* (John 8:36).

FOURTH, THIS STORY BRINGS A LOAD. Yes, a burden for the souls of men. This we must have. We must declare the Gospel everywhere. The story must be shouted to the whole world.

David Hume, a Scottish deist, once wrote an essay on the sufficiency of the light of nature and reason. A certain Doctor Robertson, an evangelical theologian, answered Hume's essay by writing on the necessity of divine revelation and pointing out the insufficiency of the light of nature.

One evening Hume visited Robertson and the time was spent in conversation on the subjects about which both had written. Friends of both who were present that night said that Robertson reasoned with unusual clearness and power.

Whether Hume was convinced by Dr. Robertson's reasoning or not, we are not told. At any rate, he did not acknowledge his conviction. As Hume arose to leave, he bowed politely to those in the room and then caught sight of Dr. Robertson reaching for a lamp to show him the way out of the house and down the stair. Hume immediately said, "Pray, don't trouble yourself, sir. I find the light of nature always sufficient."

But as he left the house, Hume stumbled in the dark passageway and pitched down the steps into the street. Running after him with the lamp, Dr. Robertson held it over him and whispered softly, "You had better have a light from above, Mr. Hume!"

Yes, man needs light. Man needs Jesus Christ who is "*. . .the light of the world*" (John 8:12). We must shout this message to the whole world, for the world is in darkness and only Jesus Christ can give life and light.

## THE STORY MUST BE GIVEN TO THE DYING

"*And as it is appointed unto men once to die, but after this the judgment. . . .*"

— (Hebrews 9:27).

We are all in the ranks of the dying. We die moment by moment but I am thinking especially of those who may be on the threshold of death.

Death may be near for someone in this service tonight. I do not know, nor do you. Therefore, it behooves me to give the story to you with an urgency.

Two thieves were crucified alongside of Jesus on Calvary's hill. One thief looked upon the Lord Jesus Christ and acknowledged Him as Saviour and said, "*. . .Lord, remember me when thou comest into thy kingdom*" (Luke 23:42). That dying one heard Jesus say, "*. . .Verily I say unto thee, Today shalt thou be with me in paradise*" (Luke 23:43).

It is imperative that the message be given to dying men. Some time ago Tommy Manville, the playboy of Manhattan, died. He died at 73 years of age after several years of poor health. At the time of his death, "Marrying Manville," as he was called was living with his eleventh wife, a 26 year old German girl whom he married in 1960. Manville inherited ten million dollars from his father. His other assets included lots of shares of the Johns-Manville Company, which his father had owned before his death. The flamboyant millionaire playboy once said he spent over a million and a quarter dollars on his divorcees.

The story might have some interest to newspaper readers, but as far as I'm concerned, Tommy Manville died as a poor sinner of the world. As far as we know, he died without any faith in Christ. He died with his sins upon his soul. I am sure the story must have been given him; but doubtless in his wealth and weakness he turned away from it.

I repeat, the story must be given to the dying. Dr. Blanchard, one-time president of Wheaton College, gave this remarkable testimony:

> "Some few years ago an engineer on the Pennsylvania lines became very ill and was taken to the hospital in pain. As his illness continued he wasted away to less than 100 pounds. Finally doctors pronounced him dead.
>
> "The wife strongly insisted her husband wasn't dead, or if he was, God would bring him back from the dead. 'For,' she said, 'I have prayed for his conversion for twenty-seven years. God is faithful. Do you think God would let him die now after I have prayed for him for twenty-seven years and he is not saved?'
>
> "A screen was drawn around the hospital bed to separate the living from the dead. So great was the wife's insistence that her husband was not dead that other physicians were brought in. One after another, they made their examinations and confirmed the verdict that the patient was dead.
>
> "The wife still believed that God would not fail her, so

> she knelt by the bed in expectation. A nurse placed a pillow under her knees for comfort. One hour, two hours, three hours passed. The screen still stood by the bed. Four hours, five hours, six hours, seven hours, thirteen hours passed, and in spite of loved ones and friends and doctors, she refused to move from the side of the bed. 'No,' she said, 'He has to be saved.'"

Dr. Blanchard said that at the end of thirteen hours, the husband opened his eyes and she said, "What do you wish, my dear?"

He said, "I want to go home."

Dr. Blanchard said that the husband was restored to perfect health and was soon converted and became a strong witness for Jesus Christ.

An Associated Press story told about Pastor Rees Evans, 80 years of age, preaching his own funeral sermon. There were 1,000 people who turned out to hear him.

The coffin was placed at the front of the auditorium. On the pulpit stand was a tape recorder. The sermon had been recorded five years previously. Only his middle-aged son knew about it, and he was sworn to secrecy.

The sermon lasted for an hour and was interspersed with hymns which the pastor had composed himself.

At the end of the sermon, he addressed a special message to his widow and the family who sat on the front row: "We shall meet again —."

The story is interesting, but actually we are preaching our funeral sermons day by day. Paul preached his own funeral. He said, *"For I am now ready to be offered, and the time of my departure is at hand. I have fought a good fight, I have finished my course, I have kept the faith: Henceforth there is laid up for me a crown of righteousness, which the Lord, the righteous judge, shall give me at that day: and not to me only, but unto all them also that love his appearing"* (II Timothy 4:6-8).

My dear friend, what is the message that you are preaching to the world through your life? Are you telling people of your faith in Jesus Christ? When you come to the time of death, will men be able to stand and say that you were a Christian?

There is one way to settle this matter, and that is to repent of your sin of unbelief and believe in Jesus Christ as Saviour.

The jailor said, "*. . .Sirs, what must I do to be saved? And they said, Believe on the Lord Jesus Christ, and thou shalt be saved. . .*" (Acts 16:30,31). Come to Him now!

# Part Two
# Keep It Burning

# 14
# This Little Light of Mine

> *"Let your light so shine before men, that they may see your good works, and glorify your Father which is in heaven.."*
>
> —John 3:16

Charles Haddon Spurgeon said, "He is wisest who reads both the world-book and the Word-book as two volumes of the same work, and feels concerning them, 'My Father wrote them both.'"

In Psalm 19 David pictures the heavens as preaching. He said, *"The heavens declare the glory of God; and the firmament sheweth his handywork. Day unto day uttereth speech, and night unto night sheweth knowledge. There is no speech nor language, where their voice is not heard. Their line is gone out through all the earth, and their words to the end of the world. . ."* (Psalm 19:1-4).

One person said, "The preaching of the heavens is wonderful in three respects; first, as preaching all the night and all the day without intermission; second, as preaching in every kind of language; third, as preaching in every part of the world, and in every parish of every part, and in every place of every parish."

Another has said, "Though all preachers on earth should grow silent and every human mouth cease from publishing the glory of God, the heavens above would never cease to declare and proclaim His majesty and glory. Though nature be hushed and quiet, when the sun in his glory has reached the zenith in the azure sky — though the world keep her silent festival, when the stars shine brightest at night — yet says the Psalmist, they speak, aye, holy silence itself is a speech provided there be the ear to hear it."

The witness of the heavens is never interrupted. It is continuous, going on day and night. Instruction is given without a single break. What power and what glory! Their line is gone out through all the earth, and to the ends of the earth their words. It is a universal witness, extending everywhere.

As the heavens preach, so are we commissioned by the Lord to preach. he said, "*. . .Go ye into all the world, and preach the gospel. . .*" (Mark 16:15). Then again He said, "*But ye shall receive power, after that the Holy Ghost is come upon you: and ye shall be witnesses unto me both in Jerusalem, and in all Judaea, and in Samaria, and unto the uttermost part of the earth*" (Acts 1:8).

As David said of the heavens, "*. . .their line is gone out through all the earth. . .*" (Psalm 19:4) so must this same thing be said of our church. We are to extend lines — life-saving lines throughout all the earth, and we are to send the Word of God to the end of the world.

Jesus said, "*Ye are the light of the world. . .let your light so shine. . .*" Paul said to the Philippians, "*Ye are to shine as lights in the world, holding forth the word of life*" (Philippians 2:15b,16a).

Now, may we repeat three simple things.

## THE LIGHT OF THE LOCAL CHURCH IS TO SHINE TO THE ENDS OF THE EARTH

Through the missionary programs, the sun should never

set on the work of the local church. We thankGodthat we can say this today of the Highland Park Baptist Church. We have missionaries around the world who are giving forth the Gospel.

Thank God the work never ceases. When we sleep, the missionaries on the other side of the world are awake and working. When we arise to work each day, they are able to get a little sleep.

Our field is the world. Jesus said, *"For God so loved the world, that he gave his only begotten Son. . ."* (John 3:16). As God loved the world of men, so are we to love the world of men, and to do all we can to bring them the message of God's love and of Christ's death.

Much of the world is still in heathen darkness. Many millions have never heard of Jesus Christ for even the first time. As a church, may we hear the cry of those who are dying and sinking into eternal darkness.

Let us realize our responsibility to the people of China, of Japan, of Africa, India, Europe, South America, the islands of the sea — yea, to the whole world.

Openyour ears to hear the cry of those who have no hope. Think what it would be like to be without Christ. Try to imagine the emptiness of living without Him, and of having only fear of death and eternity.

At this time we are supporting through our church and the World Wide Mission Fund, 560 missionaries. The number should be much increased.

May we set ourselves to pray and to give that more might be done.

## YOUR LIGHT AS AN INDIVIDUAL CHRISTIAN IS TO SHINE TO THE ENDS OF THE EARTH

You say, "My light is so small. I cannot project it to the uttermost part of the earth." In this you are wrong. God has so made a way that you can shine, even as the sun, to the ends of this earth.

FIRST, BY FERVENT PRAYER YOUR LIGHT CAN SHINE. How much we miss by not realizing the power of prayer! how drastically we fail our missionaries by not praying for them! How terribly we hinder the work of missions by not praying definitely for the salvation of souls in all parts of the world! Almost every prayer should include the work of missions around the world.

Paul wrote to the churches and constantly asked for their prayers in his behalf. Though the people in Thessalonica, Corinth, and Ephesus remained in their local communities, by prayer they could send forth the light to many cities, towns, and villages.

SECOND, YOU CAN GIVE FORTH YOUR LIGHT TO THE ENDS OF THE WORLD BY THE GIVING OF MONEY. The amount of your giving will depend on the burden which you may have. How little we give to missions! The American people spend billions for pleasure, but give only pennies for missions. All Christians in our land, that is, professing Christians, did not average giving as much as one stick of chewing gum each to the work of missions last year.

How should you give? It is my conviction that the work of missions should be carried on through the local church. This church must be missionary-minded. As you place your money here, you can give to missions around the world, and you can pray for the individual missionaries we support. If you have a special sum that you want to give to missions, and you desire to designate it to a certain cause or field, this can be done through the church. We are here to help you make your light shine to the ends of the earth.

THIRD, YOUR LIGHT AS AN INDIVIDUAL CHRISTIAN CAN SHINE TO THE ENDS OF THE WORLD, IN SOME CASES, BY YOUR GOING TO THE ENDS OF THE EARTH. This will not touch all of us, but it will touch some. Thank God for those who are going to carry their God-given lights to lands of heathen darkness. They are willing to sacrifice, to leave home, to suffer loneliness, in order that the Gospel might be taken to others.

Missionary volunteers, rejoice that God has called you! Do not turn back for a single moment. Go straight forward. The road may be hard, long, and dusty, but travel it, and Christ has promised to go with you.

A few days ago, I had a most unusual experience.I walked into a strange church during the song service, and sat down near the end of a bench. As I sat there, I glanced to one side,and saw the shiniest pair of shoes I think I have ever seen. they were beautiful shoes, unscarred, and unmarked. They were men's shoes. I thought to myself, "This is a very neat person." In a moment I looked again to the person sitting near me, and I saw that he was seated in a wheel chair. Later I discovered that he was paralyzed from the waist down. A little later he said that he wanted to talk to me, and he told me of his great desire to serve God, but he said, "What can I do? I am paralyzed. I cannot be a missionary. I cannot go to distant lands. I cannot carry on the work of a pastor. What can I do?"

His shoes were shiny because he could not go. Some of you have shiny shoes because you refuse to go. My friend, if God has called you, and your health permits it, go to the mission field. Let your feet carry you along pathways untouched by missionaries. Take with you your light as a Christian, and let it shine in the darkness.

There is no escaping our responsibility to shine to the ends of the earth. Christ has spoken. The commission has been given, and we must obey. Some of you will recall that Dr. W. B. Riley chose Billy Graham to be his successor as president of Northwestern Schools in Minneapolis. According to the story, he told Billy very definitely that he wanted him to take up the work to carry on for him. I do not know for certain, but it is likely that the young man gave his word to Dr. Riley that he would take the work. As you know, he did so for a while, and then God began to use him as an evangelist. He felt that he could not carry on the work of the school and be gone continuously in revival campaigns. Therefore, he resigned as president of the school and severed all connections with it. I have no word of criticism to say to this. I am sure that God has been leading in it all. But here is the point I wish to make: Billy Graham can escape from the responsibility of the Northwestern Schools, even though Dr. Riley had requested that he carry on in his stead. But neither Billy Graham nor you can escape the responsibility of shining to the ends of the earth.

## YOUR LIGHT MUST SHINE ALSO RIGHT WHERE YOU ARE

Jesus gave an exhortation that we should let our lights shine, and it is implied that there is a danger; yes, the danger that your light might be hidden.

Some lights have been placed under a bushel so that they cannot shine unto all that are in the house.

There are many bushels that hide the lights of Christians. The bushel of neglect and indifference has hidden the light of many. The bushel of sin and worldliness has covered other lights. The bushel of greed and avarice has hindered other lights from shining.

Remember, hiding your light is dangerous, both to you and to others. It is dangerous to you because it means failure to obey Christ, and will take away the joy of the Lord from your heart. It is dangerous to others because of the hiding of your light, souls will be left in darkness, and will go to hell. If you love your Lord and you care for the souls of men, let your light shine.

Live so that your light can shine.

Speak and let others know of your faith in Christ.

Be a testimony for God wherever you go. In the home, let your light shine. In your office, in the school, on the streets, everywhere, let your light shine before men.

Perhaps right now you are conscious that some things are hindering the outward shining of your light. Confess and forsake the wrong that you may shine for Christ.

# 15
# Visionary and Missionary

*". . .Lift up your eyes, and look on the fields, for they are white already to harvest."*

—John 4:35

The Son of God was both visionary and missionary. His eyes were open to the perishing multitudes. He saw them as sheep having no shepherd. His heart understood their great need, but Christ was also a missionary. He did something for those who had such great spiritual need.

Today we have many Christians who are neither visionary nor missionary. They do not see and they do not act. Then again, we have some who see the need, but do nothing about it. They know that every hour hundreds of sinners are dying without Christ, but they do not give themselves, nor do they give their money for the spread of the Gospel.

There are three words I want you to consider in this chapter.

## VISION

The author of Proverbs says in chapter 29, verse 18, *"Where there is no vision, the people perish. . ."*

Jesus said to his disciples, *"Lift up your eyes and look on the fields, for they are white already to harvest"* (John 4:35). This was plainly a rebuke to the disciples, for they did not consider Samaria a field for their services. Judaea and Galilee were all right, but Samaria was out of bounds in their thinking.

Our vision certainly needs to be threefold:

FIRST, WE MUST SEE A LOST WORLD. Some people have never been able to see beyond their own homes. Others cannot see beyond their communities. Some have a vision that takes in their home city. A few can think of the nation, and very, very few have a world-wide vision.

We must all exercise care that we do not lose our vision in the urgency of the work here at hand. Our vision of a lost world must take in all countries, all colors, and all races. We must see that all men out of Christ are perishing, without hope, and are lost forever more.

There must not be a discrimination in our thinking against any person because of his color, his race. The Negro needs Jesus. The Jew needs Jesus, and the Japanese and the Germans, yes, all men need the Saviour.

We cannot be a missionary unless we first catch a vision of perishing men. It is said that over two thousand people die every hour. Of the two thousand people who pass away at least two-thirds of them do not know Jesus. We need to think upon this tragic figure until we are concerned for those who die without Christ.

SECOND, WE NEED TO SEE A SUFFICIENT SAVIOUR. How hopeless would be our contemplation of a lost world if we could not also think of Jesus who has power to save to the uttermost. The children have a song which says,

"Jesus loves the little children
All the children of the world;
Red and yellow, black and white,
They are precious in His sight,
Jesus loves the little children of the world."

The Lord Jesus Christ died as much for the black man as for

the white. He died that all men might be saved who would come unto Him by faith. There is no one too hard for Jesus. There is no one too degraded for His saving power if they will but come.

THIRD, WE NEED TO SEE OUR PLACE IN THE LORD'S WORK. We must have a vision of what we can do. A Moravian church in Germany had such a vision. Pastor Harmes led his poor church to a great vision of world-wide missions. In forty years that one church had put into the field more than three hundred fifty missionaries, and supported them. One out of every sixty members was a missionary. Let us see our place in the Lord's work.

## ACTION

It is not enough to have a vision of the lost world and a sufficient Saviour and our own place in the Lord's work. We must go into action for Jesus.

The Saviour said, *"As the Father hath sent me, even so send I you"* (Mark 16:15).

We must obey our great Captain. Christ commands us to go, and we must go. Christians need to be active in His service. No one can be a missionary without having a vision, but above all, we must not stop with the vision, but must go into definite missionary action.

Who is a missionary? A missionary is one who goes across the street, or across the sea, to talk to a soul about Christ. Some of us may leave our home land, but we are not less missionaries if we are willing to cross the street, or cross the city, to tell others about Jesus.

The early church was both visionary and missionary. They did not need a Missionary Society — the entire church was a missionary society. The men and the women, the boys and girls, who were followers of Jesus, considered themselves as missionary interests to a small band of women in the church. The men do not think of missions. The young people are not educated along missionary lines, and the church becomes as dead as the Dead Sea.

The work of missions is two-fold. It is given to us here in John 4, in these words of our Master:

> *"And he that reapeth receiveth wages, and gathereth fruit unto life eternal: that both he that soweth and he that reapeth may rejoice together.*
>
> *"And herein is that saying true, One soweth, and another reapeth."*
>
> —John 4:36,37

In the work of missions, it is true that some sow the seed and others come to reap. A pastor may faithfully preach for six or twelve months and after this time an evangelist comes who has the joyous privilege of reaping the harvest. But according to the Word of God, he that soweth and he that reapeth have the same wages. Therefore, we must not disparage those who spend their time in sowing. The important thing is to get out the Word of God and to beseech men to be reconciled unto God.

Let us pray each day that God will give this church a vision, and then will stir within us the desire to do something with our vision. May the day soon come when at least one hundred of our members are on the mission fields, telling the story of Jesus. May God keep us busy during the day here in our city and homeland, and when night falls and we retire to our beds for sleep, may we have missionary representatives in China who arise to do business for the King.

Let us remember this: When Christians are like Jesus, they will be missionary minded. The anti-missionary Christian has no part with the Saviour who left heaven's glory to come into this world to die for sinners.

## SALVATION

The object of vision and action is the bringing of people unto Jesus.

The words we are studying were spoken to the disciples just after Jesus had led the woman at the well to salvation. The woman went away to tell others about Christ, and while she was gone, the disciples returned to the Master, and brought Him food, which he refused, saying "*. . .My meat is to do the will of him that sent me, and to finish His work*" (John 4:34).

What was the will of the Father who sent Jesus into the world? Surely it was to deliver lost sinners from the hands of the devil, and to bring them from death into life. Christ came for the purpose of saving people. This was the Father's will and this was the Saviour's work.

The disciples often had their attention drawn to some other object in life. They sometimes forgot their high calling, and began to quarrel among themselves. They behaved as normal, average, every-day Christians behave now. But Jesus had only one aim in life — the salvation of others.

May the day soon come when many of us shall have such singleness of purpose as did our loving Saviour. You may have to work in the office, the shop, or the plant, to make a living, but the whole purpose of your life wIll be to bring others to Jesus. And yet again, there are many who feel that God would have them in full time service for Him. They will therefore renounce all ambition and worldly gain and separate themselves to the work of the Gospel.

May God give us a vision of a lost world. May we do something for others and may the object of all our work be the salvation of the lost.

"Sudden, before my inward, open vision;
  Millions of faces crowded up to view;
Sad eyes that said, 'For us is no provision,
  Give us your Saviour too.'
"'Give us,' they cry, 'your cup of consolation,
  Never to our out-reached hands 'tis passed
"We long for the desire of every nation,
  And, 'Oh, we die so fast.'"

# 16
# Stirring Up Dust

*". . .Either what woman having ten pieces of silver, if she lose one piece, doth not light a candle, and sweep the house, and seek diligently till she find it?"*

—Luke 15:8

There are three main reasons why Christians do not obey the command of Christ and seek the lost.

FIRST, THEY DO NOT KNOW THE WORTH OF A SOUL. If ever we understand the preciousness of one eternal soul, we will go after it. If we can understand that one soul is worth more than all the wealth of a city, we will seek to rescue that soul from eternal loss.

SECOND, CHRISTIANS DO NOT FULLY BELIEVE THAT ALL MEN ARE LOST AND BOUND FOR HELL WITHOUT CHRIST. They read the words in the Bible, but the full meaning does not grip their hearts. We will never be soul winners until we understand that a soul away from Christ is lost, doomed, and damned.

THIRD, MOST PEOPLE ARE SELFISH. Paul said, *"For all seek their own, not the things which are Jesus Christ's* (Philippians 2:21). The average Christian is content with what he has. There is no tug at his soul to go after others. Too many Christians seek their own ease. Going after the lost is work, hard work, and they do not want to work.

Jesus gave three parables to illustrate the love of God for lost men. In the first parable there were a hundred sheep. One was lost. The shepherd left the ninety and nine and went after the lost one. He found it, laid it upon his shoulders, and came home rejoicing.

In the second parable, a woman had ten pieces of silver. She lost one, and immediately instituted a search for it. She lighted a candle, swept the house, and searched till she found it. And then she called in her neighbors and said, "*. . .Rejoice with me; for I have found the piece I had lost*" (Luke 15:9).

In the third parable there were two sons. One son decided to leave home. He took his portion of the inheritance and went to a far country. There he wasted all in riotous living. He began to be in want, and lowered himself to feeding swine. While in this condition, memory began to work, and he came to himself. He came home and the father received him joyfully.

*"For this my son was dead, and is alive again; he was lost, and is found. And they began to be merry"* (Luke 15:24).

Taking them together, these parables of our Saviour present three thoughts.

## THE MISERY OF A LOST SOUL

The sheep, away from the fold, out in the wilderness, was surely miserable and unhappy. The same was true of the boy in the hogpen. He was hungry, lonely and conscious of his sin.

There is no abiding happiness without Christ. Never be deceived by the actions or words of people. A person may appear lighthearted and gay, but without Christ there is no real happiness.

I have seen men who appeared to be self-sufficient, perfectly poised, confident, and happy. They were successful business men. But when I began to talk to them, I found misery in their souls.

God says there is unrest, dissatisfaction and unhappiness in the souls of the lost. Isaiah 57:20 tells us, *"But the wicked are like the troubled sea, when it cannot rest, whose waters cast up mire and dirt."* Paul tells us, *"Tribulation and anguish, upon every soul of man that doeth evil; of the Jew first, and also of the Gentile"* (Romans 2:9).

There is no mechanical meter to measure the misery of a lost man. Only God can know the recesses of men's hearts. He knows the agony of the lonely hours when men face the fact of their sin. Although we cannot measure misery, we do know what brings it to the hearts of the lost.

FIRST, SEEKING PEACE AND FINDING IT NOT. *"There is not peace, saith my God, to the wicked"* (Isaiah 57:21).

Christ is the source of peace. Zacchaeus had no soul until he met Jesus. The Apostle Paul, though occupying a high position among the Jews, was a man of misery until he accepted Christ.

Fame and fortune do not give peace. Position and power cannot give rest. This world cannot satisfy. The great goal of man is contentment, peace, and happiness. But so few look to God. Too many seek peace in the things of the world, and failing to find it, add to the misery of their lost souls.

SECOND, FACING AN UNCERTAIN FUTURE BRINGS MISERY. It is recorded that the brilliant, witty Frenchman, Voltaire, who scorned the light of divine truth, when death was in prospect, exclaimed, "Now, for a fearful leap in the dark."

Nothing brings fear like uncertainty. Christians face death and the future without fear because they know where they are going. The lost do not know and the misery of the soul is the result.

THIRD, CARRYING A BURDEN OF SIN BRINGS MISERY. The unsaved person, wth a consciousness of unforgiven sin, cannot have peace. He may try to lose his sins in the revelry of the world, but will fail. He may try to forget his sins by delving into the accumulated knowledge of men, but again, he will fail. He may try to lose his sins by travelling to the far corners of the earth, but this will not give him peace.

There is no way for man to lose his burden of sin except by coming to the cross of Chrsit.

Confess today the misery of your soul. Come to yourself as the prodigal son in the far country. Compare your destitution with God's plenty, and today come to the Lord.

## THE MISSION OF A SAVED SOUL

Our mission is to seek others.

In the parable of the sheep, the shepherd went after the lost one. It is our business to follow in the steps of the great Shepherd, Jesus Christ.

In the parable of the woman we have illustrated our mission. She had ten pieces of silver. She lost one of them. She did not sit down and say, "I am contented. I have nine other pieces of silver." No, she began to search for the lost coin. She did three things in order to find the lost.

FIRST, SHE LIGHTED A CANDLE. The houses of that day were not too well lighted with large windows; therefore, a light was necessary. The picture is plain. We are in a world of darkness. If we are to seek the lost, we must have a light. The candle can represent the Word of God, for His Word is a light. We must not try to seek the lost without the Word. Again, the candle can represent the Holy Spirit, for we cannot find the lost, or win them to the Saviour without His aid.

SECOND, SHE SWEPT THE HOUSE. Jesus was doubtless thinking of one of the houses of Palestine. The light was necessary because of the darkness within, and the sweeping was necessary because the coin might be covered over with dust.

She swept the house. This sweeping would raise a dust and commotion. But it was done in order to find the lost coin.

Souls are in the dust and dirt of this world. If we win them to Christ, we will stir up dust. This is one reason why we do not win more people to Christ. We are afraid to stir up the dust of this world. We do not like opposition and persecution. Therefore, we seek to be quiet and easy, and in so doing, we fail to find the lost.

The four men who carried the palsied man to Jesus were not afraid to stir up dust. They determined to bring their friend to Christ, and to do so, they had to tear up the roof, and cause considerable commotion, but they succeeded.

Let us not be afraid to stir up dust in order to find the lost. It is better to stir up dust and win souls than to live peacefully and see our loved ones and friends go to hell.

Paul stirred up dust everywhere he went. In every town he had a revival or a revolution — quite often both. Let us consider this matter and begin to stir and win.

THIRD, SHE KEPT ON SEARCHING TILL SHE FOUND. This is persistence. The same persistence is given in the parable of the sheep, for the shepherd went after the lost until he found it.

Here again, we see the reason for our many failures. We lose heart and stop our efforts to win. Our mission is to seek the lost and in this task we should be persistent, night and day, year in and year out. Most of us are sorely lacking in patience and persistence.

A missionary once testified in our church that he had spent four years in Africa before he saw his first convert. But today there are thousands of converts. Four years is a long time to wait for the harvest. Most of us would have quit and returned to the comforts of home.

Adoniram Judson spent almost seven years on the mission fields before he saw one person saved. When his mission board questioned him regarding the work, and the prospects, he answered, "The prospects are as bright as the promises of God." He had persistence, and today hundreds of churches and thousands of Christians are working for Christ because he refused to quit.

Our mission is to seek the lost. May we not fail our blessed Saviour.

### THE MIGHT OF OUR MASTER

It is ours to go and to witness.

It is His to save.

Jesus reveals two truths about God we need to notice.

FIRST, THE LOVE OF GOD FOR THE LOST. He does not love our sins, but He loves us. There are many verses which present this truth. *"But God commendeth his love toward us, in that, while we were yet sinners, Christ died for us"* (Romans 5:8). *"But God, who is rich in mercy, for his great love wherewith he loved us"* (Ephesians 2:4). *"In this was manifested the love of God toward us, because that God sent his only begotten Son into the world, that we might live through him"* (John 4:9).

And, of course, when we think of God's love, we remember that favorite, John 3:16, *"For God so loved the world, that he gave his only begotten Son, that whosoever believeth in him should not perish, but have everlasting life."*

Parents will often say to a little child, "How much do you love me?" The answer is usually a kiss and a hug. If you put the same question to our Heavenly Father, His answer will be, "The cross." God gave His only begotten Son to die on the cross for us. Here is the love of God.

There is no way to measure God's great love. It is greater than anything we can say or think.

The story is told that when Nansen, the explorer, tried to measure the depth of the ocean in the far north, he used a long measuring line, and when he discovered that he had not touched bottom, he wrote in his record, "Deeper than that." The next day he tried a longer line, only to write again, "Deeper than that." Several times he tried, and finally, he fastened all of his lines together, and let them down, but his last record was like the first — "Deeper than that." He left without knowing the depth of the ocean at that point, except that it was deeper than many thousand feet.

Whenever we try to measure the love of God, we can simply say, "It is deeper than that."

Someone has said, "the love of God is an ocean, and no line can sound its depths. It is a sky of unknown dimensions, and no flying machine can reach its heights. It is a continent of unexplored distance, and no tape can measure its lengths. It is a width of unsurpassed country, and no survey can find its boundary. It is a mine of wealth, and no delving of man can estimate or exhaust its riches. It is a pole of attraction which no explorer can discover, and the love of God is a forest of beauty, and no botanist can find and describe its variety and glory."

This we know, that God loves lost men and women. Such a thought should break our hearts, bring us to our knees in rededication, and should send us out after those whom God loves.

SECOND, JESUS REVEALS ALSO THE POWER OF GOD TO SAVE. Whenever I go out witnessing to the lost, I do not have to say, "I trust the Lord will be able to save you," or, "I hope my Saviour can take away your sins." No, the power of God is sufficient to forgive and to save all who come unto Him. This is the might of our Master — He can save unto the uttermost.

This is my message for this hour. In heaven the angels are waiting to rejoice over one sinner that repenteth. Let us pray they will not be disappointed in you and your decision. We have tried to picture the misery of a lost soul, the mission of the saved soul, and the might of our Master to save all who will come to Him. Come today.

# 17
# Enthusiasm For Humanity

> *"For I am not ashamed of the gospel of Christ: for it is the power of God unto salvation to every one that believeth; to the Jew first, and also to the Greek"*
>
> — Romans 1:16

There are times when I lose my interest, my concern, my compassion for some members of the human race. My loss of interest may be because of personal problems, or because of some treatment which I have sustained.

But, not so with our Saviour. His compassion for men did not change, and he is *"The same yesterday, and today, and for ever."*

Christ was ever enthusiastic about men. His concern did not waver. He cared for the multitudes.

He fed the four thousand as we read the story in Matthew 15.

He fed the five thousand in John 6.

He was concerned about the great city of Jerusalem and the people in it. His heart was burdened because of their sin. He wept because of their rejection. We hear Him cry,

> *"O Jerusalem, Jerusalem, thou that killest the prophets, and stonest them which are sent unto thee, how often would I have gathered thy children together, even as a hen gathereth her chickens under*

*her wings, and ye would not!"*

— Matthew 23:37

Christ was concerned for families. How beautiful is the story given to us in Mark 1:29-31. Jesus came into the home of Simon Peter. Peter's wife's mother lay sick of a fever. Jesus came and *"took her by the hand, and lifted her up; and immediately the fever left her, and she ministered unto them."*

We see His concern for families in the great story given us in John 11. Jesus loved the family of Mary and Martha and Lazarus. The call came, death came, and finally Jesus arrived on the scene. And the Bible says very plainly, *"Jesus wept"* (John 11:35). He was concerned for his family and for their welfare.

The Son of God was concerned for individuals. There are scores of illustrations in the Bible which bring out this fact. He cared for Nicodemus, the ruler of the Jews. He witnessed to him and pointed him unto salvation through faith in the crucified Christ. He had concern for the woman at the well. He was concerned for the woman taken in adultery, the story given to us in John 8. His heart was touched by the man born blind and He healed and saved him. Jesus was concerned for the thief on the cross and gave unto this one salvation.

Yes, the Lord Jesus had enthusiasm for humanity — concern for the lost.

FIRST, THE CONCERN OF MY SAVIOUR SHAMES ME. The holy Son of God was concerned Himself for the educated and the uneducated. He desired the salvation of the Pharisees as well as the salvation of the beggar by the roadside. I repeat: His concern shames me.

Some time ago I heard a couple of young people talking about a professor in a university. They were taking classes under this man. He called himself an atheist. He laughed at the faith of Christians. When I hear about a person like that, I become somewhat stirred with an inner anger, and yet I must remember that the Son of God loves that man, and will save him the very moment that he repents and believes.

SECOND, HIS CONCERN STIRS ME. When I read about the Lord Jesus Christ and His great compassion, I want to walk after Him. I know that I need to be concerned. I need to have tears., I need to desire the salvation of others.

THIRD, HIS CONCERN SENDS ME. Everything fails unless I walk after the Lord Jesus and thereby go after souls. This means that I must be concerned about the people around me. I must also be concerned about those in far distant places. I must believe in home missions and foreign missions.

It is my conviction that enthusiasm for humanity will mean an understanding of the following:

## THE PROBLEM OF SIN

In a consideration of man and his need, we must begin with the matter of sin.

FIRST, ALL ARE SINNERS. The Bible declares, *". . .For there is no difference: for all have sinned, and come short of the glory of God"* (Romans 3:22,23). The entire human race is involved in the statement of the Apostle Paul. The world is in one single boat.

Someone tells about the two Irishmen who crossed the ocean. One of them said, "Ikey, the boat is sinking." "Well, " said Ikey, "What of it? We don't own it." Man may be unconcerned for his fellowman, but this does not change the fact — "All are sinners."

SECOND, ALL ARE HELPLESS. Man is a sinner and the Bible says that Man is *"dead in trespasses and sins"* (Ephesians 2:1).

*"That at that time ye were without Christ, being aliens*

> *from the commonwealth of Israel, and strangers from the covenants of promise, having no hope, and without God in the world:*
>
> *"But now in Christ Jesus, ye who sometimes were far off are made nigh by the blood of Christ."*
>
> — Ephesians 2:12,13

THIRD, ALL ARE CONDEMNED. John 3:18 reads, *"He that believeth on him is not condemned: but he that believeth not is condemned already, because he hath not believed in the name of the only begotten Son of God."*

FOURTH, ALL MEN NEED HELP. I am thinking especially at this time of the help that we can give to men. The Bible says, *"Ye shall be witnesses unto me."* It is ours to witness and to teach and preach. We must tell men of Christ, for all men need help.

The problem of sin is everywhere. IT IS AMONG THE WEALTHY. A Chicago paper told the story of a poor woman whose husband worked for one of the railroads of the city. He had not worked for three months because of an injury. The baby died. They put the little body in a rude pine box and she carried it to the cemetery. She took the street car out of Chicago to its terminal and walked three miles to a place where she could bury her baby. The Chicago newspapers got hold of the story. At the same time they published the story, they published also the story of one of the owners of the railroad, who had lost $150,000 in gambling resort. The newspaper said, "He took his loss like dead game sport. He lighted his cigar, smiled, and walked out as though he did not care."

Ah, but let us remember something. Sin is everywhere. It is among the poor and the rich. Man is a sinner!

SIN IS FOUND AMONG THE EDUCATED. Education has accomplished much in our world. Some years ago a man with a college degree was a rare person, but today college degrees are plentiful. All universities and colleges are packed and jammed with people. Millions and millions of dollars are being poured into the educational system every day. But you see, sin is everywhere. It is among the educated as well as among the uneducated.

Sin is everywhere! It is among the rich and among the poor. it is found in the mansions on the mountain.

It is found in the hovel in the slums.

When Dr. Faulkner and I travelled in the West Indies, we paid a visit to the little island of Anguilla. Some ten or eleven thousand people are on the island. No bathrooms, no telephones, no doctors, no dentists, no hospital. But you see they had 110 liquor stores, tiny liquor shops built in every part of the island. I repeat, sin is everywhere! The problem of sin is a great problem of the human race.

## THE PERSON OF CHRIST

Throughout my ministry I have read sermons by the great Charles Haddon Spurgeon. Many of his sermons are on the person of Christ. As I read carefully, and ofttimes with my emotions stirred, I have come to the end of the message and said, "Could anything else be said by a preacher?"

I have read many sermons by the eloquent T. DeWitt Talmadge. He was an orator, a man acquainted with beautiful words, and ofttimes as I finish reading one of his sermons, I wonder if anything else could be said about the Lord Jesus Christ.

Some years ago I heard the famous Dr. George W. Truett of Dallas, Texas. I do not believe that many men in the world have ever spoken so eloquently of Christ as did Dr. Truett. After listening to him preach, I have wondered in my heart if anything else could be said about the Saviour.

It has been my part to hear Dr. R. G. Lee, a man greatly used of God — a preacher who has spent his life in telling the story of Christ. I listened to him one day preach on John 20. I do not think I have ever heard such a message, and when he had finished, I thought in my heart, "Could anything else be said about Christ?"

Oh, my friends, let men speak as they will. We can never exhaust the subject of Christ! We can never come to the end of our discussion of His worthiness, His loveliness, and his power.

Here is the one who can reach out to some poor sinner in a far distant land and save him and transform his life.

Our thoughts are centering on the subject of missions. Who is a missionary? A missionary is one who has been saved and called of God to tell the story of Christ to those who have not heard.

A poor man who had just been liberated from the penitentiary after serving his sentence met a boy with a cage of birds for sale. He bought them and opening the cage door, he let each bird fly away. The astonished boy said, "Sir, what made you pay for them and then turn them loose?" "My boy," he said, "If you had been in jail as long as I have, and had suffered what I have, you would not ask me why I let the birds go."

Ah, yes, it is Christ who can set the sinner free. It is Christ who can take away the chains and give man liberty. We must speak of Jesus, the Son of God, the Saviour of the lost world. He is the One for lost sinners.

He is the One for distressed saints. Many are the problems which confront us daily. Heartaches are the common lot of man. Sorrows will come to all of us. Death will invade our homes and take away our loved ones. Here is the One who can give us peace, even the Lord Jesus.

HERE IS THE ONE FOR DISTURBED YOUTH. Young people are disturbed by the questions of today. They are disturbed by the wickedness of present society.

They are disturbed by the doubts of an intellectual world.

They are disturbed by the weakness of professing Christians. Young people, look to the Saviour! Be disturbed no longer, but be believing. Look to Christ, believe in Him, and trust him.

When I think about humanity and its need, I am forced to think about my Saviour. I must point people to the Lamb of God who takes away the sin of the world.

## THE PROPOSITION OF FAITH

The Bible plainly says, *"Verily, verily, I say unto you, He that believeth on me hath everlasting life"* (John 6:47). Men are saved by simple faith in Christ.

FIRST, SALVATION IS FOR MEN WHO SEE THEMSELVES AS SINNERS. Jesus said, *"For the Son of Man is come to seek and to save that which was lost"* (Luke 19:10). But very strangely, some people will not see themselves as lost and undone. They are trusting in their self-righteousness.

But our Saviour declared emphatically that He came to give salvation to all who recognized themselves as sinners.

SECOND, SALVATION IS BY GRACE THROUGH FAITH. Let us turn in our Bibles to Ephesians 2:8,9.

> *"For by grace are ye saved through faith; and that not of yourselves: it is the gift of God. Not of works, lest any man should boast."*

The Lord Jesus said, *"I give unto them eternal life, and they shall never perish."* Salvation is a gift of God. It is received by grace through faith.

THIRD, SALVATION IS FOR "WHOSOEVER WILL."

> *"And the Spirit and the bride say, Come. And let him that heareth say, Come. And let him that is athirst come. And whosoever will, let him take the water of life freely."*
>
> — Revelation 22:17

Every Christian is to be a soul winner. We are to see first the problem of sin, second, the person of Christ, and third, the proposition of faith. It is our duty to tell men of Christ. If they do not accept Him, the responsibility is upon them. But we must be sure to free ourselves of their blood by declaring the message of salvation. Ezekiel cried out,

> *"When I say unto the wicked, Thou shalt surely die; and thou givest him not warning, nor speakest to warn the wicked from his wicked way, to save his life; the same wicked man shall die in his iniquity; but his blood will I require at thine hand."*
>
> — Ezekiel 3:18

In our concern for others, WE MUST BE CAREFUL OF BITTERNESS. Man is deceptive and unfair. Man will cheat and lie. Sometimes we may fail to present our Saviour as we should because of bitterness of heart.

SECOND, WE MUST BE CAREFUL OF INDIFFERENCE TOWARD OTHERS. Paul lamented this fact of selfishness on the part of the people in Philippi, when he said, *"For all seek their own, not the things which are Jesus Christ's"*. Beware of selfishness that takes away your concern for souls.

THIRD, BE CAREFUL OF FORGETFULNESS ABOUT MAN. Remember that man is an eternal soul. The Bible tells us that his soul is worthy of rescue. It matters not how he dresses or how he speaks or how he acts — we must be interested in his soul and seek to bring that one to Christ.

I believe there is a story in every man's heart. The story of need, of longing, of desire for the highest and best. Let us pray that God will help us to look upon the men and women in a different way and with a longing for their salvation.

**THE PERMANENCE OF SALVATION**

Jesus said to the woman at the well, *"But whosoever drinketh of the water that I shall give him shall never thirst; but the water that I shall give him shall be in him a well of water springing up into everlasting life"* (John 4:14).

> *"He that believeth on the Son hath everlasting life: and he that believeth not the Son shall not see life; but the wrath of God abideth on him."*
>
> —John 3:36

> *"And whosoever liveth and believeth in me shall never die. Believeth thou this?"*
>
> —John 11:26

Our Saviour is not an Indian giver. He gives eternal life. He doesn't snatch it away. Through your faith in the Son of God you become a new creature in Christ Jesus.

> *"Therefore if any man be in Christ, he is a new creature; old things are passed away; behold, all things are become new."*
>
> —II Corinthians 5:17

The life which he has given me is for eternity. I received Christ as my Saviour and He does the rest. John wrote, *"But as many as received him, to them gave he power to become the sons of God, even to them that believe on his name"* (John 1:12).

In Christ, we have life everlasting and this life sustains us through all hours and all events.

Some time ago there was a man in Kilby Prison in Montgomery, Alabama, by the name of Bill Bowen. Bill

Bowen, crazed by drink or drugs, or both, had killed a woman with a knife. He fled from the scene. Later he came to his senses and turned himself in to the police. At his trial he said that he deserved to die for what he had done. The judge and jury agreed.

Someone asked Rev. James S. Cantrell, pastor of the Third Presbyterian Church of Birmingham, Alabama, to visit Bill Bowen. Brother Cantrell went to see Bill Bowen.

He found a stocky, blue-eyed individual with thinning blond hair. He was sharing a cell with another condemned murderer. He was awaiting the day of his execution.

But, Bill Bowen had a remarkable serenity and it did not take long to find out why. He had been saved. He was a new creature in Jesus Christ.

Bill Bowen, just thirty-two years of age, condemned to die, was a great witness for Christ. He witnessed to his friends in the penitentiary.

He donated the corneas of his eyes to blind persons — the eyes to be given after his execution. He wrote to Brother James Cantrell many times and the final letter asked that Brother Cantrell be with him when he died.

As James Cantrell arrived at the prison and was brought to the cell, Bill Bowen asked him, "Did you bring the doctors for my eyes?" He was then taken upstairs to the execution chamber. Brother Cantrell said, "The warden was carrying a length of rope." He asked him why he had it and he said, "Well, sometimes the prisoners struggle and we have to tie them down." No one had to tie Bill Bowen. He came in quietly led by his guards. There was no tension in him at all. He spoke to the warden, urging him not to feel badly for what he had to do. He walked over and sat down in the chair under the harsh overhead light. The straps over his left forearm were loose. They came back and tightened them.

Before the hood was slipped over his head he made his last statement: "I am now ready to pay for the crime I committed. I have no malice for anyone. God has forgiven me. Christ has saved me. This chair will not send me to my death, but to my home."

The warden gave the signal. Brother Cantrell kept his head bowed. He said that when he raised it, Bill Bowen's brief and troubled hour on this hour earth was over.

Jim Cantrell said the next day he met a friend in Birmingham. This one said, "Well, I hear that you were with Bill Bowen at the end. Is that right?"

Brother Cantrell answered, "No, I was with him at the beginning." How right he was! Life begins with our Lord Jesus Christ. He is the Saviour. He gives us salvation and keeps us for eternity.

John Jasper was a mighty preacher of the Gospel. He had been a Negro slave, and had been called of God to preach. The people came by the thousands to hear him — the white and the colored. When his old body was about worn out, he preached a sermon on heaven. He closed his message by saying something like this:

> "When I get to heaven, the angel is going to say, 'John Jasper, do you want your robe?' And I will say, 'not yet, not yet.' And then he will say, 'Do you want to see your mansion?' And I will say, 'Angel, before you show me my harp, and my crown, and my mansion, I want to see my Jesus.'"

Christ is the Saviour! Jesus said, *"Him that cometh unto me I will in no wise cast out."* Will you come to Christ today?

# 18
# Are The Heathen Lost?

> *"Wherefore, as by one man sin entered into the world, and death by sin; and so death pased upon all men, for that all have sinned:"*
>
> —Romans 5:12

The answer to our question, "Are the heathen lost?" is found in the text. Sin did not begin with Adam, but it entered the human race with Adam. When Adam sinned, sin entered and death came on all men. *". . .for that all have sinned:"* Please notice the word, "all."

The Bible describes the condition of men. It does not show any respect of persons, for God is no respecter of persons. A few verses will establish the state of all men without Christ.

> *"What then? are we better than they? No, in no wise: for we have before proved both Jews and Gentiles, that they are all under sin;*
>
> *"As it is written, there is none righteous, no, not one:"*
>
> *—Romans 3:9,10*
>
> *". . .for there is no difference: For all have sinned, and come short of the glory of God;"*
>
> —Romans 3:22,23
>
> *"Behold, all souls are mine; as the soul of the father, so also the soul of the son is mine: the soul that sinneth, it shall die."*
>
> —Ezekiel 18:4

When Adam sinned, all men were brought under condemnation. The whole world is guilty before God.

As by one man sin entered, so by one man, even Christ, came life. The Bible is largely the story of two men; Adam, by whom sin entered, and Christ, who brought life and immortality.

Adam disobeyed and brought death. Christ obeyed and brought life. The Word of God plainly states this fact: That all men are lost without Christ. All men, all races, all colors, and nations.

In the light of these truths there are three solemn facts for us to remember.

### WE HAVE A COMMAND FROM CHRIST

Jesus said, *"Go ye into all the world."*

In Matthew 28:18-20, He gave the great commission as follows:

> *"And Jesus came and spake unto them, saying, All power is given unto me in heaven and in earth.*
>
> *"Go ye therefore, and teach all nations, baptizing them in the name of the Father, and of the Son, and of the Holy Ghost:*
>
> *"Teaching them to observe all things whatsoever I have commanded you; and, lo, I am with you alway, even unto the end of the world. Amen."*

In Mark 16:15,16, read,

> *"And he said unto them, Go ye into all the world, and preach the gospel to every creature.*
>
> *"He that believeth and is baptized shall be saved; but he that believeth not shall be damned."*

The command is recorded in Luke's Gospel and reads:

> *"And said unto them, Thus it is written, and thus it behooved Christ to suffer, and to rise from the dead the third day:*
>
> *"And that repentance and remission of sins should be preached in his name among all nations, beginning at Jerusalem.*
>
> *"And ye are witnesses of these things."*
>
> —Luke 24:46-48

In John's Gospel, Jesus commanded His disciples as follows:

> *". . .Peace be unto you: as my Father hath sent me, even so send I you."*
>
> —John 20:21

In the book of Acts, the Saviour said just before His ascension:

> *"But ye shall receive power, after that the Holy Ghost is come upon you; and ye shall be witnesses unto me both in Jerusalem, and in all Judaea, and in Samaria, and unto the uttermost part of the earth."*
>
> —Acts 1:8

On the day of Pentecost the disciples of our Lord were obeying His commission when they preached to the people and three thousand were saved and baptized. I believe that the three thousand went to their many countries and there told the story of Jesus in obedience to His command. We can see at once how the great commission was reaching out.

The book of Acts is a record of God's people obeying the command of Christ. For example, in Acts 8, a deacon obeyed the Lord's command and became a mighty missionary and evangelist.

In Acts 9 a bitter Pharisee was saved and immediately

began to obey the command of Christ to tell the story to the whole world. He became the world's greatest missionary. He believed that all men were lost without Christ. He did not believe that ignorance would save anyone. The highly educated Paul would not have given his life to the work of missions if he had not believed men were in a lost state.

Yes, we have a command from Christ. This command is to be obeyed.

Dr. R. A. Torrey said that one time when speaking in Minneapolis, he noticed a young lawyer in the audience. When the meeting was over, he went to him and said, "Are you a Christian? The lawyer replied, "Well sir, I consider myself a Christian." Dr. Torrey said, "Are you bringing other men to Christ?" He answered, "No, I am not. That is not my business. That is your business. I am not called to do that. I am called to practice law. You are called to preach the Word."

Dr. Torrey said, "If you are called to be a Christian, you are called to bring other men to Christ." The lawyer replied, "I don't believe it." Dr. Torrey said, "Look here." And he opened his Bible to Acts 8 and read, "*. . .they that were scattered abroad went everywhere preaching the Word.*"

"Oh, yes," said the lawyer, "but these were the apostles." Dr. Torrey said, "Will you be kind enough to read the first verse of the chapter?" And he read, ". . .and they were all scattered abroad throughout the regions of Judaea and Samaria except the apostles."

Yes, every believer is to be a witness and the command is to all of us.

## WE HAVE A COMPANION

Jesus said, *"Lo, I am with you alway, even unto the end of the age."*

The promise is for going Christians. This promise of companionship is not for disobedient, lazy, silent Christians. It is for those who go with the message of Jesus.

This was the favorite verse of the great missionary, David Livingstone. While receiving an honorary degree at the college in Scotland, he was asked to give his favorite verse of Scripture, and he replied humbly, "My favorite verse is, 'Lo, I am with you alway.'"

The presence of Christ gives courage. We need not fear to go anywhere if Christ is with us.

A missionary told of going to the heart of Africa. He began his work with companions as eager as himself. One by one they succumbed to the terrible climate. Three he buried — the others he took to the coast and sent home. Then he turned back to stand utterly alone in the midst of hundreds of thousands of men who had never heard the name of God. Again and again he tramped the blistered plains with his tongue so swollen that he could not speak. Thirty times he was stricken by fever with no one to care for him. Lions attacked him. Natives ambushed him. He lived upon everything and here was his conclusion, "I know the great joy of walking with Jesus Christ in the midst of all things. I stand ready at this moment to go through it all again for the joy I have had in flashing the word, SAVIOUR, into the darkness of a heathen tribe."

The Apostle Paul had courage, for Christ was with him.

William Carey did not go alone. Christ was with him.

Our missionaries now on foreign fields are not alone. Christ is with them.

Miss Mary Mahl, who was a missionary to Arabia, did not go alone. Christ was with her. He is with her now as she recovers from a serious illness in a London hospital.

The presence of Christ gives courage. *"If God be for us, who can be against us?"*

The presence of Christ gives peace. How often the Saviour spoke to his terrified disciples, *"Peace be with you."* It is the presence of One who is mightier than all enemies that gives us peace.

The presence of Christ gives patience in the midst of trials. The loving Saviour endured everything for our sake. He patiently bore the cross. He imparts unto us patience as He walks by our side.

We have a companion. Can we say that He walks and talks with us? Do you have courage and peace and patience because of His presence?

## WE MUST HAVE COMPASSION FOR OTHERS

It is necessary that we recognize the command of Christ and that we make sure of His companionship, but we will never be missionaries nor missionary-minded unless we have the compassion of Christ for lost men.

When the time came for Christ to leave His disciples and to return unto the Father, His great yearning soul was reaching out toward a world lost in sin. It was then that He gave the command that the Gospel should be preached to all men. Back of the "Go ye" is the compassion of Christ.

We must have love and compassion for others or we will not go.

First, let us take inventory of the blessings we have because of Him. What joy surges through our hearts because we are the children of God.

When I think of the great blessings Christ bestows upon his own, I want everyone to know Him and to share these same blessings.

We must have compassion on those who live in daily fear. Throughout the world there are men and women and children who live in a constant state of fear. Knowing Christ takes away fear, it takes away the fear of man and the fear of the future. It gives us peace.

We need to have compassion for those who are dying without Christ. Think of those in the far distant places who have never heard His name. They are waiting for us to come unto them.

Whenever we would observe the Lord's Supper in our church, it was always my custom after the giving of the bread to ask the question, "Has anyone been missed?" After we had passed the cup, symbolizing the shed blood of Christ, I would also ask the question, "Has anyone been missed?"

Over the world there are millions in China, India, Africa, South America, and Central America, yea, throughout the entire world who could raise their hands and say, "We have been missed in the distribution of the bread and the cup."

> Sudden, before my inward open vision,
> millions of faces crowded up to view;
> "Sad eyes that said, 'For us is no provision,
> Give us your Saviour too!
> "Give us,' they cry, 'your cup of consolation,
> Never to our outreaching hands is passed.
> "We long for the desire of every nation,
> And, oh, we die so fast!'"

God grant us a compassion which will make us go to the ends of the earth with the message of Jesus.

Perhaps today someone is asking the question. "How can we go?"

FIRST, WE CAN GO OURSELVES. God may be calling some of our finest young men and women to go to the foreign fields. If God calls, do not hesitate to obey.

SECOND, WE CAN GO BY LETTING OTHERS GO. Someone near and dear to you may feel that God is calling them. Don't be selfish. Don't place a hindrance in the way of that person, but let him go. A Christian layman at a missionary convention prayed earnestly, "O Lord, send laborers into Thy harvest fields." Then as the Spirit carried him along, he prayed, "O Lord, send someone from our State Convention into Thy harvest fields," paused a moment, and then continued, "O Lord, send someone from our church into Thy harvest fields." Again, there was a pause, longer this time, and an inward struggle seemed to be taking place. At length, he prayed, "I have a daughter, just one daughter, O Lord, if it be pleasing to Thee, send her into Thy harvest field."

THIRD, WE CAN GO BY GIVING. Many of us cannot go ourselves, but we can give our money so others can go. The way to have a real interest in missions is to give something. There will be no blessing for our hearts until we catch a vision of how we can go to the foreign fields by giving.

FOURTH, WE CAN GO BY PRAYING. We must pray for missionaries and the work of missions. God is able to answer prayer anywhere. We may send up a prayer from our home and the answer come in China. We must not forget the power of prayer.

And I believe as we pray, our love and compassion will grow. Our gifts will increase, and volunteers will answer God's call.

We have a world task. It begins in Jerusalem — our home town, and extends to the most distant place in the world.

May our compassion be for all lost people, at home and afar. As we pray, and give to foreign missions, let us not forget the lost ones in our own household. Jesus said, *"Ye shall be my witnesses."*

# 19

# The Damned DO Cry

*"There shall be weeping and gnashing of teeth, when ye shall see Abraham, and Isaac, and Jacob, and all the prophets, in the kingdom of God, and you yourselves thrust out."*

— Luke 13:28

There is coming a day when people will know the meaning of the words, "saved" and "lost." Today the world laughs if you talk about salvation, the new birth, damnation, and hell.

There is coming a day when we shall all know the counterfeit from the real. Today the confusion is so great that we scarcely can distinguish between the spurious and the genuine. True and false churches stand side by side. Believers and professors worship together, but the day of separation and full revelation is coming.

There is coming a day when men will come to their senses and realize the error of their ways. Today they travel on blindly and carelessly, but one day they shall awaken — but it will be too late.

There is coming a day when men shall cry to God — but in vain. Men may brag and flaunt their sins in the face of God now, but one day tears and crying will supplant boasting and defiance.

There are those who brazenly declare that they will take their chances on eternity. They say that whatever God hands out, they will take and not complain or cry. In this they are wrong. "The damned do cry."

Bold and defiant speech belongs to sinners now, but after a while tears and crying will come.

I want to give three reasons why the damned do cry, and why all who go to hell will be brought to tears.

## THE DAMNED DO CRY BECAUSE OF EXCLUSION FROM HEAVEN

Jesus said to the people, *"There shall be weeping and gnashing of teeth, when ye shall see Abraham, and Isaac and Jacob, and all the prophets, in the kingdom of God, and ye yourselves thrust out."*

A man may laugh at the teaching of heaven and despise God's way of salvation, and reject the only way of life, but one day he will be brought to weeping and gnashing of teeth when he realizes that he is excluded from Heaven.

Those who reject Christ are condemned already, and when death comes, they go directly to the place of torment and punishment.

Please note there is no lapse of time between death and the beginning of hell. The rich man died and in hell he lifted up his eyes. We do not have indicated any period of time between his death and the beginning of his suffering. It was a hard and harsh awakening for the rich man to suddenly discover himself in the place called hell. We do not wonder that he lifted up his eyes in torments and cried.

Again, notice there is no passage between heaven and hell. The rich man cried for Lazarus to come and dip the tip of his finger in water and cool his tongue, but Abraham made reply, and said, *". . .there is a great gulf fixed: so that they which would pass would pass from hence to you cannot; neither can they pass to us, that would come from thence"* (Luke 16:26).

Since there was no passage between hell and paradise,

there was no hope of release from that awful place for the rich man. No one can pass from one to the other.

When he died lost, all hope of heaven vanished. He was separated from God, the angels, and the saved, and there was no chance given to him for a parole, or a release from the awful prison house of hell.

Almost two thousand years have gone by since Jesus gave the account of this rich man. He has suffered about 2,000 years and the sad part of it all is that the suffering is just beginning. The eternal ages roll on and on, and there will be no alleviation and no release.

## THE DAMNED DO CRY BECAUSE OF THE TERRIBLE PUNISHMENT OF HELL

The rich man in hell cried because he was in torments. In verse 23, it is said of him, "*. . .being in torments. . .*" In verse 24 he cried and said, "*. . .I am tormented in this flame.*" In verse 25, Abraham repeated the matter of his punishment by saying, "*. . .thou art tormented.*"

In many places we have the teaching that hell is a place of weeping, tears, and torment. But here is the only view that God has given to us of the suffering of hell. The account reveals many remarkable things.

First, the rich man retained his mind, for he recognized Lazarus, and he remembered his brothers. He had the same bodily desires, for he longed for a drop of water on the tip of his tongue.

The suffering of hell will be mental, for memory will be retained. Abraham said to him, "*. . .Son, remember that thou in thy lifetime receivedst thy good things, and likewise Lazarus evil things: but now he is comforted, and thou art tormented*" (Luke 16:25). In hell men will have plenty of time to remember every sin they ever committed. They will remember every opportunity to be saved. They will remember every church service, every prayer, every gospel song, and every invitation given by loving Christians.

The rich man doubtless remembered his ingratitude to God. Riches had been his, but he had not used them in a right way.

My lost friend, memory can be a blessing or a curse. In hell it will be a curse to you. There will be nothing to do but remember. You will remember that Christian who placed a kind hand upon your shoulder and said, "Don't you want to be saved?" Today men get angry and refuse to return to the church, but one day their anger will be turned to tears when they realize that they are in hell forever.

The suffering of hell will also be physical. The rich man went to hell. His body was placed in the grave, but one of these days there will be a second resurrection. The graves of the lost dead will open, and they will stand before the Great White Throne Judgment. Let us read this solemn passage:

> *"And I saw a great white throne, and him that sat on it, from whose face the earth and the heaven fled away; and there was found no place for them.*
>
> *"And I saw the dead, small and great, stand before God; and the books were opened: and another book was opened, which is the book of life: and the dead were judged out of those things which were written in the books, according to their works.*
>
> *"And the sea gave up the dead which were in it; and death and hell delivered up the dead which were in them: and they were judged every man according to their works.*
>
> *"And death and hell were cast into the lake of fire. This is the second death.*

> *"And whosoever was not found written in the book of life was cast into the lake of fire."*
>
> — Revelation 20:11-15

Lost souls are now suffering consciously in Hades, but after the judgment of the Great White Throne, both soul and body will be cast into the lake of fire.

The suffering of soul and body in hell is clearly taught by the Lord. Notice in Matthew 10:28, *"And fear not them which kill the body, but are not able to kill the soul: but rather fear him which is able to destroy both soul and body in hell."*

The suffering of hell will be eternal. *"And these shall go away into everlasting punishment; but the righteous into life eternal"* (Matthew 25:46). Hell is eternal, just as heaven is eternal.

Yes, the damned do cry in hell because of the awful punishment — punishment and suffering which includes mental suffering, soul suffering, and one day bodily suffering. Men shall weep and wail because this torment is eternal.

## THE DAMNED DO CRY BECAUSE OF A SCOURGING CONSCIENCE

The rich man died and went to hell because he did not repent. On the earth he turned from God, and in hell he still was unrepentant. He went to hell because he loved darkness and hated the light.

We have nothing to indicate that this rich man was immoral or worse than other men. It does not even say that he was any more covetous, but we do know that he failed to repent of his sins, and take God's way of salvation.

In the flames of hell there were two things which concerned him; first, his own suffering, and secondly, his five brothers.

It seems that his conscience was giving him a hard time in hell because the five brothers were lost, and he knew they were headed for the place where he now found himself.

There were six boys in the family. He died a lost man and went to hell. Five brothers were left, and they were all lost. What an awful picture this is. Down in hell the rich man was troubled. He knew that he had failed in his responsibility. His own example had been wrong, and the five brothers were on their ways to hell.

One in hell — five more on the way.

Hell will be a place where the conscience will torment men and women year in and year out through eternity.

Some of you have chosen the way of sin. Death is coming, and hell immediately. In hell you will be troubled not only for your own condition, but for the condition of those who followed you back on the earth.

Bob Ingersoll, the atheist, is having a rough time in hell now, for he can clearly see the result of his evil and damnable influence. Aroung the world there are foolish people who read the foolish statements of Ingersoll, Voltaire, Tom Paine, and others. They are foolish enough to follow such blind leaders. In hell the atheists, the skeptics, the infidels, can clearly see the result of their deeds.

In our colleges and universities there are teachers who bankrupt the faith of young people. They sneer at the Bible, and salvation by blood. The professor dies. In hell he is able to see the young people he led astray, trooping down the broad way into everlasting hell. His conscience will be a scourge to double the pain of hell, and the tears of remorse will flow.

Let us not forget the tears of the damned will not avail to change their condition. Their place is set. Nothing can be done.

But, this picture of the tears of the damned should stir us to a greater compassion for the lost about us. We cannot help those who are already gone, but we can help the living about us. Our hearts should be moved as surely the heart of God is moved.

If you think that God wants sinners to go to hell, then you need to read your Bible again. Because of God's love, we have the Bible, His message to mankind. Because of His love, we have the Holy Spirit to bring conviction to hearts. Because of God's love for sinners, we have Calvary with its bloodstains. Because of God's love, we have preachers and teachers who are circling the globe to tell others of Jesus and salvation. Yes, our hearts need to be moved to compassion for the lost.

Not only should we have compassion, but we should be moved to activity. Witnessing should be our daily business in the light of the awfulness of hell.

Not only compassion and activity, but we should be moved to unceasing prayer in behalf of lost sinners. The fearfulness of hell should keep us on our knees, praying unto God for convicting power, to seize those who are lost, and to bring them to salvation.

In closing, lost sinner, your heart should be moved by the tears of the damned. The word indicates the awful state of the lost. Let this vivid picture stir you to action, and to repentance and faith.

The rich man did not need to go to hell. He had Moses and the prophets. If he had repented, his soul would have been saved.

You do not need to go to hell, for God's message is before you. Repent of your sins, believe on Jesus Christ. ". . .*except ye repent, ye shall all likewise perish*" (Luke 13:3). ". . .*Believe on the Lord Jesus Christ, and thou shalt be saved. . .*" (Acts 16:31).

# 20
# The Heart of Every Church

*"And with great power gave the apostles witness of the resurrection of the Lord Jesus: and great grace was upon them all."*

— Acts 4:33

The heart of the early church was missions. The church in the minds of the first century believers existed for one purpose — the spread of the Gospel. They heard the voice of the Saviour and now they gave obedience to His command.

The church that is near to the heart of God will always be interested in missions. Therefore, it is not difficult to tell when a church is away from the Lord — there is no concern for missions. The interest is centered in things temporal instead of things eternal. The church seeks for earthly approval. There is a looking for man's approbation instead of divine commendation.

Trace, if you will, the great missionary ventures of the early church. Note the greatest of men were missionaries. Give heed to the fact that the Bible record of early Christianity is a story of missions.

The heart of great churches of the past has centered in missions. Whether in Antioch, Jerusalem, Rome, Ephesus, or Corinth, the interest has been in missions. Churches fail when missions are ignored. The work of missions is the work of

God.

It is my belief that missions will do three significant things for every church.

## MISSIONS WILL MAKE THE CHURCH COURAGEOUS

The Lord Jesus told the disciples to go. After the giving of the commission on the mount of ascension, they were prepared to move out until Christ urged them to remain in Jerusalem until the Holy Spirit should come upon them. But after the coming of the Holy Spirit we note the boldness of these men. Simon Peter, who seemed a bluff, a coward, a loud talker without faith, became the mighty Apostle Peter on the day of Pentecost. There was granted unto him a boldness which came from the Holy Spirit.

I notice in my Bible that the word "boldness" occurs three times in Acts 4. First, it appears as a commendation from the enemy:

> *"Now when they saw the boldness of Peter and John, and perceived that they were unlearned and ignorant men, they marvelled; and they took knowledge of them, that they had been with Jesus"*
>
> —Acts 4:13

In Acts 4:29, we find the disciples praying that God would grant unto them boldness.

> *"And now, Lord, behold their threatenings: and grant unto thy servants, that with all boldness they may speak thy word."*

In Acts 4:31, we find the fulfillment of their prayers. Boldness was granted unto them and they spoke the word of God. Let us read this verse:

> *"And when they had prayed, the place was shaken where they were assembled together; and they were*

> *all filled with the Holy Ghost, and they spake the word of God with boldness."*

As we study this account, we must come to this conclusion that the filling of the Holy Spirit will give a person boldness. Boldness is not the braggadocial clamorings of a coward, but boldness is the courage granted to one who depends upon the Spirit of God.

FIRST, THE EARLY CHRISTIANS HAD COURAGE TO SPEAK AGAINST SIN. In their compassion to make Christ known to men and women everywhere, they spoke out against the evil which they saw. The Sanhedrin did not hinder them from this divine business. The fact of suffering and death did not turn them from the business of speaking against sin.

It will be the missionary spirit which will make our churches courageous and will make us bold in the faith of Christ. Missions will enable us to see the awfulness of sin and the need to speak against it.

SECOND, THEY HAD COURAGE TO STAND FOR THE RIGHT. It is one thing to speak against sin — it is also necessary that we stand for righteousness. One is negative, the other is positive. If a thing is right, then we must be for it. If it is wrong, we must be against it. If it is sinful for men to sell and drink liquor, then we must be against it. If it is right to stand for sobriety, then we must be for sobriety.

THIRD, THEY HAD THE COURAGE TO OBEY THE LORD. We find the Apostle Peter saying, . . .*"We ought to obey God rather than men"* (Acts 5:29). Such a statement implies that God has spoken to His servants and they were giving their obedience to Him. In like manner we must recognize that God has spoken to us. His command is that we go . . . *"into all the world, and preach the gospel to every creature"* (Mark 16:15). In this we must not fail. We must give our obedience unto the Lord.

I repeat, missions will make the church courageous. In a time when churches are trembling and faltering and failing, there is need for courage. May God grant us courage to stand for right, to speak against evil, and to give our obedience unto Him in all things.

## MISSIONS WILL MAKE THE CHURCH CONSECRATED

The Bible tells that we must hate the world, despise the flesh, and abhor Satan. Let us read in I John 2:15-17,

> *"Love not the world, neither the things that are in the world. If any man love the world, the love of the Father is not in him.*
>
> *"For all that is in the world, the lust of the flesh, and the lust of the eyes, and the pride of life, is not of the Father, but is of the world.*
>
> *"And the world passeth away, and the lust thereof: but he that doeth the will of God abideth for ever."*

We are admonished by the Bible to turn from all things of the world. We are to have no affection for that which is evil. Separation from the world is a high essential for the church that desires to be a Bible church.

This stand will not be popular with all people, but it is God's way. God has called for His people to come out and be separate and touch not the unclean thing. Separation from the world is a scarce commodity among churches.

I made a special note on a recent 2000-mile trip. All men and women smoked with the exception of one man. Cursing was a common thing in restaurants, on trains, on planes. I checked very carefully to note if any people returned thanks when meals were served. I found no one. Now, the question comes, were all of these people unchurched? Were all of them unsaved? It would be my guess that many are professing Christians and doubtless some of them were saved. But the theme of separation had missed their minds completely.

The tragedy of this hour is that so many churches are compromising with the world. They seek the favor of a sinful world. I have found this to be true in every church I have pastored. The people were running after the things of the world —dancing, card playing, drinking, smoking were all common acts of the people. When we began preaching separation, many became angry. Some turned away from the church, but God gave the victory. As a result, souls were saved and lives were transformed by the power of God.

Separation we must have! The world may criticize, but we must take our stand for the Lord Jesus Christ and for the way of separation from the world.

The number of separated people will always be small, but God will give victory. It was when Gideon reduced the number of his men to three hundred that God said, *"I will give you the victory over the Midianites."* When Gideon still felt some misgivings about the forthcoming battle, God sent him down to hear what the people had to say. The Scriptures point out to us in Judges 7:11-14, that Gideon put his ear near to the tent of the Midianites and listened to one of the men telling his companion that he had a dream about a cake of barley bread tumbling into the host of Midian, and overturning a tent. The friend said,. . .*"This is nothing else save the sword of Gideon the son of Joash, a man of Israel: for into his hand hath God delivered Midian, and all the host."* When Gideon heard this, he went back to Israel and worshipped God, and said, *". . .Arise; for the LORD hath delivered into your hand the host of Midian."*

Christians, we must hear what this world has to say, but we must not let it trouble us, but stand for Jesus Christ. Sometimes the world may speak in a hostile fashion, but again it may speak in a forlorn and desperate way. We must keep our definite stand for the Lord Jesus.

Missions will make a church consecrated. It will bring us out from the world and will cause us to be separate from the things of evil. Let us keep our hearts set on obeying God and sending the Gospel to the ends of the earth and the blessing will come down upon us.

## MISSIONS WILL MAKE THE CHURCH COMPASSIONATE

Our Saviour was compassionate! It was Jesus who looked upon the multitudes and wept over them. It was Christ who was moved with compassion because he saw the people fainting and scattered abroad as sheep having no shepherd. It was Christ who wept over the city of Jerusalem when He saw the open rejection of the Pharisees.

No man is like Christ who does not care for the souls of men. Let us not give any false impressions. We are not like Christ unless we are concerned about souls.

Some years ago, I was speaking in a conference in a certain city. One of the Bible teachers in the conference brought a glowing message on the love of God. The message was well outlined, well illustrated, but the entire sermon was lost to me when the man in charge of the conference made this statement: "I am sure that you enjoyed the message of Dr. So and So. He is an excellent Bible teacher. There is but one thing wrong with him. I have never known him to speak to a man about Jesus Christ. He has little compassion for others." The message of the man was lost, for he was not following in the steps of Jesus. His heart was not moved with divine compassion.

FIRST, LET US REMEMBER THAT COMPASSION WILL PRODUCE GENEROSITY. When we love souls, there will be no difficulty in the opening of our purse strings. When we love the work of our Saviour, we will never complain about offerings of the church. We will rejoice in every opportunity to give as we are able.

Some time ago, one of our members told of talking to another member of our church and this member was complaining about the church always asking for money. I would like to check the giving of that complaining individual. I think that I would find that the amount given would be very small and the compassion almost, if not completely, nil.

We will never complain about giving when our hearts are moved with compassion. The only complaint that we have to offer is that we have so little that we can give.

SECOND, COMPASSION WILL GIVE A WORLD-WIDE INTEREST. The Gospel must be given to the whole world. Jesus gave His command to us and this command we must obey.

During a recent war a regiment received orders to plant some heavy guns on the top of a steep hill. The soldiers dragged them to the base of the hill, but were unable to get them farther. An officer, learning of the state of affairs, cried, "Men, it must be done! I have the orders in my pocket."

The Church of the Lord Jesus Christ has definite orders to get the Gospel to every creature. We must be moved by a divine compassion to see that this job is carried out.

THIRD, COMPASSION WILL GIVE A CONCERN FOR THOSE AROUND US. There is something wrong with the person who exhibits an interest in missions, but never cares about folks at home. Our giving to missions should never take the place of an interest in those around us. We must not miss the ones who live close to us and who have such deep soul need.

Compassion for others — this will aid us in speaking to them. This will cause us to put aside all foolish inhibitions and give the Gospel with clarity to their hearts.

An old soldier had been disabled in the wars. When he had no means of support, he was endeavoring to play his violin on a main thoroughfare. His dog was trained to hold his hat, but no one dropped anything into it. The old soldier was tired and hungry. He had not the strength to play. In despair he sat down. A passerby noticed him and stopped, looked at him, and said, "You take the money and I'll play." And then he began to play. The people stopped to stare at a gentleman playing a violin out in the streets, and remained to listen, delighted with the strains they heard. The crowd grew larger and larger. The hat filled up so fast, not only with small coins, but with silver and paper money, that the dog began to growl, for the hat had never been so heavy to hold. The old man was told to empty its contents into his pockets, which he did, and the hat began to fill again. After a while, the gentleman handed back the violin and disappeared before he could be thanked. Everyone was saying, "Who is it? Who was the man who was playing?" Finally, the answer was given. he was a famous violinist. He had seen a friend in need and he stopped to give his aid. He had a compassionate heart. Such compassion should move us that we give the Gospel to those around us that they might hear of Jesus and be saved.

To the sinner friend, we live in a land where the Gospel is being preached on almost every corner. Every radio station carries religious programs which tell the story of Jesus. I regret that all of them are not true to the message of our Christ, but many are. Yet, in spite of all of these advantages you are still without the Saviour. Will you not today open your heart's door and let Christ come in? Let Him be light and life to you. Let Him be strength and power and rejoicing and hope to you.

When George Wing was ninety-four years old, he was very sick. Early one morning he sent for his pastor. When he arrived, the old man greeted him with these words, "I had a vision last night. It was dark and I was in trouble and needed help. I did not want to call for help, but I did. I called to God and it was light and it is still light." And with a smile on his face, he added, "And it will never be dark again." And then he urged the pastor to try to preach so that people will know that God is more important than all else.

The vision remained with the old man until his death. Each time the pastor called, George Wing would smile and say, "It has not been dark since, and it will never be dark again. My faith is in Jesus Christ." Faith in God will give light to the young and to the old. If we put our trust in the Son of God, the light of heaven will shine upon our hearts. The darkness will vanish and light will be ours because God is with us.

Friend without Christ, it need not be dark upon your way if you will let Jesus come into your heart. Look up into the face of the compassionate Son of God and say, "I receive Him now as my Saviour."

# 21
# How Far Have We Gone?

*"And when they were come, and had gathered the church together, they rehearsed all that God had done with them, and how he had opened the door of faith unto the Gentiles."*

—Acts 14:27

Barnabas and Saul were sent out as missionaries from the church in Antioch. They witnessed for Christ on the isle of Cyprus and on the mainland of Asia Minor. Their first missionary journey brought to pass many remarkable events. For example:

A sorcerer was made blind because of his opposition to the Gospel.

John Mark deserted the missionary party.

The Jews opposed Barnabas and Saul in Antioch and Pisidia.

In Lystra Barnabas and Saul were thought to be gods and came down among the people. Paul dissuaded the people and said, ". . .We also are men of like passions with you, and preach unto you that ye should turn from these vanities unto the living God, which made heaven, and earth, and the sea, and all things that are therein."

Paul was stoned in Lystra and taken out of the city as a

dead man.

After a time Barnabas and Paul returned to Antioch and gave a report of their activities. That brings us to the text of this message — "*. . . They rehearsed all that God had done with them. . .*" We come now to rehearse some things that God has done for us as we ask the question, "How far have we gone?"

**WE HAVE NOT GONE FAR ENOUGH**

Our failures are evident, our selfishness is apparent, our indifference is manifest.

FIRST, WE HAVE FAILED IN THE MATTER OF A BURDEN. This is a day calling for light burdens, for ease, for vacations, for good salaries, for little concern. This is a time when religion is merely a by-word and soul-compassion is unknown. We have failed to have a burden for others!

The Apostle Paul cared! I have repeated this again and again and I repeat it once more. Paul said,

> *"I say the truth in Christ, I lie not, my conscience also bearing me witness in the Holy Ghost,*
>
> *"That I have great heaviness and continual sorrow in heart.*
>
> *"For I could wish that myself were accursed from Christ for my brethren, my kinsmen according to the flesh."*
>
> — Romans 9:1-3

We have not gone far enough in this matter of having a burden for others. In this regard our failures are evident. Let us pray that God will forgive, but let us remember that His forgiveness will only be granted if we intend to have a burden in the days ahead.

SECOND, WE HAVE FAILED IN OUR GIVING. I mention here

a sacred matter—the giving of the tithe. And yet many Christians have never learned the joy of giving. Churches have failed in this regard. Many believers do not tithe. Because we have failed in giving, we have failed to get the Gospel out to the ends of the earth.

A short time ago I picked up a missionary magazine coming from India. In the pages of this magazine I saw an article on giving. It said, "The person who has never learned to give has never learned to live, and the Christian who has never learned to tithe has never learned to do the Lord's will in the matter of giving. He has never learned to rightly relate his material substance to the kingdom of God." The article went on to speak of tithing and why this person believed in tithing. "I practice tithing because it is God's plan. He has a plan for every life. In a matter so important as the giving of oneself, He surely has a plan. He gave the tithing plan to Israel and she used it through the centuries. If the Jew under the rigid law gave a tithe and beyond, certainly I can do no less under the liberality of His grace."

But the article went on to speak of tithing. "I practice tithing because it is systematic and sensible. It puts every giver on the same basis. No one is asked to give more in proportion than another. The man who makes hundreds of dollars per week and the widow who makes five dollars per week are giving the same amount proportionately. It solves the individual giver's problem. He always knows just how much he has to give and knows how to respond to the calls that are made on him. If he uses the old haphazard way of giving, he never knows where he stands. Tithing does away with uncertainty in giving and puts it on a systematic and sensible business basis. I believe this is pleasing to God."

At the end of this article, to my surprise, I saw the name of

William Herschel Ford. Dr. Ford had preached in our church many times. His article on tithing had been carried in some magazines of this country and then had been copied by a leader of the Lucknow Christian College in India.

Let me give emphasis to the matter of tithing. FIRST IT IS GOD'S PLAN, AND SECOND, IT IS SYSTEMATIC AND SENSIBLE. God will not fail if we are honest in our tithing. He will give us blessings far beyond anything that we might imagine. In this matter of missions we have failed in our giving.

THIRD, WE HAVE FAILED IN THE GIVING OF OUR YOUTH. Has youth failed to respond? I doubt it. We have failed to challenge them and we have failed to give them to the work of missions. This means that mothers and fathers must relinquish their claims upon their children and say with joy, "I send my child to the mission fields if he feels that is where God wants him."

A mission secretary said to a gentleman who was taking leave of his son who was going to a foreign mission land. "Is it not a great trial to you to part with your eldest son?"

The man replied, "Yes, it is a great trial, but I have been expecting it for a long time. The day my son was born I attended a missionary meeting and was greatly impressed with what I heard. When I went home, I took the babe out of the bed and, holding him in my arms, I said to my wife, 'Will you give this boy to the work of missions?'

"She replied, 'Yes, I will.'

"From that time I have been expecting my boy to go to the mission field. I gave him, my wife gave him, if God wanted him."

In too many cases we have been holding on to our children. Our affection has led us into gross selfishness until we have not been open hearted in the giving of our youth.

I say to you that we have not gone far enough in the work of missions. We have failed in the matter of having a burden for souls. We have failed in the giving of our youth.

## WE REJOICE IN THAT WHICH HAS BEEN DONE

FIRST, EVERY CHILD OF GOD WILL REJOICE IN THE SOULS SAVED THROUGH THE WORK OF MISSIONS IN THE DAYS GONE BY. We are glad that God has saved our souls and we are glad that He has saved the souls of others. It is a mark that we have been born again if we rejoice in the salvation of other individuals.

SECOND, WE REJOICE ALSO IN THE WORK OF MISSIONARIES OF THE PAST. We cannot fail to be happy that God has used so many in the great work of spreading the Gospel around the world. How we thank God that David Livingstone went into Africa and gave the Gospel to many, and explored that great country and did a work which blessed missions to this hour. It was Livingstone who wrote in his journal on May 13, 1872, "He will keep His Word, the gracious One, full of grace and truth. no doubt of it! He said, '. . .*him that cometh to me I will in no wise cast out*' (John 6:37), and '. . .*whatsoever ye shall ask in my name, that will I do. . .*' (John 14:13). He will keep His Word! Then I can come home and humbly present my petition, and it will be all right. Doubt is here inadmissible surely." The great Livingstone believed in missions and he believed that God would pour out His blessing upon him.

We rejoice in the work of the great William Carey. In a time of adversity Carey sailed for India, believing that God had the power to save souls and to do a transformation in the lives of multitudes.

Thomas Bridges, that boy who was picked up on St. Thomas Bay between two London bridges, went to

Patagonia to live and preach and teach and to love the people to Jesus Christ. It is common knowledge that when Darwin first went to Patagonia, he found not a Christian, but when Charles Darwin (one who was not a Christian) went to Patagonia the second time, he found most of the people had accepted Jesus Christ and were walking in His steps.

Adoniram Judson went to the land of Burma — a land of darkness, idolatry, and cruelty. The hilltops were crowned with Buddhist temples. A savage king ruled whose will was law. It was Judson who labored for seven years before he saw his first convert. But, he kept on and for thirty-two years he literally gave himself to preach Christ, the Saviour of the world. At his death there were thousands of converts in India. I say to you that we rejoice in that which has been done. The work of missionaries of the past gives us encouragement to press on.

THIRD, WE REJOICE IN THE MISSIONARIES OF THE PRESENT HOUR. In 1957, I sent to New York City for the exact number of missionaries at that time in the world. I received a wire telling me that there were at that time 34,692 missionaries — Protestant missionaries. Of this 34,692, 23,432 were from North America.

The world population in 1957 was about three billion people. If you would take the ratio of missionaries to people, you would find there was one missionary for every 85,714 persons (based on estimated figures in 1957).

There are not enough on the fields, but we rejoice to know of the ones who are there, and we praise God that souls are being saved and the work is going on. Let us join in prayer that God will send out more to the fields, that the message of missions — the message of Christ's saving power — might reach the untold thousands who are yet in darkness.

## WE DEDICATE OURSELVES TO THE TASK BEFORE US

FIRST, WE HAVE A TASK. It is a world wide task. It is the task of reaching the billions of people — six billion by the year 2,000!

We have a task also in our nation. Church membership figures of some time ago reveal the following: There were 63,000 Buddhists in America; 36,700 who belong to Old Catholic and Polish National Catholic Churches; TWO MILLION, THREE HUNDRED EIGHTY SIX THOUSAND were Eastern Orthodox.

5,500,000 were Jewish people.

Roman Catholics numbered 33,396,000.

Protestants numbered 58,448,000.

This gives a total of approximately 100,000,000 people in America who belonged to some kind of church. This was about 59% of the population. You will be interested also to know that in the following year, Roman Catholics increased 3.5% and Protestants increased 3.9%.

We have a task — a task in this world — and a task in America. The fields are white unto harvest. We must not fail to go with the Gospel.

SECOND, THE TASK IS DIFFICULT. It is not easy. The enemies are strong. The world, the flesh, and the devil are fighting. There is constant opposition.

We must constantly remind ourselves that our first business as followers of Christ is to give the Gospel to those who have it not. If we are not missionary Christians, then we are missing Christians in the day when rewards are given. We should be asking ourselves daily, "What does God want me to do?" Perhaps some are hearing the call now to go to the mission field. Others are being called upon to give of their means. All of us should be praying for missions.

We have heard the Gospel but many have not. We owe much to the heathen people. Let us pay our debt and give them the Word of God. This means the giving of ourselves and the giving of our funds.

THIRD, THE TASK IS JOYOUS. Any achievement brings joy. The saving of souls will always give us joy.

The companionship of our Lord will give us joy. Why did Jesus come down to this earth? Why did He make this long sojourn amidst poverty and scorn? Why did He give His life in a toilsome ministry in Galilee and Judaea? Why the journey to Jerusalem and the trail of rejection and cruel death? The answer is given in a verse of Scripture, *"For the Son of man is come to seek and to save that which was lost."*

We are the recipients of the grace of God and the salvation of our Lord. Now that we are saved, we have His companionship with us. May we not be selfish, but may we share Jesus with others who know Him not.

FINALLY, HIS COMMENDATION IS JOYOUS AND CERTAIN. If we are faithful, then He will commend us. When we stand before the judgment seat of Christ, we will hear Him say, *". . . Well done, thou good and faithful servant. . ."* (Matthew 25:21).

Are you faithful in the work of missions? Are you giving your money? Do you spend time in prayer? Do you recognize the call of God unto us? The time is ripe. Let us go now and do what God has commanded us.

Robert Moffatt, the great African missionary, led a man called "Africaner" to the Lord Jesus. This man was a notorious Hottentot chief. He was the scourge and terror of that country. The people did not believe it possible that he could be converted, and after he became a Christian, many wanted to see him and to see him in the company of the missionary. A more bloody man never tasted the power of Christ to save.

It is said that this chieftain went with Mr. Moffatt to Capetown. On the way he mentioned the fact of Africaner's conversion, and a Dutch farmer said, "I can believe almost anything you say, but that I cannot credit. There are seven wonders in the world — that would be the eighth."

Mr. Moffatt assured the farmer that the desperado had become a changed man. The farmer said, "Well, if what you say is true, I have only one wish, and that is to see the man before I die. When you return, as sure as the sun is over my head, I will go with you to see him, though he killed my own uncle."

At this word the missionary conducted the farmer to the wagon and pointed to the chief and said, "There he is." The farmer was astounded. Starting back, he said, "Are you Africaner?" The chief doffed his hat in a respectful bow and said, "I am." Then he testified to the truth of the missionary's statement regarding his conversion. Then the farmer cried, "Oh God, what a miracle of thy power! What cannot Thy grace acomplish?"

We must believe that this Gospel message can save souls anywhere if people will receive it and will take the Lord Jesus Christ.

We must not hesitate to give it here in our own land. We must not hesitate to tell men and women everywhere that Jesus can save. I want everyone who has not believed on the Lord Jesus Christ to know that Christ can save you. He waits to save you. Will you trust Him now? Yes, Jesus, the Son of man *". . .is come to seek and to save that which was lost"*

# 22
# "Churchy" Chattanooga and a Lost World

*"But when he saw the multitudes, he moved with compassion on them, because they fainted, and were scattered abroad, as sheep having no shepherd."*
—Matthew 9:36

Chattanooga is a city of churches. You cannot drive far in any direction without seeing a church. We have churches of all denominations, many of them large and flourishing.

The city is well evangelized, but by no means converted. According to the figures of a few years ago, there were but 65,000 church members in all churches of all denominations. Compared with the population we can see there is still much to do in Chattanooga.

Although I love our city, if I were making a choice of a place to serve, this would be my last choice. The finest people in the world are found here. God has blessed me and my ministry, but if I had my choice, I would choose a place where the opportunities for evangelism were greater than in this location. I would want to be in that place where the true Gospel is not preached, or where the Gospel has never been heard at all.

But God has placed me here and here I stay until He moves me. But whether in Chattanooga, Chicago, or China, I can have a missionary outlook on the world. I can by my prayers and my giving have a part in the winning of souls wherever missionaries go.

"Churchy" Chattanooga is doing far too little toward sending the Gospel around the world. There are three things which hinder.

FIRST, A COMPETITIVE SPIRIT AMONG CHURCHES. This is deplorable. The competition among local churches means a lessening interest in world wide missions. God knows and you know that this church has never engaged in competitive work. We do our very best, but we are not endeavoring to beat another church. No one can point to the occasion when I said, "Let's work hard and beat such and such a church". I fear such a thing, for it is of the flesh. I say again, the competitive spirit, for it lessens the interest of people in the salvation of souls around the world.

SECOND, THE COOPERATIVE SPIRIT HINDERS MISSION WORK. Some churches are so bound by the cooperative idea that they cannot see the mission fields. We need to cooperate, but we need also the spirit of enterprise — launching out into new and untouched fields for the sake of lost mankind.

THIRD, THE CONCENTRATION OF TOO MANY WORKERS AND TOO MUCH MONEY IN ONE PLACE HINDERS MISSION WORK. We need the spirit of the church at Antioch when they were impressed by the Spirit of God to send out Barnabas and Paul as missionaries. They sent away from their local church the very best they had.

We need the spirit of the early Christians who lost all love for earthly things, and sold their possessions and gave the money to the apostles. We are spending too much money in one place while the world is bleeding and dying. Especially those of us who believe in the soon coming of Jesus should be careful how we put all of our money in brick and mortar and decorations to satisfy the flesh.

There needs to be a scattering as it was in the early days of persecution. That is the program of this church — to scatter the message just as far as we can. Because of that we support through the World Faith Mission Fund over five hundred and sixty missionaries.

As we think of this city of churches, beautiful buildings, fine equipment, and hundreds of workers, a three-fold prayer should come to our lips.

## O GOD, GIVE US A VISION OF THE WORLD!

Roughly, here is the world picture: Seventy per cent of the world is without Christ. Approximately one billion, five hundred million people do not know our Saviour.

Your heart will be made to ache whenever you read of the terrible darkness of this world. Thousands dying every day who have never heard the name of Jesus. Africa, the open sore of the world, with her one hundred and fifty million, calling for laborers. India, the land of little widows and child wives, with her six hundred million stretching out weary hands for the light. China, with eight hundred million helpless, lost people.

This is only a small part of the world picture, but it should be enough to make our hearts burn within us, and to make our faces burn with the consciousness of our failure.

Yes, we need to pray for a world vision — which will give us an interest in the soul of the man farthest away as well as the one closest to us. The people in the back rows of the world need to hear as well as the ones in front. America, sitting in the front rows, is fat, full, and rebellious. But there are those away back who have never heard for the first time.

The fields are white unto harvest. The time is right and ready. We need to hasten to the fields, to those who wait for our coming.

The knowledge of Christ in our hearts, and a vision of a lost world, will make us want to go and tell others. There is an interesting story in II Kings 7. The Syrians had laid siege to Samaria. The people were starving and hungry. Outside of the camp of the Syrians, there were four lepers. They said, "*. . .Why sit we here until we die?*" (II Kings 7:3). They reasoned that they might as well go inside the camp of the Syrians and take their chances on the mercy of the enemy, for they were starving to death. They arose and came inside the camp, and found that the Syrians were gone, but they had left everything behind them. Food was in abundance. They began to eat and when they had feasted upon all the good things, they said one to another:

> "*. . .We do not well: this day is a day of good tidings, and we hold our peace: if we tarry till the morning light, some mischief will come upon us: now therefore come, that we may go and tell the king's household.*"
>
> —II Kings 7:9

**O GOD, GIVE US A WILLINGNESS TO GO.**

Persecution scattered the early Christians and they went everywhere preaching the Word.

We do not have persecution to scatter our people today; therefore, there must be placed into our hearts by the Holy Spirit a willingness to go to those who need Christ.

God has already called many to be missionaries who are unwilling to go.

Too many seek the ease and comfort of home. Too many men are looking for a place of prestige and leadership, and are unwilling to take the lowly place of a missionary.

Someone has said that there are fifteen thousand students in one hundred divinity schools of America. Only a few will ever respond for foreign mission service. At the present time

Without a burden for souls, we will never be missionary minded. We must have a concern for souls of men.

Christ had a burden for all. There was no respect of persons with Him. Some people have a burden for certain ones. They would endeavor to win some to Christ, but would pass others by. This is surely not the burden for souls which we have.

A burden, a crying concern for the souls of others is the thing which will make us pray and give and witness. May we as Christians pray for concern which will send us to those near at hand and give us an interest also in the souls of those far away.

A friend of mine told this story in one of his sermons:

> A little girl was dying. She sent for the preacher to come to see her. Her father was a man who had never cared for religion, the Bible, the church, nor salvation. When the preacher got there, he tried to comfort her. He wanted to pray for her, and he said, "Wouldn't you like to get well again?" She said, "I don't think so, sir."
>
> The preacher didn't know what she meant. He asked her why she said that. And then she told him about her father and said, "Preacher, I have tried over and over again to get my daddy to go hear you preach, and he wouldn't do it. And I think that if I die, you'll preach my funeral, won't you?
>
> The preacher hardly knew what to say, but he told her he supposed he would. And then waited to see what she would say next. She said, "Preacher, when I die, and you preach my funeral, my daddy will go to the funeral. I've tried so many times to get him to go hear you preach, and he wouldn't. But if you preach my funeral, he'll go then, and he'll hear you preach.

there are ten young women who present themselves to mission boards for every one man. Southern Baptists have 32,000 churches. These are pastored by more than 25,000 ministers. How easily we could spare a thousand of this 25,000 to go as missionaries.

Perhaps the Lord is speaking to you. Pray that God will make you willing to go. We need volunteers.

Volunteers who love Christ supremely. You will not be much of a missionary unless you love Christ more than you love the things of the world.

Volunteers who will risk their lives for the sake of the Gospel. There must be a forgetting of self and a willingness to go anywhere for Christ.

We need volunteers who will stick to the business of preaching Christ. We have enough missionaries now sitting behind college desks. The call is for those who will go out and preach the Gospel.

Our Heavenly Father was the first to enter the advertising business. Centuries ago he advertised for a man in this way: "*. . . Whom shall I send, and who will go for us?. . .* (Isaiah 6:8).

*From out of the ranks stepped Isaiah, and answered "*. . .*Here am I; send me*" (Isaiah 6:8).

The Lord is calling now to all of you, "Who will go for us?" God grant that many will answer, "Here am I; send me."

We need to make it a matter of prayer that workers will be sent into the harvest fields, for Jesus said, *"Pray ye therefore the Lord of the harvest, that he will send forth laborers into his harvest"* (Matthew 9:38).

**O GOD, GIVE US A BURDEN FOR SOULS**

Without a burden for souls, there will be no volunteers for the mission field.

And I'd rather die six times if I can only get my daddy to hear the Gospel one time."

The preacher left and when the little girl finally died, he was sick himself and could not conduct the funeral service. But sometime later on, a man came to his office and said, "You don't know me, do you?"

"I don't believe I do," said the preacher.

"I'm the father of little Mary, the girl who died the other day." And I heard how she said before she died that she would die six times if she could get me to hear the Gospel. It broke my heart, and I want to be saved."

Yes, he found salvation that day. Why? Because of the concern of his little girl over his salvation.

Let us pray for a burden for souls which will make us willing to give and pray and go, yes, and die, if by so doing, others can be saved.

# 23
# Scattered

*"Therefore they that were scattered abroad went every where preaching the word."*

—Acts 8:4

In the years that followed the flood all men spoke one language. They dwelt together and feared but one thing — "*. . .lest we be scattered. . .*". They said, "*. . .Go to, let us build us a city and a tower, whose top may reach unto heaven; and let us make us a name, lest we be scattered abroad upon the face of the whole earth*" (Genesis 11:4).

In order to scatter them God sent a confusion of tongues. They could no longer build, because they could not understand one another. "*So the Lord scattered them abroad from thence upon the face of all the earth. . .*" (Genesis 11:8).

The scattering process has always been feared by man. Today instead of scattering to the ends of the earth to accomplish great things for God, the denominations are trying to come together. Many denominations have already united, simply to increase their size and to make a name for themselves.

Before Jesus ascended unto the Father, He told His followers to scatter to the ends of the earth, and to witness regarding Him. Instead of scattering, they joined themselves together in Jerusalem. They seemed to fear separation from one another.

But when the great persecution arose, at the time of the

stoning of Stephen, the Christians were scattered — "...*except the apostles*" (Acts 8:1) — they still stayed close to the home base. Philip was one who was thrust out. He went to Samaria, and conducted a sweeping revival. When God was finished with him in Samaria, he sent him into the desert to speak to a single soul, and to lead that one to Christ. The flood scattered God's people at one time and persecution scattered them at another time. We are concerned about this second scattering.

Why did God want His people to scatter? In order that they might spread abroad the message of love and salvation.

Three things confront us as we face the necessity to scatter the message.

## THE GREAT COMMISSION

Men have been commissioned to do almost everything, but the greatest commission ever handed to man was given by the Lord Jesus. In Matthew 28 we hear Him say, *"Go ye therefore and teach all nations, baptizing them in the name of the Father, and of the Son, and of the Holy Ghost: Teaching them to observe all things whatsoever I have commanded you: and, lo, I am with you alway, even unto the end of the world"* (Matthew 28:19,20).

Someone has said, "If you want to follow Jesus Christ, you must follow Him to the ends of the earth, for that is where He is going."

In Acts 1:8, our Lord said to his disciples, *"But ye shall receive power, after that the Holy Ghost is come upon you: and ye shall be witnesses unto me both in Jerusalem, and in all Judea, and in Samaria, and unto the uttermost part of the earth."*

The commission of Christ to us was given to be obeyed. We have no alternative — there is no option. The great commission is given to all — there are no exceptions and no exemptions.

It can be obeyed in three ways.

FIRST, BY THE GIVING OF OUR MONEY. I pity and sympathize with that person who has never known the joy of giving his money in order that someone might take the story of Jesus to the lost and dying heathen. We cannot all go to foreign fields in person, but our money can help to send others.

SECOND, WE CAN GO BY PRAYING. This great avenue of blessing is open to all. It is sad that such a few avail themselves of it. Daily pray for missionaries by name. Pray for mission work around the world, and though we be thousands of miles from some mission fields, God is able to hear and to answer.

THIRD, WE CAN OBEY THE GREAT COMMISSION BY GOING. It is the plan of Christ that many shall hear the call and respond by giving themselves. Someone must go and tell the story of redemption.

It was said of Christ that after His resurrection when He went to heaven in victory and power, the whole angelic host came out to welcome Him. The archangel, the head of the parade, was the spokesman. He said, "Lord, you have finished the redemptive work on the cross. Is it enough to save the world?"

The Lord answered with a note of victory, the same loud cry which came from the cross, "*. . .It is finished. . .*" (John 19:30). The archangel seemed to be satisfied with the answer. But another question came up as to how the world might know of this Gospel, to which the Lord answered, "I have told my disciples, 'Go ye into all the world, and preach the Gospel to every creature.'"

But the archangel queried again, "The world does not

know. Suppose your disciples become busy with their own work, and Peter goes back to fishing, or Levi goes back to the customs office, and they forget to preach the Gospel. What will you do?"

There was a pause. The Lord looked straight into the face of the archangel, and said with determination, "They must, for I have no other plan."

The story may be imaginary, but the point of emphasis is true. Christ left no other plan save the going of His people to tell the story.

The great commission is before us. It was given by Christ, and it was given to be obeyed. We can obey by giving, by praying, and by going. Have you obeyed the great commission?

## THE GREAT TEMPTATION

Christ said, "*. . .Go ye into all the world. . .*". Again, he said, "*. . .and ye shall be witnesses unto me in Jerusalem, in all Judea, and in Samaria, and unto the uttermost part of the earth.*" What, then, is the great temptation?

FIRST, TO DELAY OBEDIENCE. Every sincere Christian recognizes the call of God, but it is easy to say, "Not now." The great temptation in mission work is to delay, to procrastinate.

SECOND, IT IS TO SEEK THE EASY PLACE. Going into destitute and lonely places with the Gospel is not a pleasant task. It is easier to stay at home. It was easier for the disciples to remain in Jerusalem. Although there was opposition, it was easier to remain in the field where the pioneer work had already been done. Beware of the easy place. Don't allow selfish ease to tempt you into disobedience.

THIRD, THE GREAT TEMPTATION IS TO BE SATISFIED WITH PAST ACCOMPLISHMENTS. The apostles must have been satisfied with the results of Pentecost, and the days thereafter.

They were not in any hurry to seek out new fields. They succumbed to the temptation to remain at home. And the Scripture tells us that even when many disciples were being scattered abroad throughout Judea and Samaria, the apostles still remained at home. Let us never be satisfied with what we have done in the past, or with our present accomplishments. As long as men are lost, let us not cease our efforts to win others.

FOURTH, THERE IS A GREAT TEMPTATION TO SEEK OUR OWN AND NO MORE. To a certain extent we are all guilty of this. We want our families, our loved ones, our close friends saved, but we are not too much concerned about those we do not know. I have noticed that many wives are concerned about winning their husbands, but as soon as the husband is saved, they show no further concern for anyone else. Parents are often concerned for their children, but as soon as the children are saved, they do not show anxiety for other lost people.

This is a great temptation. We realize the truth and the urgency of the great commission, but we are sorely tempted to delay our obedience, to seek the easy place, to be satisfied with our accomplishments, and to seek our own. For Christ's sake, for souls' sake, let us war against this temptation, and seek to be obedient to our Master's call.

## THE GREAT COMPULSION

We have noted the great commission, given by Christ to be obeyed by every Christian. We have noticed also the great temptation to disobey. Now, may we consider the great compulsion — the things which compel, yea, even drive us to obedience.

FIRST, THERE IS THE CONSCIOUSNESS OF MAN'S NEED. We will never be missionaries in heart and action until there is given us a real consciousness of man's need of Christ. We must come to realize that people without the Saviour are lost and hell-bound. We must know that hell is an eternal place, and those who go there will have no opportunity for release.

After seeing the lost condition of man, we need to pray that God will give us a compassion for all people, of all races, kindred, and tongues. Someone has written an estimate of the world's condition:

> "Is it nothing to you that Japan, with her 80 million people, only has one hundred fifty missionaries?
>
> "Is it nothing to you that 500 thousand Indians in Brazil have not heard the Gospel?
>
> "Is it nothing to you that 40 million will die this year without ever having heard the Gospel?
>
> "Is it nothing to you that two-thirds of the population of the world is unevangelized?
>
> "Is it nothing to you that 27 mission children in America are spiritually illiterate?
>
> "Is it nothing to you that there are ten thousand villages in the U.S.A. without a church, and 30 thousand without a resident pastor?
>
> "Is it nothing to you that in America only one out of three children attend Sunday School?
>
> "Is it nothing to you that two-thirds of the Indians have not heard the Gospel?
>
> "Is it nothing to you that only 8% of the population of our country goes to church on Sunday morning, and only 2% on Sunday evening.?
>
> "Is it nothing to you that souls are perishing, and that among them are your own loved ones, neighbors, and friends?

May God give us a vivid picture of man's need, and of this world's need. Rev. W. W. Martin said, "I had put over the clock in a certain mission, '83 A MINUTE'" At last a committee came to the pastor and said, "Will you kindly take that down. It haunts us." They knew it meant that eighty-three souls a minute were passing into eternity, into the dark, who had never heard of Jesus Christ.

Study and pray until this fact of man's need becomes a burden to your heart and then you will be interested in missions at home and abroad.

SECOND, LOVE FOR OUR FELLOWMAN SHOULD MAKE US MISSIONARIES. If we love people, we will not be happy to see them wait and wait to hear about Christ, and die in darkness, and go to hell.

A person's heart must surely be made of stone, if it is not moved by this statement by an old Mohammedan woman: "How long is it since Jesus died for sinful people? Look at me. I am old. I have prayed, given alms, gone to the holy shrines, become dust from fasting, and all this is useless. Where have you been all this time?"

Whose heart would not be moved by the cry of a man in the snow heights of the Andes: "How is it," said he, "that during all the years of my life I have never before heard that Jesus Christ spoke those precious words?"

A Moor in North America said to a Bible seller, "Why have you not gone everywhere with this Book? Why do so many of my people not know of the Jesus whom it proclaims? Why have you hoarded it to yourselves? Shame on you!"

These are but a few of the cries which have come from the world — from people who finally heard the Gospel after years of delay.

Dr. S. D. Gordon once told this story with peculiar missionary emphasis:

"It happened in one of our Southern cities, during the time before the Civil War. Sanitary conditions were very poor. A plague came to a city — a plague of disease, and wrought havoc. The city death cart was rolling in the streets almost all the time, and hardly a home but had a tear, and a vacant chair. Into one very poor home the disease came and did rapid work. They were all carried out one after another, until there remained a mother and her baby boy of about five or six years.

"The story says that he crept on his mother's knee, with his baby face very close to hers, and he said, 'Mother, father's dead, and brother and sisters are dead. Suppose you die. What will I do?'

"What could she say with the face so close to hers? She must keep brave. Her heart had thought of it, but what could she say? She was a Christian woman, and as she swallowed hard, she said, 'My boy, if I should die, the Lord Jesus will come for you.'

"The answer satisfied his heart. He had been trained from earliest life to know about Jesus, and how good He was. The boy went about his play on the floor thinking, 'It is all right. If mother should die, Jesus will come for me.'

"The disease did quick work. The mother died, and they carried her away. The little lad followed and saw where she was laid. He came back to the house, and in the excitement of the town, he was forgotten, and he was left alone in the poor, humble home. He tried to sleep that night but couldn't, so he arose and dressed himself as best he could. He found his way down the street, and out upon the road to where they had laid her. Finding the spot, he threw himself down upon the freshly thrown-up earth, and went until nature kindly stole away his consciousness in sleep.

"Early in the next morning, just at the break of day, a Christian gentleman, coming down the road, past the graveyard, saw the boy, and quickly guessed some story of a heart-breaking kind. He called to him and said, 'My boy, what are you doing there?'

"The boy raised himself, rubbed his eyes, and said, 'Well, my father's dead, and brothers and sisters are dead, and now mother's dead. She said that if she did die, Jesus would come for me. But He hasn't come, and I am tired of waiting.'

"The man was greatly touched and then said quietly, as he tried to control his voice, 'Well, my boy, I've come for you.'

"The boy looked up with his eyes big and said, 'You've been a long time coming.'"

Jesus said, "*. . .Go ye into all the world. . .*" (Mark 16:15). How many are saying now, "You have been a long time coming to us." Millions will die and never hear. Surely love for our fellowman and his eternal soul will make of us missionaries at home and abroad.

THIRD, OUR LOVE FOR CHRIST SHOULD BE THE STRONGEST COMPULSION OF ALL TO MAKE US MISSIONARIES. Jesus paid the supreme price that we might be saved. It is not enough to sing, "O, how I love Jesus." We must show that we love Him by obeying His command.

Let us begin now to scatter this blessed Gospel everywhere

we go. In the home, in the office, in the school, on the street, in the buses, in the factories, in the stores — everywhere, we should be busy scattering the Word, even as the farmer scatters the seed over the field.

We have a great commission to obey — a great temptation to fight, and a great compulsion — our love for Christ, to send us into the harvest fields.

# 24
# The Field of Missions

*"Say not ye, There are yet four months, and then cometh harvest? behold, I say unto you, Lift up your eyes, and look on the fields; for they are white already to harvest."*

—John 4:35

Many people live to eat. Their god is their stomach. Such is almost the picture of John 4. The disciples left Christ and went into Sychar of Samaria to buy food.

The Saviour sat down at Jacob's well. A woman came to draw water. Christ engaged her in conversation. As a result of the kindly but probing words of Jesus, the woman accepted Him as Saviour. She went away to tell others about Christ.

When the disciples returned from their expedition to buy meat, they urged Christ to eat. But the Saviour said, "*. . .I have meat to eat that ye know not of*" (John 4:32). The disciples thought that someone else had brought Him food, but Jesus said, "*. . .My meat is to do the will of him that sent me, and to finish his work*" (John 4:34). Then we find the words of our text, "*Say not ye, There are yet four months, and then cometh harvest? behold, I say unto you, Lift up your eyes, and look on the fields; for they are white already to harvest.*"

In this chapter on missions, we are discussing the fields — the fields that are white unto harvest.

### THE FIELDS ARE ROUGH

The way was rough in the day of Jesus. Our Saviour felt the

opposition of man, the hatred of many. He saw His disciples weakly turn away from Him. The record is given in John 6:66, *"From that time many of his disciples went back, and walked no more with him."*

It is hard to find a day in the life of our Saviour that was not filled with anguish and heartache. And yet, Jesus looked upon the crowds and saw in them the people for whom He had come to die, and He gave Himself without reserve to the business of pointing them to salvation in Him. But, let us keep this before us — the fields were rough. There was nothing easy in the task given to our Saviour.

The early disciples felt the roughness of the fields. When we come to the book of Acts and see Peter preaching on the day of Pentecost, we discover mockers in the crowd. Throughout the entire book of the Acts, we find the record of suffering and death. As a matter of fact, all the disciples died in some violent way with the exception of John. Paul, who counted himself as one of the apostles, suffered greatly. Listen to him:

> *"Of the Jews five times received I forty stripes save one.*
>
> *"Thrice was I beaten with rods, once was I stoned, thrice I suffered shipwreck, a night and a day I have been in the deep;*
>
> *"In journeyings often, in perils of waters, in perils of robbers, in perils by mine own countrymen, in perils by the heathen, in perils in the city, in perils in the wilderness, in perils in the sea, in perils among false brethren;*
>
> *"In weariness and painfulness, in watchings often, in hunger and thirst, in fastings often, in cold and nakedness."*
>
> — II Corinthians 11:24-27

The Apostle Paul saw the fields white unto harvest, but he also saw the roughness of the fields. He was conscious of the suffering which attaches itself to everyone who walks with the Lord Jesus Christ. Let us remember that the suffering endured by the Apostle Paul was endured by many others who were faithful servants of the Lord Jesus in the first century.

The fields are rough today. There is so much around us that brings adversity and suffering. It is not easy to give the Gospel to men. The doors do not swing open. Invitations of "Welcome" are not spread out. The giving of the Gospel is often the hardest task that can be assigned to a man.

Catholicism has closed many doors on the mission fields. In South America many have died because of the persecution brought against missionaries by Catholicism. Missionaries are not allowed in some countries. They cannot walk down the street and preach the message of Jesus Christ. The hierarchy of the Catholic church has brought a roughness into many fields of service.

Communism has also caused difficulties on various mission fields. The doors in China are closed. Missionaries can no longer go into that great mass of mankind and preach the Word of God. The only work in China today is that which is carried on by native people. In various parts of the world communism is closing in and turning people away from salvation through Jesus Christ.

The roughness of this day is also increased by the fast living. People have no time for God. The speed in which we live has ruled out the consideration of the needs of the eternal soul.

Again, plain, open, bitter sin is also increasing the roughness of this day. In the vast category of present day sins, one is quite prominent because of its opposition to missions: I speak of the sin of selfishness. Selfishness fights against the giving of money and of lives to get the Gospel to the ends of the earth.

Let us remember that the man who opposes missions is opposing Christ. When men believe in Christ, they must believe in missions, for our Saviour was a missionary.

Let us be conscious of difficulties and the problems in the present time, but let us remember that there have always been problems in getting out the Gospel. The fields have always been rough. Satan is opposed to missions and will do all that he can to hinder the work of God-called men and women who march forth with the message of Christ.

## THE FIELDS ARE RECEDING

When Jesus gave the great commission, the world was a tremendous place. Travel was slow. Much of the world was undiscovered. Men lived within the confines of certain well-known areas, but today — the world is small. In a matter of hours a jet plane can go around the world. In a few days one can be on many fields of the world.

Yes, travel has made our present world a small place. But let us not forget something — though the world may be small, as considered in the realm of present day travel, it is still a place largely unreached by the Gospel of Jesus Christ. The map lines may recede, but still, multitudes are without the Saviour.

Let us set ourselves to utilize every channel of communication and travel to get the Gospel to all men.

Let us send our missionaries, but let us use radio, television, the printing press, and various other avenues of expression. Let us make sure that the man in the farthest corner of the world hears of the Gospel of Jesus Christ. Let us not withhold from him the message of our Saviour when that message can be sent to him with ease if we will simply give ourselves, our time, and our money.

Someone tells the story of the transmission of messages in Africa. If a certain chieftain wishes to send a message hundreds of miles across the jungle, he summons the village drummer and gives him three pieces of information — the message, the name of the addressee, and the name of the drummer five miles down the line who is to relay the message.

The drummer then hastens to the center of the clearing, picks up his sticks and commences to beat out the message. The drum is a bit of hollowed out log. It has high and low tones and the use of the drummer's code makes it possible to transmit messages of relative intricacy from point to point.

The notes of the drum echo and re-echo through the jungle. Miles away another village drummer is out in the forest hunting; ever on the alert he recognizes his drum name, listens to the message, drops his hunting net, and runs back to his town to relay the words in the direction of the one for whom the message is intended. Thus from drummer to drummer the message is carried until in due course it reaches its destination.

Two thousand years ago God sent His Son into the world to die upon the cross that men might be saved. Jesus died, rose again, and ascended to the Father. But He put in our hands a message to be given to the whole world. We have his commission to go into all the world and to preach the Gospel to every creature.

In every day God has raised up men who have answered his call, understood the message, realized that it was intended for a lost race of men, and sounded it forth with notes of clarion clearness. They were drummers for God. They were sending out this message into a lost and needy world.

The fields are receding today, but the message must go out.

God has given to us effective ways for the transmission of the good news. May we not fail Him to get the Gospel to men and women every where.

## THE FIELDS ARE READY

First, I said the fields are rough.

Second, the fields are receding.

Third, the fields are ready. Yes, not only ready, but ripe! I restrained myself from using the word "rotten." Some might misunderstand, but in too many cases, we have failed to go with the message of our Saviour, and the rottenness of sin has overtaken whole areas, and even whole nations. Why? Because we failed to go. The fields were ready. The time was right, but we did not respond.

The fields were ready in the day of Jesus Christ. That is the reason Jesus could say to the disciples, "*. . .Lift up your eyes, and look on the fields; for they are white already to harvest*" (John 4:35). He was saying, "*Go, give the message, do the work — the time is at hand.*"

The fields were ready in the day of the Apostle Paul. He saw the fields and went out as the first missionary from the church in Antioch. He might have stayed at home and sought a place of ease and luxury; but instead he went out into the fields which brought privation and suffering. Why? He saw the ready fields. He saw they were white already to harvest and he went with the message of our Christ.

The fields were ready in the day of William Carey. He saw the fields and answered God's call. He was just a cobbler, humble and unknown, but God made him one of the world's greatest linguists. He translated the Bible into thirty-five languages and dialects. He published six grammars and compiled three dictionaries.

The fields were ready in the day of David Livingstone and

he responded to the call of God. Livingstone was just a humble weaver, but he went into Africa and opened up that dark and unknown continent. With persistence he travelled from place to place until a new map was drawn and the Gospel preached in the most isolated villages.

The fields were ready in the days of Dr. Peter Parker. He was the first medical missionary to China. It was said of him,

"He opened the gates of China with a lancet, when western cannons could not heave a single bar."

Peter Parker specialized in eye diseases. China was a country where many were blind. He answered the call and went out as a medical missionary.

The fields were ready in the day of Robert Moffatt, one of the great missionaries to Africa.

The story is simply told of a mother and son walking along a winding country road near Fife, Scotland. They were soon to part for the first time and their hearts were heavy.

"Robert," said his mother, "I have just one thing to ask you and I want you to promise me before I ask."

Robert was reluctant to answer before he knew what he was promising, but after some persuasion he gave his word.

"Promise me," she said, "that every night before you to to sleep you will read a chapter in your Bible and pray."

The youth kept his promise. Because of that promise his knowledge of Jesus as Lord and Saviour grew and led him to be a missionary in Africa. The work still goes on. The fields were ready, and he responded.

Dear friend, the fields are ready in our day. We must give and go and pray. We must not hesitate to do all that we can to bring people to the Lord Jesus Christ.

Dr. Clovis Chappel tells the story of a man who was said to be more familiar with Chinese affairs than any other man in his time. Because of this a great oil company sought to obtain his services. It sent a representative to offer him a salary of ten thousand a year. When he refused, the representative went up to twenty-five thousand. Then he invited him to set his own salary. In reply, this missionary said, "The salary you offered first is large enough. I am making only twelve hundred a year. It is not your salary that's too small — it is your job! I have a bigger job than you can possibly offer."

The fields are ready, for men are lost and dying. Without our Saviour, they perish forever. Without Jesus, they drop into the pit of hell for eternity. The commission has been given to us. May we not fail our Saviour, but may we go with this gospel message.

# 25
# The Enemy of Missions

*"Forasmuch then as the children are partakers of flesh and blood, he also himself likewise took part of the same; that through death he might destroy him that had the power of death, that is, the devil."*

—Hebrews 2:14

Every good work of God is fought by Satan. He is a liar, a schemer, and a destroyer. He never rests, never takes a vacation, never ceases his efforts to tear down the work of the Saviour.

We thank God that His Word reveals the end of Satan; but the fact that Satan is coming to an end by no means curtails his fiery endeavors at this time. He is now working in the hour which is his. He is the prince of the powers of the air. He is the god of this world.

Satan sought to defeat our Saviour. In Matthew 4 we have the account of the time when the devil tempted the Lord Jesus. Christ gave the answers from this infallible book, the Bible. Satan was turned away and the angels came and ministered unto Christ.

Please notice that if Satan did not hesitate to work upon the Son of God, then he will not hesitate to try to defeat your life. You are in constant danger. The Word of God points out this danger and tells you to beware.

Satan seeks to blind the minds of people. We read in II Corinthians 4:3,4:

> *"But if our gospel be hid, it is hid to them that are lost:*
>
> *"In whom the god of this world hath blinded the minds of them which believe not, lest the light of the glorious gospel of Christ, who is the image of God, should shine unto them."*

Satan contends with the saints of God, for Paul said in Ephesians 6:12:

> *"For we wrestle not against flesh and blood, but against principalities, against powers, against the rulers of the darkness of this world, against spiritual wickedness in high places."*

Ananias and Sapphira felt the full force of Satan's deception, and by their lying they tempted the Spirit of the Lord. As a consequence they both died suddenly and were buried by the young men of the church in Jerusalem. There is one who is opposed to all missionary work. That one is Satan.

Let us study about this enemy for a few moments.

## THE CHARACTER OF THE ENEMY OF MISSIONS

The blackest of words could no wise describe fully the vile and deceptive character of Satan. From the Garden of Eden to the present time there has been no change in this evil one. There is not one good thing that can be said for Satan. He is against God, against Christ, and against all righteousness.

All selfishness originated in the devil and is passed on to us. It does not matter whether the selfishness appears in saints or sinners, it is from Satan.

The early church in Jerusalem heard the command from our Lord Jesus, but did not hasten to go out into the mission fields. Here we see the devil's power in blocking missions. He brought an indifference to the people; consequently, the missionaries were sent out — not from Jerusalem, but from Antioch. Barnabas and Saul were selected by the Holy Spirit and sent forth to give the glad tidings to people everywhere.

Whenever you find a person who fights missions, you can be confident that individual is following in the steps of Satan. He does not have the mind of our Saviour who wept over sinners. He is not concerned, as is God, our heavenly Father, who sent His Son into the world to be the propitiation for our sins and to establish forever that work which is wisest and best — the telling of the story of Jesus. I repeat — Satan is back of all selfishness.

Satan is the father of all subtle, sinful allurements. I am referring now to those things which steal the interest of people and keep them from entering wholeheartedly into missionary endeavors. How nicely Satan can tie up a person in some worldly business and tell him to enjoy life and to give whatever money may be necessary to the church. It sounds good, but it does not bring peace and satisfaction.,

Notice for a moment how Satan works. First, he removes the good seed. Look at Matthew 13:19:

> *"When any one heareth the word of the kingdom, and understand it not, then cometh the wicked one, and catcheth away that which was sown in his heart. This is he which received seed by the wayside."*

Not only does he remove the good seed, but we find that he sows bad seed. Look at Matthew 13:38,39:

> *"The field is the world; the good seed are the children of the kingdom; but the tares are the children of the wicked one;*
>
> *"The enemy that sowed them is the devil; the harvest is the end of the world; and the reapers are the angels."*

Could any words be clearer than these? Can you not see

how Satan works and that he is the enemy of all missions?

But again, I want you to notice that Satan is working to defeat God's people; consequently, Simon Peter said,

> *"Be sober, be vigilant; because your adversary the devil, as a roaring lion, walketh about, seeking whom he may devour:"*
>
> — I Peter 5:8

The work of the Christian will never be easy in this present age. Satan will see that you will have a difficult time.

We have tried to give briefly the character of the enemy of missions. Let us remember that the work of missions will always feel the furious onslaughts of this evil one.

## THE COURAGE OF THE ENEMY OF MISSIONS

The devil will walk into any situation. He will tackle any job. He will face any person. The devil has courage!

FIRST, HE WILL WALK INTO ANY CHURCH AND SEEK TO MAKE IT SELFISH. He will cause the church to turn away from missions. He will bring about dissension in the midst of God's people. The devil will always invade the church that is active and seeking to do something for Christ and missions. The church that is missionary-minded will never cease to have its problems, for Satan will see that this is so.

Someone tells the story of an artist who was once asked to paint a picture of a decaying church. To the astonishment of many, instead of putting on the canvas an old tottering ruin, the artist painted a stately edifice of modern grandeur. Through the open portals could be seen the richly carved pulpit, the magnificent organ, and the beautiful stained glass windows. Within the grand entrance was an offering plate of elaborate design for the offerings of the fashionable worshippers. But — and here the artist's idea of a decaying church was made known — right above the offering plate there hung a square box bearing the words, "For Foreign Missions." And right over the slot through which contributions ought to have gone, he had painted a huge cobweb.

Let us keep in mind that Satan does not care how beautiful or big the church may be if we forget about missions. He makes it his task to see that the church gives up the work of missions and turns to the regular humdrum civic life which is the plague of so many churches today.

SECOND, SATAN WILL WALK INTO ANY HOME. He will come into the home to kill missionary zeal. He will come into the home to turn fathers and mothers against missions. He will come into the home to hinder children from surrendering themselves to the mission fields. He will seek to turn mother and father away from the idea of missions. He will cause every handicap to be thrown before young people to keep them from the work of the Saviour. Does Satan hesitate to do this? Not at all. He has the courage to work into any situation, into any home, and to insert himself into the life and thinking of any people.

THIRD, SATAN WILL WALK, NOT ONLY INTO ANY CHURCH AND ANY HOME, BUT ANY LIFE. Keep in mind that if he tried to tempt the Saviour, then he will try to pull you down. This means that the Christian must openly, deliberately, and devotedly fight against the evil one.

The Bible says, *"Neither give place to the devil"* (Ephesians 4:27).

Again, we are told, *"Put on the whole armour of God, that ye may be able to stand against the wiles of the devil"* (Ephesians 6:11).

Again we read, *"Submit yourselves therefore to God. Resist the devil, and he will flee from you"* (James 4:7)

The enemy of missions is alert. He never sleeps, never

rests, never takes a vacation.

The enemy of missions is able. He has shown his power against the finest and fairest. he has destroyed the best of missionary programs. He has reduced the lives of some of God's great servants to mere shadows of former endeavors.

The enemy of missions is aggressive. In the ministry of the Apostle Paul he never ceased to fight against Satan. He gave his warnings to God's people everywhere against the devil. Satan brought heartache to Paul, but Paul did not vary in his belief in the Lord. Satan defeated Paul in certain places, but the apostle went on.

The devil works to blind the mind of God's people. He contends with the saints of God, even as he begged for the opportunity to tempt Job and to pull him down.

Satan will work upon you. He will try to keep you from the highest of Christian living.

Satan will try to stop the church that goes into missionary work.

After one of my meetings in a state north of here, a young preacher came up to me with tears in his eyes and said, "Last evening my deacons voted that nothing would be given to any missionary endeavors until we had built and paid for an educational building." This young pastor stated that he had told his men that this was the quickest way to defeat the work of the Saviour, but they had insisted that what they were doing was right and that missions should begin at home and that not a penny would be given until the building was erected and free of debt. The young man asked me what he should do. I told him that he should go back to his church and preach the Word of God and pray that God would either give a revival or a revolution.

A church is not a church that does not have a missionary

program. A church without a missionary program is no more than a civic club.

It is missions which makes a New Testament church.

But again, I remind every missionary candidate that Satan will try to defeat you. He will try to deter you from preparation and seek to loosen your intent to go to the field. Here is an illustration:

> A young man and his wife announced they were going to Africa. They raised quite a few hundred dollars to put themselves on the field; and then suddenly, the wife decided that she would not go. This young couple came to see me. I talked and prayed with them. I later received a letter stating that the wife had given here agreement to go to the field and that she would be a missionary along with her husband. Satan had tried to defeat them, but the Lord had given the victory.

With courage and power and sly and subtle effectiveness Satan is working in this day. Many countries are feeling the effect of his damnable heresies.

All foreign missionaries have been pulled out of China.

They are leaving India and the doors are closing in some places.

There are yet millions in India who have never heard the Gospel of Jesus Christ. In some parts of South America it is difficult for the missionaries to enter.

In Africa there are definite movements against missionaries in certain fields.

Let us not be unaware of the devil's tracks, but let us give ourselves wholeheartedly to this work of getting the Gospel to the ends of the earth.

## THE CONQUEST OF THE ENEMY OF MISSIONS

What I am saying now about Satan's effectiveness in various fields will one day be over. Satan's power will come to a close. Our Saviour will reign!

But, let us thank God that Satan can be defeated now. He can be defeated by aggressive action, by faithful prayer, by humble obedience.

Satan loses every time a man says "Yes" to God and determines to walk in His steps. The devil is defeated whenever a young man or a young woman gives way to the Holy Spirit and surrenders himself or herself to the field of missions. Consider this:

"I said, 'Let me walk in the fields,'
He said, 'Nay, walk in the town.'
I said, 'There are no flowers there.'
He said, 'No flowers, but a crown.'

"I said, 'But the skies are black;
There is nothing but noise and din.'
And He wept as He sent me back,
'There is more,' He said, 'There is sin.'

"I said, 'I shall miss the light
And friends will miss me, they say.'
He answered, 'Choose tonight,
If I am to miss you or they.'

"I pleaded for time to be given;
He said, 'Is it hard to decide?
It will not seem hard in heaven,
If you have followed the steps of your Guide.'

"Then into His hand went mine,
And into my heart came He;
And I walked in a light Divine,

The path I had feared to see."

Satan can be defeated now if you will but say "Yes" to the Lord Jesus. Christ is waiting for your affirmative answer. Hear what He says and do it now.

Finally, we repeat that one day Satan will be defeated completely. This is given to us so plainly in the Word of God. First, we find in Revelation 20:2, that Satan will be bound and cast into the bottomless pit for a thousand years. Second, we find in the tenth verse of the same chapter that the devil will be cast into the lake of fire and brimstone where the beast and false prophet are. What am I saying? Simply this: Satan is fighting a losing battle. The winning side is not the devil's side, but Christ's side. I am glad that I have aligned my life with Him and His cause. I am glad that though there may be heartaches and difficulties, one day with my Lord I am going to walk triumphantly on the streets of new Jerusalem.

Are you on the side of Christ or on the side of Satan? Remember, the Bible says, *"He that is not with me is against me. . ."* (Matthew 12:30). Take your stand for Christ at this time and know the joy of fellowship with the One who shall lead us into victory now and victory for eternity.

The story is told of a strange but interesting morning in the San Francisco police court when some thirty men, red eyed and dishevelled, were lined up before a stern looking judge. It was the regular morning company of drunks and disorderlies. Young and old stood together and all hung their heads in shame. Just as the clerk rapped for order, a strong clear voice from the prison below was heard ringing out upon the air:

"Last night I lay asleeping,
There came a dream so fair."

Last night! It had been to all of them a nightmare, a drunken debauch. But the singer sang:

"I stood in old Jerusalem,
Beside the temple there."

The judge paused to listen, made a quiet inquiry of the clerk, to be told that a member of a famous opera company was in the cell below singing. As the song went on, every man in the line was moved. A boy among them broke down and sobbed, "Oh, Mother, Mother!" That stirred the men more strongly. Finally, one – more hardened than the others – said, "Judge, have we got to submit to this? We are here to take our punishment, but that song, — stop it!"

By this time the opera singer had reached the climax:

"Jerusalem, Jerusalem, sing for the night is o'er;
Hosanna in the highest, Hosanna for ever more!"

Every man in the line hid his face in his hands. Some sobbed aloud. The judge stood up, addressed a few kindly remarks and advice to the entire company, and then said, "Every case before me is dismissed." He felt that the message of redemption and heaven through the song had done more for them than spending a few hours in jail.

But wait — I ask you, "Are you ready for heaven? Do you know Christ as your Saviour? Are your feet upon the pathway that leads to the presence of God?" If you have never accepted Jesus Christ as Saviour, do so at this time.

*"For by grace are ye saved through faith; and that not of yourselves: It is the gift of God:*

*"Not of works, lest any man should boast."*

— Ephesians 2:8,9

# 26
# Fulfill Thy Mission

*"But none of these things move me, neither count I my life dear unto myself, so that I might finish my course with joy, and the ministry, which I have received of the Lord Jesus, to testify the gospel of the grace of God."*

— Acts 20:24

The Apostle Paul was a man of great determination and dedication. His will was determined to obey the Master and his life was dedicated to obey the Master and his life was dedicated to the cause of Christ. When Paul felt the hand of God guiding, nothing deterred him from obedience.

When he was closing his third missionary journey, he set his face toward Jerusalem. The Holy Spirit had revealed that he would be arrested and put in jail. The Ephesian elders met him at Miletus and tried to stop him from going to Jerusalem. The disciples at Tyre trieα to stop him from going on. At Caesarea, Agabus prophesied his coming affliction, but none of these things turned him one particle from his determination to go to Jerusalem. When the people in Caesarea besought him not to go on, he said, "*. . . What mean ye to weep and to break mine heart? for I am ready not to be bound only, but also to die at Jerusalem for the name of the Lord Jesus*" (Acts 21:13). Then Luke records the attitude of the people, "*And when he would not be persuaded, we ceased, saying, The will of the Lord be done*" (Acts 21:14).

Paul went to Jerusalem. He was arrested and finally sent to Rome, where he testified for Christ, and then one day, died on a chopping block.

Paul's farewell to the Ephesian elders is one of the most touching scenes in the entire Bible. His message to the men rings with gospel truth. He repeated again the things he had preached in their midst. His message in Ephesus had been repentance toward God and faith toward our Lord Jesus Christ. His method had been from house to house, teaching and preaching.

Now, as he said goodbye to the Christian friends of Ephesus, the Spirit had already foretold his coming bonds and afflictions.

Consider now his statement, giving his determination to do God's will.

> *"But none of these things move me, neither count I my life dear unto myself, so that I might finish my course with joy, and the ministry, which I have received of the Lord Jesus, to testify the gospel of the grace of God"*
> — Acts 20:24

This verse leads me to three comments about the great apostle.

## HE WAS RECKLESS FOR GOD

*". . .neither count I my life dear myself. . ."*

Paul did not care about his life. His concern was to please God. The prospect of suffering did not make him fear. Self was dead. His own life was worthless, compared to his desire to do God's will.

The world calls a man a fool when he gives himself wholly to the Lord. But according to the Bible, this is a good kind of foolishness. Paul was reckless for God. He was ready to face any difficulty or danger for the sake of Christ who died for him.

FIRST, HE OBEYED CHRIST. To some people this is a form of foolishness. They read the Word of God, but they do not feel any necessity to obey the Word. The Holy Spirit speaks to them, but they ignore His voice. The example of Christ is before them, but they choose their own way. Not so with the Apostle Paul. He was completely reckless in his desire to obey every single command of Jesus. When the Holy Spirit closed a door to him. He did not seek to enter. When the Holy Spirit opened a door, and called him to enter, he at once obeyed. There was a holy submission to the will of God and to the work of God.

SECOND, HE LIVED UNSELFISHLY. When Paul was saved, he gave up everything for Christ. He gave up home and loved ones, position and popularity. He became as an outcast hated by his own countrymen. And yet the great, unselfish heart of Paul was constantly yearning for the salvation of his people. Hear him as he cries:

> *"I say the truth in Christ, I lie not, my conscience also bearing me witness in the Holy Ghost,*
>
> *"That I have great heaviness and continual sorrow in my heart.*
>
> *"For I could wish that myself were accursed from Christ for my brethren, my kinsmen according to the flesh:"*
>
> —Romans 9:1-3

This is one of the most challenging, unselfish statements ever made by man. Think of it—Paul said he was willing to be separated from Christ for the sake of his kinsmen.

THIRD, PAUL LIVED BY FAITH. The apostle was not asking to see every distant scene, but was content to live and walk by faith. His heart was filled with perfect peace, for he trusted in God. Therefore, he could write to the Philippians: *"Be careful for nothing; but in every thing by prayer and supplication with thanksgiving, let your requests be made known unto God. And the peace of God which passeth all understanding, shall keep your hearts and minds through Christ Jesus"* (Philippians 4:6-7).

It is a marvelous thing to live by faith. Life is an exciting experience for that one who moves forward with a sublime trust in God. The person, a lady missionary, who gave the first money for the beginning of Tennessee Temple University, is such a person. When out of her small means, she gave a check for one thousand dollars to our school, she stated in a letter that "I have always lived by faith, and I fear that this much money would hinder my dependence upon God." This missionary, whose gift started Tennessee Temple University on its way, is still in mission work today.

FOURTH, PAUL FACED DEATH BY FAITH IN CHRIST. As he looked forward to the end of his life, there was no fear, for he said, *". . .to be absent from the body, and to be present with the Lord"* (II Corinthians 5:8).

At one time he said, *"For I am in a strait betwixt two, having a desire to depart, and to be with Christ; which is far better:"* (Philippians 1:23). There was no sting in death, for he had victory through faith in Christ.

This is illustrated by a simple story of faith. A man suggested to his wife that they visit a beautiful cemetery. He called his son, a bright little boy about four years old, and told him to get ready to go with them. The boy's countenance fell. "Don't you want to go, son?" said the father.

"Yes, father," answered the child, with quivering lips, "if you wish."

The little fellow was strangely silent during the drive, and when they got out of the carriage, he clung to his mother with a wistful look. After some time spent among the graves, and walking through the beautiful cemetery, they turned to the car, and the father lifted his little son to his seat. The child looked surprised, and inquired with a breath of relief, "Am I going back with you?"

"Of course, you are," said the father. "Why not?"

"I thought," said the brave child, "when they took little boys to the cemetery, they left them there."

The little lad had heard stories about the cemetery. He knew that bodies were carried there and left. He thought they were going to leave him, but he had faith in his father.

Let such faith grip our souls today, as we face life and death. Let us be reckless in our obedience to Christ, and in selfish living. Let the world say what it will, but may we follow Jesus.

### HE WAS RESOLVED TO FINISH HIS COURSE

*". . . That I might finish my course with joy. . ."* (Acts 20:24).

Paul did not care about fame or fortune. He did not care about sufferings of body, but he did care about finishing the work God had given him to do.

In this regard, Paul was following Jesus, for Christ said, *"My meat is to do the will of him that sent me, and to finish his work"* (John 4:34). Upon the cross of Calvary, Jesus said, *". . . It is finished. . ."* (John 19:30).

Though the people tried to keep Paul from going to Jerusalem, he was determined to finish his course. He looked upon life as a footrace. He was running to obtain a prize; therefore, he laid aside every weight, and every besetting sin, that he might finish victoriously.

Every Christian has a job to do. There are no exceptions,

and no exemptions. One task we surely know that Christ has given to everyone is to win souls. God has put you in the world for a definite business. May we fulfill the mission God has given us to do.

In the carrying out of our task, we have a Helper. Sometimes the job seems too big for us, but there is One, even Christ, who promises to help us. Here is His promise: "*. . .lo I am with you alway, even unto the end of the world*" (Matthew 28:20).

Like Paul, we should resolve not to stop short of the finish line. Whether your task be great or small, there is joy in finishing the work given you to do. We should desire, not only to finish the course, but to finish it with joy.

## HE WAS RESPONSIBLE TO CHRIST

"*. . .the ministry which I have received of the Lord Jesus, to testify the gospel of the grace of God*" (Acts 20:24).

Paul was saved by Christ, and called by Christ into the ministry. Therefore, he felt a direct responsibility for the faithful performance of his work to the Lord. He knew that Christ would examine and test his work at the coming judgment seat.

We, too, should have this thought regarding our place in God's service. It should be our constant desire to please Christ who saved us, and set us apart, knowing that one day, we must face Him and give an account of our service.

God is simply asking for your best in the place given unto you. Your job may be small and often unnoticed, but if you do your best, your reward is equal to that of the most distinguished hero, whose work is acclaimed by the world.

Someone has said, "If God should send two angels to this world, one to rule the world, and the other to sweep the streets of the smallest village, the one who sweeps the streets and does his task well, is entitled to as much honor as the one who rules the world, for he has fulfilled his divine mission."

If you feel and know that your task is a God-given one, then do it to the best of your ability. One is your Master, even Christ. It does not matter what others may say about you. Your work is for Jesus, and you are responsible to Him.

Paul was an ambassador for Christ. He felt the power of God back of his ministry, but he also felt his great responsibility to the Lord who sent him out.

Paul's heart's desire was to please Christ, and to glorify Him. He wanted to come unashamed into the presence of Jesus, and hear Christ say, *"Well done, thou good and faithful servant."*

Christ gave His best for us, yea, His own life — what have you done for Him?

On November 7, 1907, a Mexican engineer by the name of J. Garcia was at the throttle of a loaded train in a small mining town in the state of Sonora. Among the cars were several loaded with dynamite. While the train was standing in the station, fire somehow broke out in a box car. It rapidly approached the cars of dynamite. There was no way of checking it, and the explosion of those cars would wipe the village off the map, and probably destroy every person in it. Other employees forsook the scene, calling on everyone to escape. Not so Garcia. Cooly remaining in his cab, he opened the throttle and set the train in motion. Slowly he drew it out on the line away from the village. Presently there was a frightful explosion. The train was blown to atoms. The engine was reduced to scrap iron. No trace of the brave engineer was found.

They took Jesus outside the city and crucified Him. He died that we might live, and He lives in Heaven to intercede and to save.

Christian, give unto the Lord your best. Fulfill the mission God has called you to perform.

Lost man, receive the Lord Jesus now as your Saviour.

# Part Three
# Claim The Blessings

# 27
# Shine

*"And they that be wise shall shine as the brightness of the firmament; and they that turn many to righteousness as the stars forever and ever."*

—Daniel 12:3

It should be the joy of every Christian to do everything that he can for Christ. Out of gratitude for the gift of salvation, our hearts should be willing and submissive, our minds dedicated, and our entire bodies committed to the service of the Lord.

If a shining life glorifies God, then we should have shining lives. Jesus said, *"Let your light so shine before men, that they may see your good works, and glorify your Father which is in Heaven"* (Matthew 5:16). It is plainly indicated that if we shine here, we shall shine hereafter; yes, for ever and ever. I am interested in the last portion of Daniel 12:3, *". . .and they that turn many to righteousness as the stars forever and ever."*

The way to shine for God is to turn many to righteousness. When we speak of righteousness, we are speaking of our God, for He is righteous. *"Righteous art thou, O LORD, and upright are thy judgments"* (Psalm 119:137). *"The LORD is righteous in all his ways, and holy in all in his works"* (Psalm 145:17).

Therefore, the work to which God calls us is to turn men unto Himself, who is righteousness. It is not our business simply to turn people toward church membership, good habits, or clean living. It is our work to turn men to the righteousness which is in Jesus Christ, that righteousness which can be obtained only through faith in the Son of God. The Word clearly indicates that salvation is not by the work of man. Paul wrote to Titus, saying, *"Not by works of righteousness which we have done, but according to his mercy he saved us, by the washing of regeneration, and renewing of the Holy Ghost"* (Titus 3:5). And again, he wrote to the Romans, *"But to him that worketh not, but believeth on him that justified the ungodly, his faith is counted for righteousness"* (Romans 4:5). In the next verse, Paul tells us that God imputes righteousness without works.

Therefore it is the work of the soul winner to turn people unto the righteousness which is in Jesus Christ. They are to see the sinless Son of God who took our place and bore our sins on the tree, as ready to impute unto them the righteousness which is of God.

The Christian who shines here and hereafter is the one who engages in the work of turning men to God. When we turn them to God, we are turning them from sin and judgment and eternal hell. There is no greater work than this.

I want to give you seven essentials if we are to be succesful in this turning work.

## TURNING MEN TO RIGHTEOUSNESS REQUIRES AN EXPERIENCE OF GRACE

Here is a work that is shut up to men and women who know the Lord Jesus and who understand the meaning of salvation. No one is going to be successful in soul winning until he has been born again, and is made aware of the great work of God in his behalf.

Quite often I have received requests from wives who have

asked me to help win their husbands to Christ and to sober living, and upon questioning, the wives would confess that they were not saved themselves. Still they insisted that they were doing all they could to turn their husbands in the right way. Their efforts were futile and vain. Turning men to righteousness is the work of those who have themselves been turned to righteousness and have had an experience of salvation.

You may insist that there are instances where God had used unsaved people to turn other unsaved ones to salvation. Yes, I believe there are such cases, but in such a case, it is an illustration of the power of the naked Word of God as wielded by the Holy Spirit. God did not use the person, but He blessed His Word.

But he does want to use people, and He plainly says, "*. . .they that turn many to righteousness. . .*" He desires to use you and me, and as we are used of Him, we will shine for Him.

## SOUL WINNING REQUIRES CONSECRATION OF LIFE

A successful winner of souls must be a Christian, and must look and act like one. It is not enough for a person to say that he is saved — he must also demonstrate it by consecration of his life unto God.

Whenever a Christian goes out endeavoring to win souls without first preparing his own heart and life, he is sure to meet with failure. Thus we have many Christians who have turned away from active service for Christ because of early failures which resulted form lack of consecration.

The standard of the Lord is separation. When you are separated from the world, empty of self, and filled with the Spirit, you need have no worry. God will use you to turn many to righteousness.

## WINNING SOULS REQUIRES PRAYER

What kind of prayer is required? Just plain, old-fashioned, heart prayer; prayer for guidance, prayer for divine power, prayer for revival, and prayer for the salvation of the lost.

Somewhere in my reading, I came across a discussion as to why preachers of bygone days seemed to have more power than men of this day. The answer was given, "Preachers in days gone by had prayer chambers and the studies where they pondered the Word of God. Ministers of today have offices." I think the diagnosis is a good one. Prayer is an essential if we are to have the guidance of the Spirit and success in winning others.

## TURNING MEN TO RIGHTEOUSNESS REQUIRES ALERTNESS

The Lord has a place for wide awake folks. He can use a man who has a sparkle in his eye and a spring in his step.

Turning men to righteousness requires that we be on our toes. Hell is an eternal place and if people drift by us unto hell, there is no second chance.

If a bridge is out on a main highway, the highway department will put up warning lights and will place a wide awake watchman at the post.

Suppose there has been a sudden landslide on the highway going up the mountain. The road has slipped away into the valley. There is just an open chasm. A man sees the awful danger and takes his stand in the center of the highway. He waves his light and turns the people back, and away from death. But suppose he gets sleepy, and he finds a rock at the edge of the highway and sits down upon it, and begins to nod. He may sleep for a minute or two, but in that brief time a number of lives might be lost.

We have taken too lightly our responsibility to stand as

watchmen on the road of life and turn people back and away from danger, death, and eternal torment. We have manifested a tragic indifference and a woeful selfishness.

## SOUL WINNING REQUIRES DEPENDENCE ON THE SPIRIT

Turning men to righteousness is not done in human power and human wisdom. It takes the power of the Holy Spirit to convict and to convert a sinner. The Holy Spirit is the One sent into the world to convict men of sin, righteousness, and of judgment.

Not only must we depend on the Holy Spirit, but we must depend upon the Holy Spirit inspired Book, the Bible. We cannot win souls by our influence, personalities, or by tact. It is by the Word of God, empowered by the Spirit that conviction is brought about. Souls are not won by arguments. Souls are won by hearing the Word of God and being convicted of their sin of unbelief.

Anyone can win souls if he will depend on divine power.

## TURNING MEN TO RIGHTEOUSNESS REQUIRES TEARS

Nothing can take the place of a broken heart. Compassion and love will do more than anything else aside from the Spirit and the Word. We must not be ashamed to cry. Let us be disturbed that our hearts are so calloused that we do not weep more over the condition of men. The promise of God is, *"He that goeth forth and weepeth, bearing precious seed, shall doubtles come again with rejoicing, bringing his sheaves with him"* (Psalm 126:6).

The Apostle Paul was a man of tears. He said to the elders at Ephesus, *"Therefore watch, and remember, that by the space of three years I ceased not to warn every one night and day with tears"* (Acts 20:31).

Some of the best soul winners I have ever known have been humble people who loved the Lord supremely and loved souls so much that they would weep over them. The promise is, *"They that sow in tears shall reap in joy."* Our Saviour saw the people as sheep having no shepherd and had compassion upon them. He shed tears as he looked upon the sinful city of Jerusalem. He died upon the cross of a broken heart because He loved sinners.

All great soul winners have been men of tears and compassion. time would fail us to speak of Whitfield, Moody, Spurgeon, Torrey, Finney, and others.

## TURNING MEN TO RIGHTEOUSNESS REQUIRES FAITHFULNESS

Just as in any other work, we succeed when we keep at it. If we win souls, we must be instant in season and out of season. We must go in the spring, the summer, the fall, and the winter. We must go when it is raining as well as when the sun is shining. We must go in seasons of church revival and in seasons when there is no stated revival meetings.

Extensive Bible knowledge is a splendid thing, but I have seen more souls won to Christ by faithful people of limited knowledge than I have by those who had a detailed knowledge of every book in the Bible.

Again, soul winning is not a matter of talent, education, or magnetic personality. The greatest soul winners are the ones who are faithful and who persistently go after souls with compassion and love.

Christian, this is your work, and this is mine. We must spend our nights and days at the task which pays the greatest dividends here and hereafter.

Turning men to righteousness glorifies God.

Turning men to righteousness makes the Christian shine

here and hereafter.

Turning men to righteousness means the salvation of precious souls from an eternal hell.

Turning men to righteousness means they shall dwell with God forever.

This is our work. May we do it faithfully.

# 28
# The Key to Divine Blessings

> *"They that sow in tears shall reap in joy.*
>
> *"He that goeth forth and weepeth, bearing precious seed, shall doubtless come again with rejoicing, bring his sheaves with him."*
>
> — Psalm 126:5,6

The Word of God presents many promises on condition that we give obedience to God's commands.

For example, in the matter of giving, the promise of God is ours when we give obedience unto the Lord. In Malachi 3 we are told,

> *"Bring ye all the tithes into the storehouse, that there may be meat in mine house, and prove me now herewith, saith the* LORD *of hosts, if I will not open you the windows of heaven, and pour you out a blessing, that there shall not be room enough to receive it."*
>
> — Malachi 3:10

The promise is very plain. God says that He will open the windows and pour out blessings that we shall not have room to receive. But, He first says that we are to bring all of the tithes into the storehouse. The promise of His great blessing is conditioned by obedience to His command.

In Luke 6:38 we have this verse:

> *"Give, and it shall be given unto you; good measure, pressed down, and shaken together, and running over, shall men give unto your bosom. For with the same measure that ye mete withal it shall be measured to you again."*

This is a blessed promise, but the condition is that we give. Most people like to receive, but they turn away from the plain and express command of our Saviour that we are to give; and when we give, that it shall be given to us: "*. . .good measure, pressed down, and shaken together, and running over. . .*" I repeat: the promise of God is ours when we do what God commands.

Again, we have divine blessings promised to us as we read the Word of God. The Word says, "*But these are written, that ye might believe that Jesus is the Christ, the Son of God; and that believing ye might have life through His name*" (John 20:31).

Again, Jesus said, "*Search the scriptures; for in them ye think ye have eternal life: and they are they which testify of me*" (John 5:39).

The blessing of eternal life is given to us in these words of our Saviour. "*Verily, verily, I say unto you, If a man keep my saying, he shall never see death*" (John 8:51).

The Word of God gives a promise of all things that we need — salvation, peace, joy, guidance — all of these things are promised in the Word of God. Do not miss the blessing of Bible study. Someone has said, "Sodom had no Bibles, Sodom had no preachers, Sodom had no tracts, Sodom had no prayer meetings, Sodom had no churches and Sodom perished. How will America and England be spared from the wrath of the Almighty? We have millions of Bibles, scores of thousands of churches, and endless preachers, and yet what sin!"

But again, we note that the blessing of God is promised to us as we live apart from sin. The condition to divine favor very simply stated is that we forsake sin. The Word of God says,

> *"Let the wicked forsake his way, and the unrighteous man his thoughts: and let him return unto the* LORD, *and he will have mercy upon him; and to our God, for he will abundantly pardon."*
>
> —Isaiah 55:7

No one can claim the rich blessings of God and delve into this world's sin. We will lose every time! God's divine presence cannot be with us when we walk in the way of sin.

There are three things that will hinder the work of God.

THE FIRST THING THAT HINDERS THE WORK OF GOD IS COWARDICE. It is cowardice that cuts the workers down and reduces the number to go out into the fields of labor. It was cowardice that made ten of the twelve spies give an adverse report and say that the children of Israel could not take the Promised Land. It is cowardice that divides churches and keeps the people from moving forward. It is cowardice that keeps us from undertaking great things in the name of the Lord Jesus.

THE SECOND THING THAT SEEMS TO HINDER THE WORK OF GOD IS THE MATTER OF AGE AND SUDDEN DEATH. Perhaps my expression is not the best in saying that it hinders, for God always has someone ready to do the work.

But, quite often it seems that when a person is in the very best of his life that he is taken away.

The sun went down on the day of Gladstone.

The bullet cut short the leadership of Lincoln.

Spurgeon died when very young.

Mr. Moody did not see his 60th birthday.

Think of it as you will, age and sudden death give us a shock, and sometimes the work seems retarded until others can be found to go ahead.

Let us gird ourselves for renewed efforts. Let us remember that there is still much to be done: and may those of us who are living go forward and take the land which God has for us. Many of the great men of days gone by have passed on to their reward, but our day is now. When it shall close we know not, but let us do our best in the hours that God has given to us.

John Bunyan is dead, but the Christian pilgrims are still marching on toward the celestial city.

Cowper is dead, but we still sing, "There is a fountain filled with blood, drawn from Immanuel's veins."

Raikes is dead, but thousands of Sunday Schools met this morning and studied the Word of God.

Livingstone is dead, but missionaries around the world are thrilled and inspired by the record of the life of Livingstone.

BUT, THERE IS A THIRD THING THAT I MUST MENTION THAT HINDERS THE WORK, AND THAT IS SIN. The blessings of God are hindered when the people go into sin. Sin must be put out. The best that God has for us cannot be given when we tamper and play with sin. We must flee from evil. We must refuse to walk in the ways which are contrary to His will.

But may we notice the key to divine blessings: The greatest blessing will be ours when we obey our Christ — when we go as He has commanded us. I come back to the missionary theme and the soul winning theme which we are emphasizing in these days. We have a living message and that message must not remain dormant in careless hands!

Let us notice what promises are ours when we obey our

Christ.

## HIS PRESENCE

Yes, His presence is with us as we obey His command. Jesus said, "*. . .lo, I am with you alway, even unto the end of the world*" (Matthew 28:20).

There is nothing so comforting in this world as to know that He is with you.

There is nothing so disturbing in this world as to feel that God is not with you.

Be fearful of moving into any field of activity without the leadership of God. This will mean that many times you must wait upon the Lord until he reveals the path that you are to take. Wait — do not run ahead of Him. Wait, be patient, be prayerful until God says, "This is the way."

In the matter of witnessing and in the matter of missions we know what God wants, for we have His command. He has commanded us to go, and we must obey His Divine Word.

HIS PRESENCE IS WITH US IN SOUL WINNING ACTIVITY BECAUSE WE ARE CARRYING THE PRECIOUS SEED WHICH HAS BEEN GIVEN UNTO US.

This seed is precious in its origin, for it is the Word of God. It bears the express image of its great Author.

This Word is precious because of its rarity. There is nothing in heaven or on earth like it.

This Word is precious because of its effect. It brings men unto salvation. It is the instrument in the hands of the Holy Spirit for bringing conviction and bringing sinners unto everlasting life. Be assured that He will be with you as you go carrying His Word.

AGAIN, WE CAN BE SURE OF HIS PRESENCE BECAUSE WE ARE EXTENDING HIS OFFER OF MERCY UNTO SINNERS. The poor, the lost, the blind are waiting, and when we come to them with the gospel story, He will be with us. Hear His Word, "*. . .LO, I AM WITH YOU ALWAYS.*"

THIRD, HIS PRESENCE WILL BE WITH US IN SOUL WINNING AND MISSIONS BECAUSE SOUL WINNING IS HIS WORK. This was the major concern of our Saviour as He walked upon this earth. His concern was for the souls of men. It was not for the establishment of cities, the building of highways, the writing of laws — He came to seek sinners — He came to die for sinners; and now, He lives on high with the same heart passion, desiring that men might come unto Him.

There may be times when I have some doubts about some phases of our program which is so wide and varied, but about this one thing I have no doubts. I know that the work of winning souls, of getting the Gospel out to the ends of the earth, is the very work of our Saviour.

Yes, we have the promise of his presence as we go. Do not hesitate to launch out into the deep and witness for God. Be a missionary to a foreign land, for He will go with you.

**REWARD**

When we obey our Christ, then we have the promise of reward. He commands us to go, and when we give obedience and do it faithfully, then one day we will stand before Him and be rewarded for our faithfulness.

> *"And, behold, I come quickly; and my reward is with me, to give every man according as his work shall be."*
>
> — Revelation 22:12

This reward will be to all who have participated in the work of our Saviour. You may not go to a foreign land, but if you give money that others may go, then you will participate in the going. The givers will be rewarded. The prayers will receive rewards, and the goers will hear a "Well done" from the Saviour.

Christ will be with the faithful and the obedient. Be not turned aside by the skeptics or by the materialistic who would seek to keep your mind from running in spiritual channels. Do what God says. Go with His message and He will one day give a reward.

Some one hundred and fifty years ago William Carey organized the first Baptist Foreign Mission Society of the world. We are told that Sidney Smith, a witty writer, made sport of the enterprise, saying that thirteen nobodies were going out to convert India with $60.00, led by an ignorant shoe cobbler. Ah, but listen, because these men obeyed, thousands have gone to the fields and multiplied thousands have been reached for Jesus Christ. Do not worry about the reward, simply know that it is coming if you are faithful.

## DAILY SUCCESS

The third blessing that our Lord will give to you is daily success. Note I said "daily." Our labor is to be day by day, and each day the Lord will give unto us success in His service as we go in obedience to His command.

What will be a part of this success?

FIRST, PEACE OF HEART WILL BE YOURS. Jesus said, *"Peace I leave with you, my peace I give unto you: not as the world giveth, give I unto you. Let not your heart be troubled, neither let it be afraid"* (John 14:27).

There cannot be peace of heart without obedience to the Lord. Always, yea always, you will be troubled unless you are going in obedience to the command of our Saviour.

SECOND, THERE WILL BE CONSCIOUSNESS OF TIME AND MONEY WELL SPENT. We do not like to waste time and we do not like to waste money. The older we get the less we feel like wasting either of these commodities. What better success could I wish for than to feel that I had spent what little I have in the best way for the glory of God?

THIRD, I CAN HAVE THE BLESSING OF THE CONSCIOUSNESS THAT I HAVE BEEN USED OF GOD. What a marvelous truth this is! The Lord is waiting to use me and you. What an amazing and wonderful truth this is! But every man can be used of God Almighty.

I read this story somewhere: The Duke of Wellington is reputed to have knelt one day at the communion table in a church to receive the Lord's Supper, when suddenly a shabbily dressed man entered and dropped down at his side. The old minister, horrified at the sight, moved over to the poor man's side, and in a whisper said, "Move over. You are kneeling beside the Duke of Wellington."

The great soldier heard him and putting his hand out instantly to the shoulder of the man, said, "Stay where you are, my brother. There are no dukes here."

How true it is in the work of our Saviour. There are no special ones. We are all servants of the Lord Jesus. Our heavenly Father is no respecter of persons. All can be used in the great task of getting the Gospel to the ends of the earth.

Therefore, my friend, join hands with the greats of all the ages. Join hands with the prophets and apostles and move forward in this tremendous task of telling men about Christ.

God wants His richest blessings to be upon your life — this blessing can be given only when you join with Him in His work. What am I saying? Be concerned for others. Go forth with weeping and bear the precious seed and claim the promise that one day you will come again with rejoicing. There is a task to be done. May God grant that we shall do it!

And last, may I say, when you join some, there will be sadness. When you join with Christ, there will be gladness!

It was Dr. W. B. Riley who used to tell the story which he

heard from Dr. Melvin C. Eidson of the First Baptist Church of Bessemer, Alabama. Some years ago I conducted a three weeks' revival in this church. Dr. Eidson told this account:

> It was a young boy named Wesley Vincent who had been inveigled by a more experienced criminal into an attempt to live life the easy way of compelling others to provide the necessities thereof. So he joined this Richard Darrafou in a journey one night to see what he could extract from certain business houses. They were in the act of robbing the cash box of a house, when Harris, a Birmingham policeman, walked in. Instantly, the pistol which they had provided for self protection claimed its victim, and the policemen fell dead.
>
> Charged with the crime, Darrafou defeated the law by committing suicide. Young Vincent took another course entirely. It was his first crime. He saw not only the folly, but the enormity of his iniquity and confessed it all.
>
> His mother, being a Baptist, sent for Dr. Eidson and Eidson led him to Christ, and with the deepest penitence he said, "I have found peace." He said, "I can never forgive myself for the sorrow and shame I have brought to my darling mother, but God has in His great mercy forgiven me."
>
> When his mother came to comfort him just before he was to be led from the death cell, he begged her not to cry. He admitted his guilt. He deplored the awful gravity of it. He said, "My punishment is perfectly just, but I have sought and found both pardon and peace."
>
> He walked unassisted to the big electric chair. He

> subjected himself to the straps that bound him to the death-dealing electrodes, and with a smile he bade his mother and Dr. Eidson good-bye.
>
> The daily press report gave his last words which were addressed to the executioner: "I am looking at you now, but my eyes are actually on Christ, my Substitute, my Saviour."
>
> A few moments later the physicians stepped forward and put a stethoscope against his breast and said, "He is dead."

In one way we can see the result of joining hands with evil, and on the other hand we can see the result of one who joined hands with the blessed Christ.

I cannot do a better thing nor a bigger thing than to say to you, "You need Jesus now as your Saviour." There is but One who can save you and keep you and that One is the Lord Jesus Christ. He died in your place on Calvary's tree and we come to beseech you to receive Him as your personal Saviour.

> *"Jesus said unto her, I am the resurrection, and the life: he that believeth in me, though he were dead, yet shall he live:*
>
> *"And whosoever liveth and believeth in me shall never die. Believest thou this?"*
>
> —John 11:25,26

# 29
# The One Business That Cannot Fail

*"And I thank Christ Jesus our Lord, who hath enabled me, for that he counted me faithful, putting me into the ministry."*

—I Timothy 1:12

The business of our God is to visit this world and to take out a people for His name. The Lord's purpose will not fail of full accomplishment. Therefore, God's business is missions and evangelism.

The church that stays in the Lord's business will never fail. God will see to it that success is given if the proper emphasis is given to missions and evangelism. But, if the church is selfish and turns away from the mission program and ceases to win souls, that church is out of God's business and cannot claim His blessing. This church will never fail as long as we stay on the main line — as long as we make the winning of souls our major work.

Tennessee Temple University will never fail as long as we keep the emphasis on the main business. We cannot claim God's blessings upon or schools if we are simply in the business of education. We are providing education with a purpose and that is to send forth missionaries, pastors, and evangelists to win precious souls. As a Christian school we have no right to expect God to bless unless we stay in the main business.

God will bless the individual who stays in His work. If you show a vital interest in the souls of men, you need not fear — God will give guidance and direction in your life. The winning of souls is the work nearest to the heart of God. Therefore, it receives the fulness of His approval and blessing.

The Apostle Paul said,

> *"And I thank Christ Jesus our Lord, who hath enabled me, for that he counted me faithful, putting me into the ministry."*
>
> — I Timothy 1:12

He recognized that this is the greatest work of our Lord. Of whom is it expected?

## SOUL WINNING IS THE BUSINESS OF EVERY CHRISTIAN

There are no exceptions and no exemptions, God has spoken once and for all upon this subject. He tells us, *". . .ye shall be witnesses unto me. . ."* (Acts 1:8).

The quiet person can be used to win souls as well as the eloquent person. The uneducated can win souls as well as the educated. The prerequisite is a knowledge of Christ as Saviour and a love for the souls of men.

In the years of my ministry I have been amazed again and again at the people God uses in the winning of the lost. The most unlikely people are the greatest soul winners. The ones that I would expect to win souls are the ones who do nothing at all. In every church it is the people of ordinary, every day ability who get a burden for the souls of men and do this major work.

God can use young people in this as well as older ones. Many years ago I held a meeting in the state of Florida. On the first night, a lad of some twelve or thirteen years of age sat on the first row. He was poorly clad and barefooted. On the second night he was back in the same place. At the close of the service I gave an invitation. This boy walked back and spoke to another young man, some years older than he was. In a moment both of them came down the aisle. The barefooted boy said, "Brother Roberson, this boy wants to be saved." I spoke to the older young man and he was interested in his soul. I asked him, "Who has been witnessing to you?"

He said, "This boy, Nick." In a few moments he was converted.

Every night throughout the two weeks' meeting the barefoot boy led souls down the aisle. At the close of the services, it was easily realized that this lad had led more people to Jesus during the meeting than anyone else. He had only been saved for a short time. His mother and father were not Christians. But, a barefoot boy with no home encouragement, had led more souls to Christ in the revival than the pastor and the deacons put together. How wonderful it is that God can use anyone in this greatest of all works.

The quiet person is just as effective in soul winning as the eloquent person. You have all heard the story of the revival meeting where the evangelist made this announcement, "If there is someone in this service who led you to Christ, I want you to go and stand by that one." There was considerable moving for a while. Some people came and stood by the pastor, some by the evangelist, some by Sunday School teachers, others by deacons. But, over in one corner of the building a small crowd was assembling. They stood around a dear old lady who was seated on the bench. Some seventeen people came to stand by her side that day to say that she had been used of God to bring them to the Saviour. She was not a teacher, a public speaker, but only a faithful Christian who witnessed for the Lord.

## SOUL WINNING SHOULD BE THE BUSINESS OF EVERY SUNDAY SCHOOL TEACHER

What a mighty army of Sunday School teachers we have throughout the world. What tremendous results could be obtained if every teacher was a winner of souls.

In our own church we have far over 100 Sunday School teachers who need to be engaged daily in the greatest work. And yet, some seem to feel that their task is simply teaching the lesson on Sunday morning! If there is a lost one present, then the teacher reasons that it is best not to be too urgent.

Sunday School teachers, awaken to your responsibility. God is holding you accountable for the souls of the ones who sit before you. If they slip out into eternity, lost forever, their blood will be upon your hands.

On one of my trips to the north, a pastor, broken hearted and troubled, came to me. He told me of the indifference of his church toward the souls of others. he told how the Sunday School teachers refused to try to win boys and girls to Christ. Out of a Sunday School enrollment of one thousand, less than four hundred were professing Christians. He stated that this people had taken the position that no one could be saved under twelve years of age, and consequently, it was hard to reach many after they passed the age of twelve.

It was a Sunday School teacher who first pointed me to the Lord Jesus. Her plain, simple teaching of the way of salvation brought me to realize my need of Christ, and eventually to my acceptance of Him.

What a joy for teachers to win souls! What a wonderful reward will be waiting for those who have been faithful to this task.

I can never forget Miss Abey Burr of Springfield,Tennessee. I conducted a revival in a little chapel where she worked as a Sunday School teacher. She had left the First Church and gone down to the mission, feeling that she could render better service. Throughout the revival I noticed the activity of Miss Burr in soul winning. She was quiet but effective in her witnessing. While still a comparatively young person, Miss Burr became ill and died. I had part in the funeral service. After I had finished my brief part, the pastor rose and said, "Before I begin my message, I would like for the ladies seated here at the front to stand, please." Fifty-four ladies stood to their feet. The pastor continued, "These ladies have come here today to pay tribute to the life and influence of Miss Abey Burr. All of them witness to the fact that they were led to Christ by this departed one."

Wouldn't you like to come in heaven and know that fifty-four people were there that you had led to the Lord? What a joy and what a crown of rejoicing! That's what Paul said about it in I Thessalonians 2:19 and 20, *"For what is our hope or joy, or crown of rejoicing? Are not even ye in the presence of our Lord Jesus Christ at his coming? For ye are our glory and joy."*

Andrew Allen, Sunday School leader, used to recount the story of the wealthy man who picked up his friend for a ride one day. He went by a florist, bought a beautiful wreath of flowers. He drove to the cemetery and requested his friend to remain in the car. The friend watched him walk across the grass and stop beside a grave. The flowers were tenderly placed upon the grave. Then the wealthy man stood with uncovered head in what appeared to be a few moments of prayer. After this he returned to the car and they drove on. The friend was curious about it all. He said, "I suppose that that was the grave of one of your parents." The wealthy man said, "No, it is not." He said, "Then I suppose it must be some member of your family." The man replied, "No, it is not." He said, "I wonder if you would tell me who is buried there." The outstanding man replied, "That is the grave of the Sunday School teacher who led me to Jesus Christ."

## SOUL WINNING IS THE BUSINESS OF MOTHERS AND FATHERS

Parents take great pride in doing the best they can for their children. They endeavor to give them good food, good shelter, good clothes, and a good education. But how many parents have failed in winning their loved ones to Christ. Our nation is full of unsaved people whose parents were professing Christians, but never spoke a word to them.

Even in the homes of Christian leaders, there is a great neglect in soul winning. The children of pastors, deacons, and teachers are often neglected.

## THE REWARDS FOR SOUL WINNING NEVER END

Here is the marvel of winning others to Christ. It is like tossing a stone into a pool. The ripples go on and on in ever increasing circles. The person who won me to Christ has had a part in all the souls that I have brought to the Saviour. Andrew brought Simon Peter to Jesus. Simon Peter preached on the day of Pentecost and three thousand souls were saved.

What a marvelous business this is that continues to pay off in this life and the life to come.

No one can measure the joy which comes to the soul winner's heart when he sees a loved one or a friend brought out of darkness into light. This is a joy which never fails, for a soul saved for eternity and the reward will be eternal.

## SOUL WINNING IS OPPOSED BY MAN'S GREATEST ENEMY

The devil will become busy against you when you enter into the Lord's work. He hates God, he hates the souls of men, and he will endeavor to stop those who cooperate in the work of God.

A thousand doubts will come to your mind when you enter the work of soul winning. The devil will want you to doubt your own salvation. He will try to make you doubt the power of Christ to save sinners. He will cause you to even have doubts regarding the Word of God itself.

Not only doubts, but discouragements will come to you. The devil is the author of discouragement. It is his chief weapon to stop us from doing the greatest work. Our failures will seem like mountains. We will wonder if we can do anything at all.

Satan will cause you to delay until opportunities are gone. The most unpleasant memories in all of my ministry are the memories of opportunities lost. I delayed to speak to men, and while I tarried, the hand of death took them away. Only recently this was true.

Let me repeat an experience of years ago which I can never forget. I was conducting a revival in a First Baptist Church of a Kentucky town. A lady came to me and asked that I go and speak to a young man who worked at a store in the city. I took the name and address and assured the lady that I would go to speak to him. The days of the meeting rushed by. A number of times each day I walked from the hotel to the church, and from the church to the hotel. Each time I passed by the business house where this young man worked. When the meeting was nearly over, I was standing one morning in the church office. The phone rang. The secretary answered. The conversation was brief, and she turned to me and said, "Mr. So and So died a few minutes ago." I reached in my pocket and pulled out the name of this young man. He was twenty-seven years old. He had gone home to eat his noon day meal with his wife and baby. As he sat down at the table, he suddenly fell forward, and was dead before his wife could reach him.

Only twenty-seven years old! How sudden and tragic it was! But how terrible that I had failed to speak to him even once. I had passed by the store again and again, but had delayed to make my call. Everyone said that he was a lost young man. He did not read the Bible, had never gone to church, had refused to show any interest in spiritual things whatsoever. And then came death and eternity.

Do not let Satan cause you to delay the carrying out of this important business.

You can win souls. God will enable you to do so. Will you begin at once doing your part in the business that cannot fail?

# 30
# This One Thing We Know

> *"For the Son of Man is come to seek and to save that which was lost."*
>
> —Matthew 18:11

This we know — Christ has commanded us to go with the Gospel. We know that we are commanded to take it unto the ends of the earth. Doubts may invade our minds at many points, but doubt has no part here. The language of our Lord is plain. The repetition of the great commission is proof of its importance. We have been commanded by our Saviour to do a great and momentous task. We must either obey or be guilty.

May we consider three facts about the great commission.

## THE BASIS FOR IT

The great commission rests upon a three-fold foundation.

FIRST, GOD'S LOVE FOR MEN. It should take but a little while to give proof of the love of God for men. First, the Word of God tells us that He loves us.

> *"For God so loved the world, that he gave his only begotten Son, that whosoever believeth in him should not perish, but have everlasting life."*
>
> —John 3:16

> *"Herein is love, not that we loved God, but that he*

loved us, and sent his Son to be the propitiation for our sins."

—I John 4:10

Not only does the Word of God tell us of His love, but our own experience makes us know the love of God. In spite of our failures, mistakes, and sins, God showers His love upon us every day. We are the recipients of the choicest blessings — blessings that we in no wise deserve.

Therefore, when Jesus said, *"Go. . .and teach all nations. . ."* (Matthew 28:19), He was expressing the love of God for a lost mankind.

A SECOND BASIS FOR THE GREAT COMMISSION IS THE LOST CONDITION OF MEN. If men are not lost in their sins and bound for an everlasting hell, then it is clearly a worthless expenditure of time and money to send missionaries around the world. If men can be saved in any way aside from hearing the Gospel, then, too, it is a useless waste to encourage missions.

But, let it be established once and for all in the minds of all people: Men without Christ are lost and bound for an eternal hell. Jesus said,

*"For the Son of man is come to save that which was lost."*

—Matthew 18:11

*"He that believeth on him is not condemned: but he that believeth not is condemned already, because he hath not believed in the name of the only begotten Son of God."*

—John 3:18

Christ recognized the lost condition of men when He gave His command to go. The great commission becomes a foolish commission if men are not lost, damned, ana doomed without Christ.

THIRD, THE GREAT COMMISSION RESTS ALSO UPON THE POWER OF THE GOSPEL TO SAVE TO THE UTTERMOST. There is no need to carry the Gospel to the ends of the earth if it is powerless to save the worst of sinners. Thank God, it has the power to save all who will come unto the Lord Jesus Christ in simple faith. The Gospel is able to save all who will believe, and is only hindered in its mighty working power by the unbelief of man.

Briefly, I have given you the basis for the great commission: God's love for men, the lost condition of man, and the power of the Gospel to save to the uttermost. What a tragedy that we have paid so little attention to the great commission. Christian people have been outstripped by the business world. We have a message of the greatest importance but we have done so little to give it to all men.

I was reading the story of a prominent Christian merchant who once arose in a missionary convention and gave the following experience. He said,

> I stood on the edge of one of the great Chinese provinces. I asked my guide, "How many men are there beyond us who never have heard the name of Jesus Christ?" The answer was, "Thirty million." But he said, "We must go back. We are already in dangerous territory here. We must go back." The man said, "As I stood aside to bow my head, lift up my heart in prayer for that great body of men and women without the message of the living Christ, I heard the creaking of one of the unspeakable Chinese wagons. I turned. The miserable vehicle pased. It was drawn by a weatherbeaten camel, driven by a coolie, and loaded with cans of oil. Underneath it hung a crate of lamps marked — *Made in Connecticut, U.S.A.* We would

send them lights for their homes, but we have not sent them Light for their hearts."

That business man was right. Millions and millions of dollars are spent every year by various enterprises. Their representatives are to be found in all parts of the world. The manufacturers of cars and gadgets and *Coca-Cola* and other things have covered the world. But as Christians, we have failed to carry out the great work of our Saviour. We have failed to realize that we are ambassadors of God.

**THE BURDEN OF THE GREAT COMMISSION**

Let us consider again the command given by our Lord. He said to His disciples,

> *"Go ye therefore, and teach all nations, baptizing them in the name of the Father, and of the Son, and of the Holy Ghost:*
>
> *"Teaching them to observe all things whatsoever I have commanded you: and, lo, I am with you alway, even unto the end of the world. Amen"*
>
> —Matthew 28:19,20

At the close of Mark's Gospel we find the commission recorded again. Jesus said, "*. . .Go ye into all the world, and preach the gospel to every creature*" (Mark 16:15).

In Luke's Gospel we find it recorded in this way,

> *"And that repentance and remission of sins should be preached in his name among all nations, beginning at Jerusalem."*
>
> —Luke 24:47

John's Gospel gives us the commission in these words,

> *". . .as my Father hath sent me, even so send I you."*
>
> —John 20:21

In the Acts of the apostles we find the Lord speaking to His disciples and saying,

> *"But ye shall receive power, after that the Holy Ghost is come upon you: and ye shall be witnesses unto me both in Jerusalem, and in all Judaea, and in Samaria, and unto the uttermost part of the earth."*
>
> —Acts 1:8

The burden of the great commission rests upon believers. He spoke not alone to His own disciples in that day, but He speaks to us in this day. The burden to obey is ours.

FIRST, WE ARE TO GO WITH THE MESSAGE. This is the call that goes to youth: Will you go? The commission has been given. The need is everywhere. Will you surrender your life to the greatest work that could be given to any one? Will you look upon the harvest fields white already, and waiting for reapers?

Have you been puzzled for a long time about how to spend your life? Has this great thought come to you — "What is the best way to invest the time that God has given to me?" Could there be a greater investment of your life than to the ones who have never heard?

SECOND, WE HAVE A BURDEN TO GIVE! The message must go out. It is quite obvious that all people cannot go. Though we may desire to do so, there are hindering causes and reasons why every person cannot go to some distant field. But, we can give. I am prone to believe that all people can give something. The offering may not be large, but you can give something.

Here is the great advantage of a church missionary program. When we obey the Word of God to bring our tithes and offerings into the Lord's house, we are able to pool together all that we have, and to make worthwhile contributions to world missions. While I was pastor of the Highland Park Baptist Church, one-half of all offerings given in the church went to the mission cause at home and abroad.

Therefore, I would urge upon you to be a faithful tither, bringing your offering to the Lord's house on every Lord's day, remembering that with the giving of every dollar, you have a part in the world-wide mission program.

THIRD, WE HAVE A BURDEN TO PRAY. Prayer is a vital necessity for successful mission work. We should make it our daily business to hold up the missionaries in prayer.

Someone has pointed out that praying for others has a two-fold benefit — first, prayer for others lifts the man who prays out of himself and brings to view the glories of life. Second, prayer for others benefits those for whom we pray.

So few people have learned the joy of intercessory prayer. We pray for things, for objects, for material needs, but we do not pray for others.

May we begin this day to pray with renewed zeal for our missionaries. May we see and understand that prayer is the shortest route to any person. We can reach out and have a definite part in the work of missionaries by prayer. At any moment we can do so, if we will but simply pause and pray.

Dr. Herbert Lockyer writes down three principles to guide us in intercessory prayer:

1. They must have a sincere desire for the highest interest of those for whom they pray.
2. They must have the utmost faith in God's promise and sufficiency to meet the needs of those prayed for.
3. They must hold themselves in readiness to cooperate in action as an outcome of their prayers. Such prayers take feet and go to those who are interceded for.

"Make me an intercessor,
 One who can really pray;

One of the Lord's remembrances,
By night as well as day."

Yes, the burden of carrying out the great commission rests upon everyone who names the name of Christ. We have a burden to go, to give, and to pray.

## THE BLESSINGS OF OBEDIENCE TO THE GREAT COMMISSION

No one could enumerate in a few moments the blessings of doing what God says, but consider FIRST THAT OBEDIENCE BRINGS BLESSINGS TO CHURCHES AND TO INDIVIDUALS. The churches that are excelling in this day and hour are missionary churches. They are churches that have a concern for a world lost in sin. Because of their world-wide vision and world-wide giving, they are doing a more excellent job in the local field.

I have discovered in my travels that churches engaged in active missionary endeavors at home and abroad always have the supply of their material needs. The churches that struggle and fret and worry about money are the ones that are withholding from God that which should be given to Him.

It is sad that we have many churches that call themselves *Missionary Baptist Churches* that do nothing for missions. The pastor of such a church came to see me some months ago in one of my extension meetings. He said,

> *"On last evening my deacons voted that no money would be given to missions until they had built and paid for an educational building."*

He stated that if they should begin the building at once, it would take over five years to build it and to pay for it. And then came this question, "Should I remain the pastor of a church that does not give to missions?" I gave a positive "No". But I advised him to go back to the people and preach the Word of God and see if the selfishness could not be broken down, and if men and women would not begin to manifest an interest in missions.

There are not only blessings to churches, but blessings to individuals. Since God burdened my heart for missions, I have had without question the greatest spiritual and material blessings of all my life. I will say to any child of God, "If you want joy and peace and a sense of obedience to Christ, then begin giving to missions and have a daily concern for this work."

If we should follow the Bible, we would find that the normal Christian life would be as follows: Tithing, daily Bible reading, prayer, personal evangelism, obedience to the commands of Christ and an interest in world-wide missions. This should be just the normal life for the child of God who takes the Word of God at face value.

But instead of this, we find selfishness of time, talent, and tithe. We find carelessness and indifference on the part of God's own people; therefore, you will have to overcome the barriers to obedience. Selfishness must be put down. The wrong use of your time must be concquered, and indifferent hearts must be activated to real concern.

SECOND, OBEDIENCE BRINGS HIS PRESENCE. Jesus said to His disciples, "*. . .lo, I am with you alway, even unto the end of the world. Amen*" (Matthew 28:20). This was said to be DavidLivingstone'sfavorite verse.I am sure that it must be the favorite of almost every thoughtful missionary. How wonderful to have the presence of Christ with us as we give obedience to His commands!

We need to be reminded that this promise of His presence is given to the ones who obey His command. The missionary who goes to the foreign field can say, "The Lord is with me."

But that child of God who sits selfishly by and does nothing to aid the lost to hear of Christ cannot claim the promise.

FINALLY, OBEDIENCE BRINGS ETERNAL REJOICING. What rejoicing we have now in the salvation of souls. I cannot forget a little lad who came forward in a meeting in Atlanta on a Friday night. He raised his hand for prayer at the first of the invitation. He was spoken to about his need for Christ, and then he came to the front on his crutches. He had had polio. He stood before me, leaning on his crutches with big tears rolling down his cheeks. He said he was happy that Jesus had saved him. What rejoicing we have in the salvation of souls!

But there will also be rejoicing forever in glory. In eternity we will come to know the result of the giving of our money, our prayers, and the giving of our children to the work of missions. We will see and know the ones who were won to Christ by our efforts, however small they might have been. What rejoicing forever in the presence of God!

Consider today the blessings which come from obeying the great commission. Begin at this moment to manifest an interest in the souls of men, at home and afar. Take to your heart the need of missions. Pray daily for missions and missionaries. Then remember to tell men and women around you of the Saviour who cares and wants to save them.

The old story is told of a steamer which came to the wharf at Norfolk, Virginia back in 1863. It had a very peculiar load of passengers. It was an exchange of sick and wounded prisoners between the Union and Confederate armies. This steamer had brought up from the south several hundred Union soldiers who had been held by the Confederates in prison hospitals.

Many of the men were in a destitute and deplorable condition. Among them was a young man under twenty who suffered from wounds and diseases which had weakened his mind. He had been reared in a refined Philadelphia home, and the life in prison and his suffering had been almost intolerable to him. His body was covered with sores and vermin.

He had had word that an older brother who was a wealthy merchant would meet him at Norfolk. He said to his comrades as he received the message, "He will not know me." Then he told his friends how beautiful and clean everything was in his brother's home, and asserted strongly that he could never be taken there. They would not have him in the house, he was sure.

"I am so changed," he said, "that William will not know me. If he did, he would not take me. I will go and die in the hospital." Then the poor boy would weep as he looked at his ragged clothes and his thin, wasted form.

As the steamer touched the wharf a well dressed young man sprang up on the deck. It was his brother, William. He had been waiting for hours for the steamer to arrive. He had a carriage, furnished with pillows and blankets to carry his brother to the train. He had secured a furlough from Washington for his brother to go to his home, and with a face full of eagerness, he passed around the deck hunting for him.

Soon he was by his side, but sure enough, he did not know him. It was repulsive to him to look upon the wrecked object before him. Sores upon the mouth and nose, face sunken and covered with dirt, hair unkempt and fastened to running blotches upon his forehead; feet were naked and clothing rags. He turned away with an involuntary shudder.

The heart of ths poor sick boy sank within him. He said to himself, "It is just as I expected. He doesn't know me. He was disgusted with me. How clean and nice he looks. He can never have me with him as I am now." So he had not the courage to speak. His brother passed along the second time, but still he dared not speak.

Once more the brother went carefully from soldier to soldier. He had come to the conclusion that his brother was not there, and feared that he had probably died upon the passage.

Making one more effort, however, he stood for the third time beside the one he was seeking. He looked at him attentively, but no sign of recognition. "Poor fellow," he said, pityingly, and was turning away when a faint cry arrested him.

"William, don't you know me?" was uttered in faltering tones from the trembling lips of the poor sick fellow.

"My dear brother, why didn't you speak before?" was the reply of the grateful man. And then he lifted the emaciated form in his arms, and carried him, rags, filth, sores, and all, to his waiting carriage. His strength, his money, his house, everything were at the disposal of his poor brother, and the possession of all these never had a higher value in his eyes than now that he could use them on his brother's behalf.

I do not need to apply the story. I simply need to say that if you are lost today, Christ is looking for you. Everything that he has, he desires to give to you. You may feel that you are low in sin and degradation. You may say that Christ will not have you, but, my friend, He will have you, and He wants you now. You may fear to call upon His name, but remember the Bible says, *"For whosoever shall call upon the name of the Lord shall be saved"* (Romans 10:13).

Come to Jesus now, just as you are. All of the blessings of heaven will be yours when you do. Again, I quote,

> *"But as many as received him, to them gave he power to become the sons of God, even to them that believe on his name."* —John 1:12

# 31
# Four Reasons Why I Believe in Missions

*"For though I preach the gospel, I have nothing to glory of: for necessity is laid upon me; yea, woe is unto me, if I preach not the gospel!"*

—I Corinthians 9:16

In a very plain and practical way I want to suggest four reasons why I believe in missions.

Four reasons why I pray for missionaries and missionary work.

Four reasons why I give to missions and missionary enterprises.

It is my conviction that Jesus meant what he said when He commanded us, *"Go ye therefore, and teach all nations. . ."* (Matthew 28:19). I am convinced that the Gospel is the power of God unto salvation to every one that believeth. I do not believe there is any greater task in this world than that of getting out the Gospel through the missionary effort.

I want to give you four reasons why I hold myself ready for any mission activity that God desires of me.

Again, four reasons why I want to help young people get ready for the mission field.

Here are the four reasons:

## THE ETERNITY OF THE SOUL

The Bible says the soul is eternal. Now, let us see what the

Word has upon this matter.

> *"Then shall the dust return to the earth as it was: and the spirit shall return unto God who gave it"* (Ecclesiastes 12:7).
>
> *"And many of them that sleep in the dust of the earth shall awake, some to everlasting life, and some to shame and everlasting contempt"* (Daniel 12:2).
>
> *"And fear not them which kill the body, but are not able to kill the soul: but rather fear him which is able to destroy both soul and body in hell"* (Matthew 10:28).
>
> *"And these shall go away into everlasting punishment: but the righteous into life eternal"* (Matthew 25:46).
>
> *"Labour not for the meat which perisheth, but for that meat which endureth unto everlasting life, which the Son of man shall give unto you: for him hath God the Father sealed"* (John 10:28).
>
> *"But now being made free from sin, and become servants to God, ye have your fruit unto holiness, and the end everlasting life"* (Romans 6:22).
>
> *"So when this corruptible shall have put on incorruption, and this mortal shall have put on immortality, then shall be brought to pass the saying that is written, Death is swallowed up in victory"* (I Corinthians 15:54).
>
> *"And this is the promise that he hath promised us, even eternal life"* (I John 2:25).

All of these verses have been given with one intent — to show you that the soul is eternal.

You are an eternal soul! Here is a fact from which you must never escape — this is something that must be faced — you are an eternal soul. Where will you spend eternity?

This fact must be driven home into the consciousness of every person — your soul is going to live on in heaven or in hell. Heaven is a place of bliss and fellowship. Hell is a place of suffering and separation. You are not like the cattle of the field or the dogs of the street. You are a soul.

Now the Word lays down in plain and definite terms this fact that the soul is eternal and the soul is going to spend eternity in heaven or in hell. The entire matter depends on what the individual does with the Lord Jesus Christ. It is because the soul is eternal that I am concerned, desperately concerned, vitaily concerned about the work of missions.

## THE VERACITY OF CHRIST

Jesus said, *". . .I am the way, the truth, and the life: no man cometh unto the Father, but by me"* (John 14:6).

The Son of God is truth, therefore, His record must be accepted.

Christ says that souls are saved or lost.

Christ taught about heaven and about hell.

Christ taught that men are eternal beings. Listen to this: *"Verily, verily, I say unto you, The hour is coming, and now is, when the dead shall hear the voice of the Son of God: and they that hear shall live"* (John 5:25).

Christ taught that He is the only source of life. This was not a matter of boasting with our Saviour — it was simply a statement of fact. Here is what the Word says: *"He that hath the Son hath life; and he that hath not the Son of God hath not life"* (I John 5:12).

Some poor men of days gone by have tossed aside the veracity of Christ. They have despised His words. They have rebelled against His admonitions, but let us remember that this Word of God says to us plainly, *". . .let God be true, but every man a liar. . ."* (Romans 3:4). Here are the things which come to us from the statements of Jesus regarding Himself.

FIRST, HE HAS THE POWER TO SAVE. Both Jew and Gentile can be saved by coming to the Saviour. We repeated on our broadcast every day the words, *"For I am not ashamed of the gospel of Christ: for it is the power of God unto salvation to every one that believeth; to the Jew first, and also to the Greek"* (Romans 1:16).

What a joy to see a Jew come to the Saviour who is able to save to the uttermost. Some years ago Dr. Jacob Gartenhaus preached in a church in Shawnee, Oklahoma. He was told that an Austrian Jew was attending a nearby university. On Monday morning Dr. Gartenhaus went to visit this man in his dormitory room. The reception which he received from the student was colder than the weather. This young man accused Dr. Gartenhaus of betraying the Jewish people. Of course, Dr. Gartenhaus told him that he was doing the best thing possible for the Jews by pointing them to the Saviour who could end all of their sufferings, then left some tracts for the student, knowing that as soon as he left they would be thrown into the wastebasket.

A few years later Dr. Gartenhaus was back in Shawnee for a Sunday night service. The pastor called on a young man to come forward and lead the evening prayer. Dr. Gartenhaus was surprised when the Jewish student, with whom he had talked on that Monday morning, came forward and led in fervent prayer. In the army this young man had been won to Christ by some ardent Christians. A wonderful change had been wrought in his life by the Lord Jesus. Yes, Christ has the power to save. He can save Jews and Gentiles.

SECONDLY, HE HAS THE WILLINGNESS TO SAVE. Hear Him as he says, *". . .him that cometh to me I will in no wise* cast out" (John 6:37). He wants to save. He yearns to save. He longs to save. He waits to save. Yes, he is waiting for you to come to Him and to receive everlasting life.

THIRDLY, CHRIST IS CONCERNED. Here we come face to face with the compassionate Jesus. Here we see the longing heart of the Son of God who looked upon men and wept over them because they were "*. . .as sheep having no shepherd*" (Matthew 9:36). The Saviour wept over Jerusalem because the people refused to repent and believe.

Our Christ is the truth; therefore, men are lost who do not come to him. Do not imagine, my friend, that salvation will be granted unto you when you have despised the Saviour. There is but one way to be saved and that is to come by the way of the Lord Jesus Christ; the way of repentance and faith in Him.

I repeat, it is because of this truth that I am interested in missions. Christ is the truth. All who stand against Him are liars. His Word must be followed. He tells us to go with the Gospel.

## THE DESTINY OF THE DAMNED

I give my third reason for believing in missions. The Bible tells me that "*. . .he that believeth not is condemned already. . .*" (John 3:18). The Word of God says, "*For the wages of sin is death. . .*" (Romans 3:18). The Bible tells me that there is a destiny of damnation for all who reject the Saviour. Christ said as He spoke of those who had turned from Him, . . ."*Depart from me, ye cursed, into everlasting fire, prepared for the devil and his angels*" (Matthew 25:41).

Where do the lost go? They go to an eternal hell. This is taught throughout the entire Word of God. We must not follow the vain and light teachings of modern men, but we must follow the truth of the Word. The Bible says that all who reject Jesus are lost.

*". . .the soul that sinneth, it shall die"* (Ezekiel 18:4). Again we read: *"For all have sinned, and come short of the glory of God"* (Romans 3:23).

The awfulness of hell, pictured by the Lord Jesus Himself. Christ was reluctant to give this task to anyone else. Oh, that we might see the tragic awfulness of the place called hell!

I once talked with a man who had been a chaplain in a state penitentiary. He said he spent three years talking to the men, but finally he said he had to leave. He said the burden was too great. He stated that some of the men seemed to grow used to the walls and the imprisonment, but some did not. And for many, it was a hell on earth to be behind the walls, to be shut away from society and friends and loved ones.

Let us think with earnestness about the picture of hell as given by the Lord Jesus. I am not going to read the scripture in Luke 16:19-31, but simply call to your attention that story of the rich man and Lazarus. The rich man died and went to hell. The beggar died and was carried by the angels into Abraham's bosom. From hell the rich man lifted up his eyes, being in torments and cried, *"Father Abraham, have mercy on me, and send Lazarus, that he may dip the tip of his finger in water, and cool my tongue; for I am tormented in this flame"* (Luke 16:24).

To this one Abraham said,

> *"Son, remember that thou in thy lifetime receivedst thy good things, and likewise Lazarus evil things: but now he is comforted, and thou art tormented. And beside all this, between us and you there is a great gulf fixed: so that they which would pass from hence to you cannot; neither can they pass to us, that would come from thence."*
>
> —Luke 16:25,26

The suffering of hell was so intense that the rich man said, "*. . .I pray thee therefore, father, that thou wouldest send him to my father's house: for I have five brethren; that he may testify unto them, lest they also come into this place of torment*" (Luke 16:27-28).

Can you not see that Christ was doing all in His power to show to man the awfulness of the place called hell? The destiny of the damned is a fact that should shadow our hearts and move our lives. After once getting a picture of hell and its awfulness, we should be constrained to move out and give the Gospel to as many as possible.

Again, we must remember that the devil and his angels will be in hell. The Word tells us that hell was prepared for the devil and his angels. One day Satan will be cast into the fiery furnace. One day all who have rejected Christ will be cast in with him.

Think, if you will, of the destiny of the damned. Let this solemn truth of the Word of God sink into your hearts. See what Christ meant when He said, "everlasting fire."

Think of the suffering of hell, when a rich man could cry for just a drop of water to cool his tongue.

## THE UNCERTAINTY OF LIFE

I give you now my fourth reason for my interest in missions and my concern for missionary enterprises.

> "*Whereas ye know not what shall be on the morrow. For what is your life? It is even a vapor, that appeareth for a little time, and then vanisheth away.*"
>
> —James 4:14

The uncertainty of life constrains us to be diligent in giving the Gospel to those around us and those in distant places.

We have no promised days. The Word of God gives you no assurance of any definite time upon this earth. The Bible says,

*"Today is the day of salvation."* When you face each day, remember it may be the last one. What a change this should make in your life and mine!

How carefully you should consider the matter of your own soul, my lost friend, when you remember that this is all the time that you have! This present moment! Therefore, the Bible tells you to repent except ye perish.

Death may come at any time. David said, *"There is just a step twixt me and death."* How near is death? Just a beat of your heart away. At any time this frail body may cease its function and death will lay hold upon you.

Not only death may come, but Christ may come at any time. The second coming of Jesus Christ should be an urgent reason why the sinner should repent and believe on Jesus Christ.

Why doesn't Christ come quickly? Perhaps the reason is stated in II Peter 3:9,

> *"The Lord is not slack concerning his promise, as some men count slackness; but is longsuffering to us-ward, not willing that any should perish, but that all should come to repentance."*

The coming of Jesus could take place at any time, but God delays because of His love for sinners and because of His desire to see them saved. Mockers may count slackness, but we should count it salvation. As God delays, we should see this opportunity for giving the Gospel to as many as possible.

Let us not hold back, but let us press forward. He may come at any time, and until He comes, let us be busy and give the message of Jesus Christ to a world lost in sin.

God does not want sinners to be lost. He does not want men to go through this life without Christ and then go down to hell at the end of the way. He wants people to be saved. He is a great, loving Heavenly Father and He has prepared a heaven big enough for every one who has ever lived. But, my friend, if you are to be saved, it must be upon the terms of the Gospel.

REPENT OF SIN. WHAT SIN? THE SIN OF UNBELIEF. . . ."Believe on the Lord Jesus Christ, and thou shalt be saved. . ." Repentance and faith are twined together. They cannot be separated!

An old teacher used to say to his pupils, "You should repent the day before you die." But they said, "We don't know when we are going to die." Then replied the old teacher, "You should repent today." We have no assurance of any moment beyond this present one; therefore, we should repent now and believe in Jesus Christ and be saved.

Judgment is coming upon this world — the judgment of the great tribulation. The only safe place for anyone is in the ark of safety with our Saviour.

Out in Vanport, Oregon, in May, 1948, there was a disastrous flood. Hundreds heard the warning signal, but paid no attention to it. They thought it was an ordinary warning, but in just a few moments the waters were rising around the people and lives were being lost. A flying instructor who was flying through the air and saw the disaster said, "There was no warning trickle, no minor hole in the dike. There was suddenly a six-foot breach in the railroad embankment and then it was sixty feet, then six hundred. It was agony to see the people fussing about, trying to save furniture and clothes."

What a sad picture of man trying to save furniture and clothing in the hour of death! How foolish is man when he risks all for a few things of this fleeting world!

The uncertainty of life urges upon you the necessity to take Christ as your Saviour today. Will you trust Him now?

# 32
# The Worth of a Soul

*"What man of you, having an hundred sheep, if he lose one of them, doth not leave the ninety and nine in the wilderness, and go after that which is lost, until he find it?"*

—Luke 15:4

"CHURCHANITY" has taken us far from the standards of Christianity.

"CHURCHANITY" is concerned about money, but Christianity is concerned about souls.

"CHURCHANITY" is concerned about worldly prestige, but Christianity about growth in grace.

"CHURCHANITY" is concerned about denominational power; Christianity about Holy Spirit power.

"CHURCHANITY" is concerned about big, beautiful buildings, luxurious 'sanctuaries,' but Christianity is concerned about getting souls ready for the mansions in heaven.

I would not give the snap of my finger for worldly "Churchanity." It is deceptive, delusive, and dangerous.

But, for Christianity, I would give my life, yes, I am giving my life with joy and peace of heart for this cause. What I am saying is real. Souls are saved by the power of Christ. Heaven is a real place; yes, and with sadness we must make mention of the fact that hell is real also.

How much is a soul worth? My friends, we cannot value a soul in money, in houses, or in lands. There is no value that could be placed upon an eternal soul of man, when Christ, the Son of God, came down to die for souls.

However, I can give you in a few words some statements which will indicate the worth of a soul. Follow with me, please:

## SOULS ARE WORTH CONSTANT CONCERN

FIRST, JESUS SOUGHT AFTER THE SOULS OF MEN. If the Son of God had an interest in the souls of others, and came from heaven's glory for one definite purpose — the winning of souls, then how much should we show our interest in the souls of others?

JESUS SOUGHT AFTER SINNERS. I am thinking of that old and familiar story of Jesus and Zacchaeus. Remember how Zacchaeus sought to see Jesus, and climbed a tree in order to do so. Remember also how Jesus called him down from the tree, went home with him, and certainly that day Zacchaeus was saved. Jesus had concern for sinners.

There is an old and beautiful legend which relates how Zacchaeus had been converted and found Christ, and after this he had a very strange custom. He would leave his bed early in the morning and would be gone for some time. His wife was curious to know where he went and what he did. Therefore, she arose one morning and followed him. At the town well he lowered a bucket, filled it with water, and passed out of the gate of the city until he came to a sycamore tree. There, setting down the bucket of water, he began to gather and cast away the stones and branches and rubbish of any kind which lay about the foot of the tree. Having done this, he poured the water upon the roots of the tree, and gently caressing the trunk of the tree with his hands, stood silent, as if in affectionate reminiscence and contemplation. His amazed wife came out from her hiding place and asked him what he was doing, whereupon Zacchaeus said, "This is the tree where I found Christ."

Yes, Jesus cared. He cared enough to call down a poor and despised man and save his eternal soul. Jesus cared and we should care.

JESUS WEPT OVER SINNERS. See Him as He wept over the city of Jerusalem, as He cried out:

> *"O Jerusalem, Jerusalem, thou that killest the prophets, and stonest them which are sent unto thee, how often would I have gathered thy children together, even as a hen gathereth her chickens under her wings, and ye would not!"*
>
> — Matthew 23:37

Jesus wept over sinners, and we should weep over those who are lost and undone, and away from God, and without hope in the world. Jesus cared and we should care.

JESUS PRAYED FOR SINNERS. Hear Him as He cried unto God in behalf of those around Him who knew Him not. Not only did Jesus pray, but He urges us to pray that God will thrust forth laborers into the harvest. Let us notice what we find in Matthew 9:36-38:

> *"But when he saw the multitudes, he was moved with compassion on them, because they fainted, and were scattered abroad, as sheep having no shepherd.*
>
> *"Then saith he unto his disciples, The harvest truly is plenteous, but the laborers are few;*
>
> *"Pray ye therefore the Lord of the harvest, that he will send forth laborers into his harvest."*

But not only did Jesus seek sinners, weep over sinners, and pray for sinners, but CHRIST DIED FOR SINNERS. This is the great center of the gospel message: "Christ died for sinners."

How wonderful and how beautiful is this tremendous thought! Let it never get away from us as we think of those who are dying around us. Christ died that He might save sinners.

SECOND, THE APOSTLE PAUL CARED FOR SINNERS. He agonized in behalf of those who were lost and undone. There is a portion of Scripture which I read many times, which never fails to touch my heart. It is found in Romans 9:1-3,

> *"I say the truth in Christ, I lie not, my conscience also bearing me witness in the Holy Ghost,*
>
> *"That I have great heaviness and continual sorrow in my heart,*
>
> *"For I could wish that myself were accursed from Christ for my brethren, my kinsmen according to the flesh."*

Can you not see the agony in the soul of the Apostle Paul, as he thought of others, lost and dying without Christ?

The apostle agonized, he prayed, yes, and remember, Paul, as a preacher, died — in the carrying out of the great message and work of our Saviour.

One of the most thrilling portions in the Word of God is II Timothy 4. It is here that we find the apostle saying,

> *"For I am now ready to be offered, and the time of my departure is at hand.*
>
> *"I have fought a good fight, I have finished my course, I have kept the faith:*
>
> *"Henceforth there is laid up for me a crown of righteousness, which the Lord, the righteous judge, shall give me at that day: and not to me only, but unto all them also that love his appearing."*
>
> — II Timothy 4:6-8

I believe that the Apostle Paul died with a burden upon his soul for others. Paul cared. He prayed, and he died in the work of Christ.

THIRD, SO SHOULD WE CARE FOR OTHERS. We should pray and weep and witness that men and women might come to Jesus Christ and be saved. What a tragedy if people should gain the impression that we do not care about their souls. The psalmist has a phrase that reads like this, *"No man cared for my soul."* How diligently do people care for the bodies of others, but how little they seem to care for the souls of others!

How earnestly men are working upon a cure for cancer, hoping that it can be perfected so that lives may be spared, but how little they seem to care for the souls of men dying and sinking into hell!

If a small child should go down the street and fall into an open well or gutter, everyone would be concerned about rescuing the lad, but how little we care for the souls of others!

May God impress us at this time of the worth of a soul! Jesus cared, Paul cared, and we should care.

## SOULS ARE WORTH FERVENT SEARCHING

When I turn to Luke 15, I find that the entire chapter concerns itself with the matter of a soul and its need of salvation. Jesus gave three parables.

FIRST, HE GAVE THE PARABLE OF THE LOST SHEEP. In this He tells of the man having a hundred sheep, and losing one of them. He leaves the ninety and nine and goes out into the wilderness until he finds the lost sheep.

SECOND, JESUS THEN TOLD OF THE WOMAN HAVING TEN PIECES OF SILVER AND HAVING LOST ONE, she sweeps the house and seeks diligently until it is found. When it is found, she urges others to come and rejoice with her in the good fortune of finding the lost coin.

AS A THIRD PARABLE, JESUS GAVE THE STORY OF THE PRODIGAL SON. How beautiful and how touching is this account! Here is pictured a lad who went away from home after securing his part of the inheritance from his father. He wasted everything in riotous living, then when he began to be in want, he came to himself. After talking to himself for a while, he arose and came home. His father received him joyfully, and said, *"For this my son was dead, and is alive again; he was lost, and is found. . ."* (Luke 15:24).

Do you not see that these parables given by the Lord Jesus Christ tell us that we are to be fervently seeking for men and women who are lost?

FIRST, THERE MUST BE A GOING. We must go after the lost sheep. We must be interested in the lost boy. We must go at home, abroad, and everywhere. We must go with the message of redeeming love, telling men of our Saviour, that He is ready to save.

SECOND, THERE MUST BE A SEEKING OF LOST SINNERS. As the shepherd sought for the lost sheep, as the woman sought for the lost coin, so there must be a seeking on our part. Jesus came seeking sinners. *"The Son of man is come to seek and to save that which was lost"* (Luke 19:10). We will follow in the steps of our Master as we seek after those who are lost and undone.

THIRD, THERE WILL BE REJOICING. Always, we have rejoicing hearts when the lost is found, This is true in all three parables. When the lost sheep was found, the shepherd said, *". . .Rejoice with me; for I have found my sheep which was lost"* (Luke 15:6). When the lost coin was found, the woman said, *". . .Rejoice with me; for I have found the piece which I had lost"* (Luke 15:9). When the son came home, the father said,

*"...Bring forth the best robe, and put it on him; and put a ring on his hand, and shoes on his feet:*

*"And bring hither the fatted calf, and kill it; and let us eat, and be merry:*

*"For this my son was dead, and is alive again; he was lost, and is found. And they began to be merry."*

—Luke 15:22-24

What is the worth of a soul? The soul is eternal and is worth fervent searching. Let us not be easy and lackadaisical in the pursuance of this task. Let us be diligent, fervent, and energetic, knowing that men, women, and children without Jesus Christ are lost forever unless we can give to them the message of redeeming love in Christ Jesus.

I remember that which happened many years ago when, as a small boy, I was lost from my parents at a park in the city of Louisville. For many hours I tried to find them and they tried to find me. The crowd was large and the park extensive; therefore, the hours went by before we were finally brought together. I cannot forget my joy to this moment when I saw their faces. I believe that joy also came into their hearts when they had found the son which was lost.

God is concerned about you. He rejoices when you come to Him through Jesus Christ. Christ is concerned about you. He died upon the cross that you might be saved. Every true Christian who knows the Word of God and seeks to follow the teachings of the Lord is concerned about you and rejoices when you come to the Saviour. Let me repeat: Souls are worth fervent searching. Let us not be careless or half hearted in this task, but let us give our best to it.

## YOUR SOUL IS WORTH EARNEST CONSIDERATION

I speak now to every member of this audience. You are an

eternal soul. We are talking about you.

FIRST, LET EVERY CHRISTIAN REJOICE IN HIS SALVATION. Make sure that you are living for God. You have been saved by grace; therefore, let your light shine.

Thank God for the salvation which is yours! Rejoice in the fact that you have been saved and made a member of the family of God through faith in Jesus Christ!

SECOND, LIVE SO THAT OTHERS MAY SEE CHRIST IN YOU. Let men and women see that you are different from others. The shame and disgrace of this hour is that so many church members cannot be distinguished from the sinful world around them. There is no difference between many professing Christians and many sinners of the world. I exhort you, live so that others may see Christ in you.

THIRD, BE CONCERNED ABOUT OTHERS. Oh, Christian, do not allow a single moment to go by without manifesting an interest in those around you. Be so concerned that you speak to every sinner you meet. Be so concerned that you never miss a service in the church. Be so concerned that you express yourself in a constant effort to bring others to a knowledge of Jesus Christ.

Jesus died for your soul upon the cross of Calvary. If you are saved, it is because you have accepted Him as your Saviour. Your eternal soul has been made secure by His shed blood. In the name of God, how can you do anything less than give your best to Him?

Sinner friend, consider your soul. It is worth more than everything in this whole wide world; therefore, give due consideration and proper evaluation for your eternal soul.

An unbeliever once went to a minister and said to him, "I know that you are a man of common sense and practice. I have read your sermons and know that you will give a man as straightforward answer. Do you believe that I have a soul?"

The preacher replied, "Yes, I do·"

"Well," answered the man. "That is an extraordinary thing for a man of your ability to think. If you go to the museum, you can see exactly what the component parts of a man are — so much lime, so much sugar, so much phosphorous, so much carbon, and so much starch." He went on to enumerate sixteen ingredients which make up a man. "You can see them all," he said, "in bottles in a museum." "Where then does the soul come in?"

The minister looked at him and replied, "Excuse me, but I must decline to continue the argument any further."

The man said, "That was just what I expected. When you cannot meet an agrument, you throw up the sponge, and will have nothing to do with it."

"But," said the minister. "I am a reasonable man, and as such I must decline to hold any argument with so many quarts of water, so much phosphorous, so much lime, and so much carbon."

The preacher was right. There is no need for us to spend time in argument with that which is composed of certain elements which can be called by earthly names. But, our consideration should be for the soul of man — that eternal part which makes him kin to the eternal God.

FIRST, SINNER, REMEMBER YOUR SOUL IS ETERNAL. The Word of God bears this out in every place. You are an eternal soul!

SECOND, YOUR SOUL WILL SPEND ETERNITY IN HEAVEN OR IN HELL. If this seems like a dogmatic statement, then you must make the most of it, for it is based upon the Word of God.

*"He that believeth on the Son hath everlasting*

life. . ."(John 3:26). Very plainly, the Word says that a man who believes in Jesus Christ is saved forever.

But again, the Word says,

> *". . .he that believeth not is condemned already because he hath not believed in the name of the only begotten Son of God."* —John 3:18

You are an eternal soul. Will you spend eternity in heaven or in hell? One of the saddest duties which I have to perform is to stand by the side of a casket containing the body of a person who never took a stand for Jesus Christ. I have had this experience many times. I have tried to give words of encouragement to members of families, but within a few feet of where I stood was a body of one who had turned his back upon Jesus Christ and his soul was out in eternal torment.

THIRD, THE MOST IMPORTANT QUESTION THAT YOU CAN FACE IS THIS ONE: "*. . .what shall it profit a man, if he shall gain the whole world, and lose his own soul*" (Mark 8:36)? If you die unsaved, your soul is lost and condemned forever.

Christian, let me exhort you to be faithful. Someone has said, "The Word is solemn — therefore do not trifle. The task is difficult, therefore, do not relax. The opportunity is brief, therefore, do not delay. The path is narrow, therefore, do not wander. The prize is glorious, therefore, do not faint.

Lost man, consider earnestly the matter of your soul. Where will you spend eternity? There is only one way to be saved, and that way is in Jesus, who said,

> *". . .I am the way, the truth, and the life: no man cometh unto the Father, but by me."*
>
> —John 14:6

Will you come to Jesus and trust Him now?

# 33
# Life's Greatest Thrill

*"And they that be wise shall shine as the brightness of the firmament: and they that turn many to righteousness, as the stars for ever and ever."*

— Daniel 12:3

A few years ago, in another city, a young man came up to me and said, "Do you know me?" I replied, "I do not think so."

He said, "I did not expect you to know me, but you led me to Christ almost twenty-five years ago. I was a boy nine years of age when you came out on the farm and talked to me about the Saviour. I am now chairman of the deacons in a church of this city. I want to thank you for telling me about Christ."

This, my friends, is the greatest thrill that can come to any heart; the thrill of knowing that you had a part in bringing someone to salvation.

IT IS DOUBTLESS A THRILL TO RECEIVE A LARGE SUM OF MONEY, but this is nothing as compared to winning a soul to Christ. There are some people who will envy the man who won $100,000 in some kind of contest, but in bringing someone to Christ you can have a greater thrill day by day.

IT IS A THRILL TO MAKE FRIENDS, but this is nothing as compared to the exquisite joy of leading a soul to a knowledge of salvation.

WE ARE TOLD THAT IT IS A THRILL TO BE A BIG SUCCESS IN THIS WORLD. But this thrill will pass away — the joy of leading someone to Jesus will never pass away.

IT IS DOUBTLESS A THRILL FOR A YOUNG MAN TO SET A NEW RECORD IN SOME SPORT. But this cannot compare to the thrill of pointing someone to Jesus and bringing that person to an acceptance of the Saviour

Just one person on earth knows the thrill of soul winning—that is a soul winner. No one can know it except the one who has had this joy.

You can pray for others, but this privilege cannot exceed the joy of soul winning.

You can give to the work of Christ and receive a certain amount of pleasure in so doing, but this cannot compare to the joy of winning someone to Christ.

You can engage in certain forms of Christian service and this service will bring pleasure to your heart, but it will never bring the joy which can come in winning a soul to Christ.

Soul winning is a divine work. We have the command of our Saviour to go and witness and tell others of Him.

This is a demanding work. It demands our best.

Soul winning is a discouraging work. Hardships and difficulties will face us; failures will be ours many times, and we will feel very discouraged.

This is a delightful work. The delight of pointing someone to the Saviour.

What are some of the biggest reasons why people do not engage in soul winning? Perhaps timidity might be offered as one reason. People are afraid to speak to others. They do not understand the importance of this work and the necessity for going ahead with it. Nor, do they understand the help that we have from the Lord and the Holy Spirit as we engage in it.

Again, indifference may keep some people from the work of soul winning. They become so interested in what they are doing and in their own ideas of life that they turn away from this major business.

Some may be too busy with affairs of this life to engage in this biggest of all works.

All of these reasons will be as puny excuses when we stand before Christ at the judgment seat. Let us now resolve that this will be our specific job as a Christian, and that we will press forward in the winning of others to Christ, whatever the difficulty and whatever the cost.

What does it take to be a good soul winner?

SALVATION, YES — YOU MUST KNOW THAT YOU ARE SAVED. We cannot be used of God unless there is within our hearts a knowledge of salvation.

DEDICATION? YES — THERE MUST BE A DEDICATION UNTO THE LORD and a separation from the world if God is going to use us in this greatest of all works.

Now, let these things be understood — salvation, dedication, consecration, all these are things that we know we must have. Every person must understand that these are necessary to the task of winning others.

But, let us go a little further. What does it take to be a soul winner? Let me give three simple things.

## AN UNDERSTANDING OF THE TASK

What is the task of winning someone to Christ? What are the things that we must understand to do this work?

FIRST, WE MUST KNOW THAT WE ARE AFTER ETERNAL SOULS. Every soul is going to spend eternity in heaven or in hell. If we fail to give them the message of Christ, then the soul may be lost.

In many places in the Word, the soul is referred to as eternal. Jesus said, "*Verily, verily, I say unto you, he that heareth my word, and believeth on him that sent me, hath everlasting life, and shall not come into condemnation; but is passed from death unto life.*" (John 5:24).

Jesus said to the woman at the well, "*. . . Whosoever drinketh of the water that I shall give him shall never thirst; but the water that I shall give him shall be in him a well of water springing up into everlasting life*" (John 4:14).

It is necessary that we understand that the soul is eternal. The soul is going to spend eternity in heaven or in hell.

SECOND, WE MUST KNOW THAT CHRIST IS THE ONLY ANSWER FOR LOST MEN. If souls are to be saved, they must come to Christ. He is the one and only Saviour. He died upon the cross that sinners might be saved. If people turn away from Him, then they must face the awful result of eternal darkness and suffering. There is but one way for people to be saved, and that is by faith in Jesus Christ. He said to Thomas, "*I am the way, the truth, and the life; no man cometh unto the Father, but by me*" (John 14:6).

THIRD, THE MESSAGE OF SALVATION MUST BE GIVEN TO ALL MEN. As far as possible, we must give the message to everyone, at home and abroad. We must not shirk our responsibility. The winning of souls is not a light and frivolous task — it is great and important. We must not fail. We must do the work which God has given unto us.

## A WILLINGNESS TO PARTICIPATE

Christ tells us in Acts 1:8 that we are to be witnesses unto him, "*in Jerusalem, Judaea, Samaria, and unto the uttermost part of the earth.*" This is a plain and definite word which means that every child of God is to engage in the work of witnessing to others; however, there must be a willingness to do the job, or else the work will not be done.

FIRST, WE MUST SEE THAT THIS IS OUR JOB. Whatever may be our age or background, we must accept the work and do what Christ has commanded us.

SECOND, WE MUST KEEP AT IT, DAY IN AND DAY OUT; EVERYWHERE WE GO — we must give unto people the plain word of salvation and point them to the Lamb of God.

THIRD, WE HAVE A CHOICE TO DO IT OR NOT TO DO IT, but remember in your hands has been placed the message of salvation. If people do not hear it, then the fault must be laid to you. If you are negligent in the carrying out of your task, then you must give an answer unto the Lord.

### A PERSISTENCE TO CARRY ON

It is sad that some Christians begin work, but soon fall away. The difficulties discourage them. Critical words cause them to fall back and refrain from going on.

There must be a persistence to do this work, whatever may be the hardships facing us.

There must be a persistence to bring to men the message of salvation, however great may be their opposition to hearing this word.

The Apostle Paul did not have an easy task. In every place he was opposed, but he continued despite all opposition to give the message to those who were lost. The Jews opposed him because they said he was speaking against their religion. In a manner he turned from the Jews to the Gentiles because of their opposition, but he never failed to give the message to both the Jew and the Gentiles because of their opposition, but he never failed to give the message to both Jew and Gentile in every place.

The message of Paul was this, *"Testifying both to the Jews, and also to the Greeks, repentance toward God, and faith toward our Lord Jesus Christ"* (Acts 20:21).

Let your determination be stedfast to tell the story of Jesus everywhere you go. Feel that you are failing in your Christian service unless you are doing this.

In Revelation 14:13, we find these words: ". . .*Blessed are the dead which die in the Lord from henceforth: Yea, saith the Spirit, that they may rest from their labours; and their works do follow them.*"

What are the works that should follow us? The work of winning souls to Christ. This is the work that we should carry on through all of life, and when death comes, the task will continue with those that we have brought to the Saviour.

How many people can say, "You led me to Jesus?"

How many can testify, "It was because of you that I found Christ?"

Someone was telling the story of JOSEPHINE OF FRANCE, who died and was carried out to her grave. There were a great many people of pride and position who went after her. But the story tells us that some two thousand of the poor of France followed her coffin. They continued to wail and cry because they had lost their last earthly friend.

Soul winning will be done by those who have an understanding of the task, a willingness to participate, and a persistence to carry on.

# 34
# Necessary For Life

*". . . To this end was I born, and for this cause came I into the world, that I should bear witness unto the truth. . ."*

—John 18:37

This chapter is designed for everyone — for the aged, the middle-aged, and the young. A word for every Christian and a closing word for the lost sinner.

It is easy for us to pick out certain things and to say that they are preeminent and necessary for life. Quite often an educator, carried away by his position, will state that education is the top prerogative for every person. Another individual possessed with the love of money will enthusiastically prescribe the making of money as the prime prerequisite for a successful life. Still others will press the importance of position and power.

This chapter is not designed to tell you how to be a success in life, but is designed to show you what is necessary for a life of usefulness and an eternity filled with blessings.

I am not going to answer all of your questions, but I trust I can start your thinking processes and bring some sparks of determination into your hearts and minds.

**A GOAL**

Study your Bible and note carefully that all worthwhile men in Bible days had goals. Paul, pressing on, could say, *". . . this one thing I do. . ."* (Philippians 3:13).

As we study secular history, we notice very much the same thing, that men were driven on by their goals. But for this message, let us consider only the necessary goals for life.

FIRST, HAVE A WORTHY GOAL. Do not sell yourself for paltry pennies. Do not waste your life seeking after that which is secondary and spiritually unimportant. Have before you a worthy goal. Study the goal to which you have set your heart.

Write down on a piece of paper the attributes of that goal. Does God approve of your goal? Is it one that Christ can bless?

SECOND, WE SHOULD HAVE UNSELFISH GOALS. There must be about us a desire to serve others and to aid them in the things of God.

Simon Peter was selfish, thoughtless, and headstrong until Pentecost. But, when the Spirit of God filled him, others became his passion and concern. His first love was for Christ, but the second love of his heart was not self, but others. So it must be for all of us. The successful life can only be lived in terms of others.

A great naturalist, Mr. Huber, tells us that if a wasp finds some honey or other food, it will return to the nest and tell the good news to his companions, who will then go in great numbers to eat the food that has been found. Here is a lesson for all of us. The Christian has found the most wonderful thing in the world. We should hasten to tell others of Christ and tell them how to live for Jesus. This is unselfishness.

THIRD, THERE SHOULD BE A HOLY DETERMINATION TO CARRY OUT THE GOAL WHICH GOD HAS GIVEN TO US. Determination will soon fade away unless it is built on a strong affinity for the Heavenly Father.

Be determined to be what God wants you to be. Let this be the goal of your life. Count all else as unimportant as related to this great matter of being what God would have you to be.

Turn from pride! We cannot reach a spiritual goal as long as we have foolish pride. There can be no inward peace for your heart nor for mine when pride is upon the throne. Do not be afraid to take a lowly place. Do not try to shield yourself from the slighting and evil words of others. Stop your pride! Be what God would have you to be.

Get rid of pretense. Be what you are without pretending to be something else. This is a world of shameful pretense. We try to hide our inward poverty from others. We do not want people to find out exactly what we are. The man of culture is haunted by the fear that he will some day come upon a man more cultured than himself. The learned man fears to meet a man more learned than he. The rich man will sweat under the fear that his clothes or his car will sometime be made to look cheap by comparison with those of another rich man. Pretense — evil and foolish!

We should put aside also artificiality. Some people never relax. They are always trying to hide what they are from others. Artificiality will drop away when we kneel at the feet of Jesus.

Have a goal for your life! Determine that you will be something for the glory of God. Keep before you the needs of others.

## A GOAD

The dictionary tells us that a goad is a "pointed rod, used to urge on a beast." Again, "Something that produces the effect of a goad; a spur."

We will never be what we ought to be unless we have a goad — something that constantly presses upon us, to be our best.

FIRST, OUR NEEDS SHOULD DRIVE US TO THE SIDE OF

OUR LORD JESUS. The empty life is the Christ-less life. The full life is the life that depends wholly and completely upon Him.

"When the way is dark and dreary, And your path would lead astray;
If you'll only trust in Jesus, He will guide you all the way.
"When your heart is sad and lonely, And your grief is hard to bear;
If you'll only trust in Jesus, He will all your sorrows share.
"Though temptations come upon you, Calling, calling day by day;
If you'll only trust in Jesus, You can never go astray."

Jesus came to the disciples and said, ". . .*Will ye also go away? Then Simon Peter answered him, Lord, to whom shall we go? thou hast the words of eternal life. And we believe and are sure that thou art that Christ, the Son of the Living God*" (John 6:67-69).

How true it is that only Jesus can satisfy the need of our lives! Let this be a constant goad to drive you to His side.

SECOND, THE NEEDS OF OTHERS CAN GOAD US. What is the primary need of this world? What is the need of Russia, of Germany, of China, of India? The need is Christ. The need of man is salvation in Jesus Christ.

We who are Christians have something — we know Someone, and that One is Christ. We must not see the needs of others and then stop, but we must go on and aid them that they might turn to Jesus and be saved.

In a wealthy residential section of Richmond, some new owners complained that the singing of a small Christian church nearby disturbed them. A petition to be presented to the City Council was circulated. The solicitors brought it for signing to a Jewish resident. He read it and said, "Gentlemen, I cannot sign it. If I believed as do these Christians that my Messiah had come, I would shout about it from the house-tops, and on every street of Richmond, and nobody could stop me."

Ah, so it should be! We have Christ. We see the needs of others, and their needs should goad us on to tell them of Jesus. We should seek to live in such a way that they can see Christ in us and we should speak to them constantly regarding their need of faith in the Son of God.

In one of the books of E. P. Roe, the story is told of a minister who faithfully and long sought to lead a worldly skeptical young woman to Christ. He bore a good witness, much better than he knew, but she was cynical and indifferent. The conditions surrounding her were altogether unfavorable to her becoming a Christian. The minister continued his witness until the time came that he was to be transferred to another field of labor. He went to the young woman and made a final appeal for her to believe in and accept Christ as her Saviour. It seemed that his efforts had failed and then suddenly the girl burst into tears and said through her sobs, "I can believe on Jesus Christ because I can believe in you. I do believe in Christ because of your testimony and your life. You are real and because of your reality, I can believe that Jesus, about whom you talk, is real."

Ah, this testimony of the young lady was certainly a high tribute to the minister. But, such should be said about every Christian. We should remind others of Jesus. Keep this as a goad in your life. Remember to show forth the Saviour at every turn.

THIRD, THERE SHOULD BE A DESIRE TO GLORIFY GOD.

This must be a goad! Christ always glorified God. Great men and women of ages past have always sought to glorify God. This must be your aim also. Not self, but Christ!

## A GUIDE

We have spoken of having a goal, a goad, and now we come to the important part — a guide.

Who is your guide? Maybe I should also say, "What is your guide?" For some are guided by things, by money, by popularity, by prestige.

Christ is the only safe guide for any life.

Christian, is Christ your guide?

The life of King David was a veritable torrent of spiritual desire. When you read the Psalms, you will notice that each one rings with the cry of the seeker and the glad shout of the finder. He was concerned always with knowing God and God's will for his life.

When you read about the Apostle Paul, you will find this as the main burning desire of his life, *"That I may know him. . ."* (Philippians 3:10). This was the goal of his heart. He wanted to know Jesus. He was willing to count all things but loss for the excellency of the knowledge of Christ Jesus.

Is Christ your guide? Remember, all others are imperfect. When you follow others, you may be following their weakest points, but when you follow Christ, then you can be sure and confident that you are following One who cannot fail. When Christ guides men, the world knows about it. When Christ guides men, they are called fools by the world. When Christ guides men, His cause is pressed forward.

God give us men willing to follow Christ; men of a fiery urge; men like McCheyne, Wesley, Knox, and Luther.

Christ has the answer. He is the one who knows how to guide you into victory. Christ has the answer to every problem in your life. He can tell you what is best for you.

Are you dead to self? Christ would have you to be. You cannot be your best for Him as long as self is on the throne.

Are you filled with the Spirit? He wants you to be. He has given the power of the Holy Spirit for everyone of His followers. If you are saved, then be sure that you know the meaning of the Spirit of God.

My friend, make Jesus the guide of your life. Let Him guide your home life, your business life, your social life; yea, let Him guide you through every day.

Sinner friend, He cannot guide until first He is your Saviour. Will you not in this moment accept Christ as Saviour and let Him become at once the guide for your life?

A chaplain in World War II was ready to preach to a regiment of soldiers just back from the front trenches. They were tired and weary. The rain began to fall. They were standing in a field under the sky to hear his message. "My text," he began, "is 'What Think Ye of Christ?'" Then he shouted, "Dismissed!"

The question for you in this hour is this one, my friend: "What Think Ye of Christ?"

Will you let Him be the Saviour, the Lord, the Master of your life?

# 35

# Walking With The Master

*"And Jesus said unto them, Come ye after me, and I will make you to become fishers of men."*

— Mark 1:17

A new convert in Africa made this remark to a missionary. He said, "The trail is hard and tangled, but there is a Man ahead of us." What the new convert had in mind was this: that now that he knew Jesus Christ as Saviour, the way was hard and difficult; there were problems, but there was a Man just ahead guiding him.

Now, my friend, that is true with all of us. If we are Christians, there is One who walks ahead of us and One who walks with us. That One is the Lord Jesus Christ, the Saviour. This we find pictured for us in Mark 1. I want you to see this; the Lord Jesus Christ, the Master in action, working, moving, going forward.

Look at chapter one again, please. Read verses 9-11 concerning His baptism. Walk with Him. Follow Him. Are you this day saved, but not baptized? You cannot put it off another single day. You would be wrong in doing so. Why? You want to walk with the Master. This is important. If you are not sure about your baptism, then get this thing established and know where you stand. Know that you are following Jesus Christ and walking with Him.

Notice His temptation and victory down in verses 12 and

13. We can have the same victory. He is calling His disciples, verses 16-20. His miracle power is shown in verse 21-34. His prayer life is in verse 35. See His compassion, verses 40-45. All of this is given to us. Walking with the Master. Walking with the Lord Jesus Christ. I want you to think about it.

He says, *"Follow me, and I will make you fishers of men."*

There are four things that I would like to do daily.

ONE, I WOULD LIKE TO INCREASE THE FAITH OF EVERY PERSON I MEET. I am afraid that some of us don't get this. Most people reading this message are, as I am — a child of God. Yet, somehow we are not seeking to strengthen people as we ought to. Instead of giving something to them to help them, we are trying to get something for ourselves. I would like to make this the goal of my life every day to increase the faith of every person I meet. If I talk to a man, if I talk to a woman, talk to a young person, I want their faith to be strengthened by the conversation.

SECOND, I WANT TO STRENGTHEN EVERY FALTERING SOUL THAT I MEET. If a man comes in touch with me, I'd like to help him if I can. I've failed so often. Sometimes I'm in a hurry. Sometimes I'm a little bit without careful forethought about what I'm going to do and say. And I fail, but I should want to strengthen every faltering soul that I meet. Some are stumbling. They need help.

THIRD, I WANT TO LIVE THE VISION OF EVERY PERSON. I want people to see this needy world and see the need for the proclamation of the Word of God and the importance of it. I want to point every soul that I meet to the Lord Jesus Christ. Now, this should be your aim and mine, always. Daily, in every way as we walk with God, we can realize these objectives: to increase the faith of people, to strengthen every faltering soul, to lift the vision of every man, to point every man to the Lord Jesus Christ. You see, that will change your life — walking with the Lord Jesus Christ.

## THE DIRECTION OF THE DAILY WALK

CHRIST WALKED WITH HIS FACE TOWARD GOD. He turned neither to the right nor to the left, but straight toward God always.

In the Old Testament, Enoch walked with God. May God help us to walk with our Saviour day by day.

Think of how He walked. He walked unselfishly. He went about doing good, always so. This is our objective. Walking with God — this kills the selfishness of our lives. The Bible says, *"For all seek their own, not the things which are Jesus Christ's"* (Philippians 2:21). We should be seeking always to live unselfishly.

AGAIN, HE WALKED LOVINGLY. His love led Him to Calvary. He died upon the cross for us that we might be saved. He loved men when they hated Him. He loved men when they despised Him. He loved men when they drove the nails into His hands and feet. He loved them just the same. You see, that's something we don't have much of in this day.

Now, it is a matter of getting even. Somebody is hurt, somebody is injured by some word, some careless thought and we try to get even. No, no, no. We are to walk lovingly.

AGAIN, HE WALKED IN FELLOWSHIP WITH GOD. Here's the prayer life in Mark 1:35.

Sometimes our prayers fail because we are not walking with God. Sin has come in. Sin has broken the fellowship. Sin has disrupted our contact with God, and we are not walking with Him. We are failing.

Think about our walk. Our walk is to be Godward, daily, strengthening, and steadfastly walking for Him, victoriously claiming every promise of God.

Our walk is to be unselfish. That is the way we are to walk. We are fighting battles all of the time. You fight them when you come to church. You fight them in an offering if you're not careful. You fight them in every way out in the world. You're always fighting. This matter of selfishness enters into the thing, if we fail to give what God wants us to give for His cause and for His work.

I think about the little story of the Master feeding five thousand people. They were hungry. He said, "What shall we do?"

Someone said, "There's a little lad here. He's got a few loaves and a few fishes."

The Lord said, "Well, all right, have the people sit down. Have them get ready."

And the boy gave the lunch. Apparently he gave it gladly, gave it without any complaint. We don't have a single thing on record there except that the lunch was placed in the hands of the Master, then divided and given to the people. The people were fed. He was just a lad, but you see a blessing came even from the gift of this boy, a blessing to thousands of people at that time. Somebody put this in a little poem:

> "We do not even know his name, his lineage or his age,
> And yet he lives in deathless fame upon the Gospel page.
> The people around the Master pressed — the sick, the poor, the sad.
> He stands distinct from all the rest, a little fisher lad.
> He waits with patient, upraised head the hungry crowd to see.
> The fish are here, the barley bread and yet what use are these?

> Still all His Lord may take and then it must be well.
> The Master took and blessed and brake and wrought His miracle.
> Again, oh glad child heart, so pure and sweet, the perfect way to choose
> Oh, happy hands that bore the gift, the Master designed to use."

You see, my dear friend, as God used the little boy in feeding this crowd of people, so God can use us if we labor unselfishly. But you see, there is your battle. To walk with God, to love others, to help others, is the direction of the daily walk. I know it is rough. I know it doesn't sound like this world at all — the world of get-all-you-can, no matter how you get it. But, here is the picture of our Saviour. Here is a picture of the Son of God walking, and we are walking with the Master, if we are doing what we ought to be doing.

I say on that direction, there is no break and no vacation. Do you know where you have your trouble? You have your trouble when you make a break in the walk with God. It is that you are living right for a year, two years, five years, ten years, fifteen years, twenty years, maybe longer, and then all of a sudden you break! The devil walks in. He is waiting for it, the second you relax your vigilance, the second you turn away from alertness of life, that very second the devil walks in.

Some lad came to me one evening — strange thing about this. He came to me and again later another boy came to me all troubled about a certain thing that happened down in the Southland. These two boys came, both of them separately and said, "We want to pray. . .pray for the situation."

There is a painful, awful situation that exists, and something that happened. It was just a matter of the devil walking in and someone who wasn't alert and wasn't walking with

God and took a little spiritual vacation, and all was gone. The work of a life of twenty-five, thirty years or more was gone in just a few days time. All was gone, every bit of it.

Now, I'm coming back to say that in the direction of the daily walk, there is no break, no vacation. Walk with God every hour.

## THE DANGERS OF THE DAILY WALK

Are there enemies? Why, sure. The world, the flesh, and the devil are always fighting. There's danger of the self life. Oh, how you have to fight. That's the reason the Apostle Paul had so much to say about this. He said, *"I die daily"* (I Corinthians 15:31). He said, *"Likewise reckon ye also yourselves to be dead indeed unto sin, but alive unto God through Jesus Christ our Lord"* (Romans 6:11). This is the matter of the self life. Self is always fighting and Paul said, *"So fight I"* (I Corinthians 9:26). I want to keep in the victory seat. I want to move forward and do the thing that's right. You see, there are dangers to the daily walk. You have got to watch yourself daily, every single day, that you might be successful in walking with God. Just one day, that is all you have. It is just one day, but if one day you fail, if one day you relax, if one day you give way, then there is suffering that has to come.

The dear four young people who got in the car at Tennessee Temple one night never had any thought in this whole world their beautiful young lives would be interrupted by an awful accident. They never thought that. It never occurred to them and yet these four, fine, vigorous, splendid young people were in a car accident. Two of them were in intensive care in the hospital for a long time and the others suffered much. The one young lady who escaped serious injury, of course, had great turmoil in her soul because of the thing that happened.

Now, what I am getting to is this matter of watching self. Watching your self-life. See how quickly these things walk in to hurt you and to discourage you and to set you aside and to make you fail. See the danger of the self-life. See the danger of sin. See the awfulness of sin.

Now, many people today laugh at sin. I want to give you a little word. I am not going to tell you to turn off your radios. I am not going to tell you to turn off your televisions. It wouldn't do any good to tell you anyway. It's not a matter of my telling you that, but I am saying this. Whatever you do, whether you listen or watch, whatever you may be doing, listen with a bit of alertness. When things are wrong and things are sinful, turn from them. Don't just drag them into your life. Don't just say, "Well, they do that. Why can't I?"

No, No. You see, the world laughs at drunkenness. They like the picture of an old drunk staggering down the street. My dear friend, there's nothing nice about a drunk. Furthermore, they like to picture immorality and freedom of the sexes.

HERE IS THE DANGER OF SIN: WHAT SIN CAN DO TO YOUR LIFE AND TO MY LIFE, AND ALL LIVES. Sin is a serious matter. It's a serious matter — sin. Sin separates the soul from God. Sin brings the lost soul down in eternal hell. Sin steals from the life of the child of God and takes away His best.

Now what can you do? Come to the Saviour, lost sinner. Come to Christ and turn from your sin. Have your sins blotted out and have your soul cleansed by coming to Him.

Christian friend, you come and say, "Oh, God, I'm a child of God, yet I've failed my God. I must claim the promise of I John 1:9 and confess this and have my heart cleansed of the sin in my life." Don't take sin lightly. Sin is a serious business.

AGAIN, THERE IS THE DANGER OF SATANIC TRICKS. You have got to watch the devil. You say, "Well, Brother Roberson, I don't know why I did so and so." I can tell you why. You know too. The weakness of the flesh and power of Satan, and that's the reason you fail.

Listen to this verse: *"Lest Satan should get an advantage of us: for we are not ignorant of his devices"* (II Corinthians 2:11). How shrewd, how subtle is Satan. He will victimize you and will pull you down as you walk with God daily. You are seeking to walk in victory. Walking with God, you are alert to the dangers that are around you. You are running from sin, resisting the devil, fleeing temptation as your Bible teaches you to do. You do not want to be a fool and say, "Well, I can walk right on the edge of it." No, no. You run away from it. Get away from it.

Some people say, "Oh, I can get right on the edge of the roof. It doesn't bother me. I can just stand right on a pinnacle up here. It doesn't bother me at all."

My dear friend, it does not take much to make a fellow fall, you know, so you flee from temptation. You turn from the devil. you resist the devil. Make him flee from you, but you stand. There is danger in Satanic tricks.

Evangelist Joe Boyd tells the story about the fellow who had one finger off his hand. His index finger was off. Somebody said, "What happened to you?"

He said, "Well, a stick and a snake."

The fellow said, "Well, that doesn't explain a thing in the world. What do you mean 'a stick and a snake'?"

Well, Joe talked to him. Joe said, "What caused the difficulty here? A finger's gone, and something happened to you."

He said, "Well, this is what happened. I had a six-foot rattlesnake. I kept it in a cage in the back of the house. One day, just to have some fun, I got my rattlesnake in the cage, and brought it in the house, into the living room where my wife was. She looked at it. She was frightened. She didn't like the thing around at all." (She is not alone. I don't either. That's the only thing that I've backed up to kill, a snake. I'll back my car up to kill them every time. I hate them.)

Wait a minute: they got the thing in the living room in a cage, a six-foot rattlesnake. Just to have fun, he opened the door to let the snake come out. His wife fled in tears, screaming and running. He saw she was frightened, so he picked up a stick and put it down on the back of the snake, right in the back of the head and pushed it down.

He said, "When I pushed down on the stick, the snake was writhing and irritated and angry. The snake was flapping, kicking back and tossing about. All of a sudden as I pushed down on the stick, the stick broke! The snake arched at once and sank his fangs into my finger. Of course, they rushed me to the doctor. They did all they could, but my life was almost lost by my foolishness. But I lost my finger. They had to take it off because of the bite and the poison that entered it."

Old Joe Boyd said, "Now that's what sin does." You go to playing around with sin. You may be saying, "Well, I'm just having some fun." You are like this fellow who said, "I just want to have a little fun." No, no. You see, sin is just like a serpent, just waiting to bite all of the time. The devil is waiting and eager just to sink his fangs into your life, to destroy you, to tear you and bring you down. There are dangers, dangers that you have to see. Have you got it — the direction of the daily walk, and the dangers of the daily walk?

## THE DEMANDS OF THE DAILY WALK

Walking with the Master is not without demands.

FIRST, THERE MUST BE CONTACT AND CONVERSION. If you want to walk with the Lord Jesus Christ, you have got to have a touch with Him. You have got to know Him. We have too many professors. I'm afraid, dear ones, that we are wasting half of our time with folks who profess to be saved, and are not saved. I'm out here trying to strengthen people. They come to see me. They are with me in meetings everywhere I go. They profess to be saved, but have never been saved. I'm trying to build them up, to strengthen them, to make them stand up on their two feet when they have nothing to stand on. I can't help the man. He has got to be saved. He has got to come to know Christ as Saviour. When he is saved, and he knows that he is saved, then he can depend upon the power of God. The shabby living of today is caused many times because there is no conversion. If it's a matter of their being converted and still living a shabby life, it's because they have lost their close contact with God through prayer and Bible study. There must be contact with conversion. That is demanded upon you in your daily walk with God.

SECOND, THERE MUST BE COURAGE. Walking with Christ takes courage. Opposition will face us. The devil is going to put it there before us and if you don't have some courage, you are sunk. You are done for. You are a quitter!

So many people start and stop. So many preachers start out to preach and then quit preaching. So many start out to be missionaries and give up mission work, turn back, and give it all up and turn away.

The world is full of cowards. The world is full of quitters. We're tempted daily to quit, tempted daily to shirk and say, "It can't be done." We're tempted to suppress the testimony of our lips. There must be courage.

THIRD, THERE MUST BE CONTEMPLATION. Walking with God takes some thought. It takes some meditation. "What am I doing? Oh, God, show me what I'm doing with my life.

Where am I going now? Oh, God, show me what I am doing with my life. Where am I going now? What is the next step that you want me to take? Let me think a while."

Paul said, *"Meditate upon these things"* (I Timothy 4:15). Think. Where are you going? If you are going to walk with God, it demands that every day you take some time to think.

I travel in meetings quite a bit and I'll be honest with you, I don't enjoy traveling a bit. I've done so much of it by plane around this country, around the world, until it doesn't entice me in the slightest. There's only one good thing that I can see about it all, only one thing. That is that when I get on a plane to fly somewhere for a meeting, I've got an hour, maybe two hours, that I can sit with my Bible before me. I can sit there and think and think and think. I can meditate upon what God has done for me, what God wants me to do. I can think of what I should be doing and the work that God would have us to do in my city and at Tennessee Temple University. I can meditate upon my life. I can think, "What is the next step? Where do I go next? What's the next job for me to do?"

You had better take some time off, my friend. You rustling, rattling people are always jumping around, never stopping, never slowing down, never thinking at all. You had better take some time for contemplation. Walking with God demands it, you have got to have it.

Walking with God demands convictions. You have got to have convictions. Convictions that come from the Word of God. Say, "This is what the Bible teaches. This is what I hold to. This is my stand." Convictions have come out of your observations of things around you. Have convictions against sin, against wickedness when you see what is done to other people. Say, "Oh, God help me to be my best for my loving Saviour."

## THE DIVIDENDS OF THE DAILY WALK

I want to testify that God pays off. I want to testify that walking with God brings dividends. I can stop right today. This could be my last one. This day could be my last day that I will ever have in this world. I want you to know right now, dear friends, that I have no sorrows or regrets in the way that God has led me.

I am sorry about my life sometimes. I haven't lived like I should have lived. But, listen, I am so happy and I rejoice so much, that if today was all of it, that this was the end of the whole business, I would testify that there's a dividend. I've been cashing in on this thing all through these years, every single year of my ministry, every year of my life I've been cashing in.

Now there is one dividend. What is it? IT IS HIS PRESENCE. He said, "*. . .lo, I am with you alway, even unto the end of the world*" (Matthew 28:20). "And He walks with me, and He talks with me, and He tells me I am His own. . ." Do you know His presence? You should. Do you sense His presence when you walk through this world? One of the dividends of being a child of God is to say that God is with you. Jesus said, "*. . .lo, I am with you alway,*" and He will be with us in every single part of life. He will guide us and direct us and help us.

I know a man who professes to be saved. He told me he was saved. He told me right to my face, "I know I'm saved." He never reads His Bible, never prays, never goes to church at all. I couldn't say anything else to him, He said, "I know I'm saved. This is my testimony. I know that I'm a child of God." But he says certain things and then he blames it on somebody else. Some of his kin folks, some of his friends did not treat him right. So, he quit it all and took it out on God. Do you know what he lost? If he is saved, he lost the presence of God.

That is the sweetest presence that you can have day by day to encourage you and to strengthen you in life — the presence of God.

There is a second dividend. I HAVE HIS PROMISES. When I live by His Word and by His Way, I can claim the promises of God. There are 32,000 in the Bible alone for every child of God. There are 32,000 promises, promises for all of us. We can rest upon the Word of God and say, "This is His promise to me." We can walk with Him.

Again, I have a third dividend. I HAVE HIS POWER. *"But ye shall receive power, after that the Holy Ghost is come upon you"* (Acts 1:8). *". . .be filled with the Spirit"* (Ephesians 5:18). Be filled with the Spirit. When you are full of the Holy Spirit, resting upon God, then God will bless you. We have His power. The fullness of the Spirit of God is for us. It's available.

Child of God, you shouldn't be content without knowing the fullness of the Spirit of God. Every single day you should know it. I should know it. I confess that sometimes I do not, but every day I should wait upon God and say, "Oh God, I want the fullness of the Holy Spirit's power upon my life."

NOW, BY HIS POWER, HE WORKS MIRACLES IN OUR LIVES. God bless your heart. I am not through as long as I am here, until Jesus comes or I go home. I'm not through. Every time I see my mail, I'm waiting for miracles to happen. Every time I answer a telephone, I'm waiting for a miracle from God. Listen! They do come. Oh yes, they've come to me. They have been around our ministry. I have watched it all. I have watched what God can do — miraculous things. By His power, He works miracles.

BY HIS POWER, HE USES US TO HELP OTHERS TO STRENGTHEN AND TO UPHOLD THE FALTERING. By His power, He makes us soul winners. He said, ". . .*Follow me, and I will make you fishers of men*" (Matthew 4:19). ". . .*he that winneth souls is wise*" (Proverbs 11:30).

Now, this is what we can have. Here is the dividend of the daily walk: the power of God upon our lives, His presence with us, His promise is with us. All of these things are ours as we simply rest upon Him and let God have His way with us.

But, my friend, if you turn coward, if you quit, if you say, "Well, I can't do anything," and let the world take over, the devil will come in and your life will be wrecked and ruined. You become nothing, worse than nothing. You are hurting other people. You are dragging people down along with yourself, husband, wife, mother, father, whoever you are, you are, you are dragging people down. Office worker, you are dragging others down when you are not living for Christ. You are hurting other people always. You are causing someone else to go to hell because of your failure in your life.

God help us to see what He wants in the daily walk. It should be a daily walk with our Lord. Walk with Him every day. He walked by the Sea of Galilee. Here we find the miracles written all the way through this book of the walk of our Saviour.

There was an old lady, a little lady, sitting on the front porch of a hotel in Switzerland. She had in her hand and up to her eyes, field glasses, and was watching a sight. There was some distance away a high mountain rising up into the clouds. But as she watched, she had her glasses fastened on four black objects. They were moving slowly up the side of them mountain. They were coming near the top of it. It was snow-covered, of course. It was dangerous and this woman was sitting on the front porch of the hotel where she was staying, and she was watching that sight. As she watched the men climbing up the side of the mountain, all of a sudden, she fell back. The glasses fell to the floor, and she fainted.

A man standing nearby grabbed the glasses and put them up to his eyes. He fastened them on that distant mountain. He too saw the four men, but he saw what was happening.

Suddenly, he discovered that there was a tragic thing taking place. The men were slipping. They were coming down the mountain. They were not far from the summit. Yet, there was something happening that was causing them to fall back. They were slipping back. All of a sudden as the man watched the scene, he suddenly saw that rope sever. Three men slipped back down the mountain to their deaths. They brought the three bodies back in the afternoon. They brought them back into the little town. The people were broken, heartbroken, by the thing that had happened. The men were known to the people in the city, and in the town.

Later that day the fourth man came back. He walked back into the hotel, but when he walked into the hotel, the people turned away from him. No one spoke to him. He tried to get a conversation. No one would listen to him. No one would answer him at all. They turned away from him.

Finally, he found a man and said, "Sir, what's wrong around this place? Why won't they talk to me? What's wrong?"

This man looked at him and said, "Sir, you may not like this, but I've got to say it anyway. They brought your three friends back down from the mountain where they fell to their deaths. They brought them with the rope. The rope didn't break. The rope was cut! These people feel that you were guilty of cutting the rope, letting your three friends drop to their deaths while you got out to safety. The rope was cut — not broken, but cut."

I read that story, and thought (my dear friend, are you listening?), "We have got an obligation." Amen? Our obligation is to climb with our Lord and walk with Him daily and to bring others with us. We have got to be soul winners. I cannot cut the rope. I cannot cut it off and say, "Well, you go your way and I'll go mine." No, No, we are tied together by human bonds of this world and I've got to seek to get people saved. I've got to get people to the Lord. I've got to help people around me as I walk with my Saviour. I've got to keep my contract.

A lot of folks and a lot of people in this world have cut the rope. They cut it off. "Well, I'll let the world go on. I'll live my life and do as I please." That's not walking with the Master. I want to walk with the Lord Jesus Christ.

# 36
# The Greatest Missionary

*"Pilate therefore said unto him, Art though a king then? Jesus answered, Thou sayest that I am a king. To this end was I born, and for this cause came I into the world, that I should bear witness unto the truth. Every one that is of the truth heareth my voice."*

—John 18:37

The greatest missionary ever to walk upon this earth was the Lord Jesus Christ. Other missionaries have patterned after Him, but none can attain His greatness. Some have suffered greatly, but not as much as did the Son of God. Some have died in the service of our Saviour, but Christ died as the eternal Son of God. Yet, we must remember that all who en gage in missionary activity are following in the steps of the world's greatest missionary, the Lord Jesus.

I have in my library a book written some years ago by Dr. J. C. Massey, former pastor of the Tremont Temple in Boston. The title of the book is *Eternal Life in Action*. The title pictures for me the Son of God, Christ Jesus, the world's greatest missionary, who came into this world to die for sinners. He was eternal life in action.

In the same way you are eternal life in action. You are an eternal being, and as one who is saved, you are a co-laborer with Christ.

I trust that in some way the Spirit of God will make you see that you are to be like Jesus.

Earthly pleasures vainly call me;
I would be like Jesus;
Nothing worldly shall enthrall me;
I would be like Jesus.
He has broken every fetter,
I would be like Jesus;
That my soul may serve Him better,
I would be like Jesus.
All the way from earth to Glory,
I would be like Jesus;
Telling o'er and o'er the story,
I would be like Jesus.

Yes, we should desire to be like Him. This should be the fervent wish of every Christian.

Now, Christ was the greatest missionary who has ever walked upon this earth. What did Jesus see and what did He desire as He walked among men?

## HE SAW A WORLD LOST IN SIN

Our Saviour was aware of the origin of sin. He knew its beginning in heaven when Lucifer rebelled against God. He knew the first sin committed upon this earth. He knew when Adam and Eve were driven from the Garden of Eden, but though Christ was aware of the history of sin, His heart was broken by the fact of sin.

Jesus saw the universality of sin.

> *"For all have sinned, and come short of the glory of God."*
>
> — Romans 3:23

Our Saviour knew that there was no righteous one who could stand and say he was without sin. Sin touched every life.

Christ knew the wages of sin.

> *"For the wages of sin is death; but the gift of God is eternal life through Jesus Christ our Lord."*
>
> —Romans 6:23

When Jesus looked upon men, He saw the complete picture of sin. He saw the awfulness of sin as we cannot see it. He saw the downward trend of man away from God.

When we look upon this sinful world, we must see the world as Jesus saw it. We must look upon the world even as Christ admonished us to look in John 4:35:

> *". . .Lift up your eyes, and look on the fields; for they are white already to harvest."*

Not only must we look, but we must also pray, for this is the admonition of our Saviour as He said,

> *"Pray ye therefore the Lord of the harvest, that he will send forth labourers into his harvest."*
>
> —Matthew 9:38

Not only look and pray, but we must give. We must give of ourselves and give of that which we have. Jesus said,

> *"Give, and it shall be given unto you; good measure, pressed down, and shaken together, and running over, shall men give into your bosom. For with the same measure that ye mete withal it shall be measured to you again."*
>
> —Luke 6:38

We must also go. We must go with the message of our Saviour. The command is repeated for us in many places in the Word of God.

> *". . .Go ye into all the world, and preach the gospel to every creature."* —Mark 16:15

We must see this lost world! We must see the need of men without Christ! These figures were given to us some years ago by a missionary.

> In Africa there is one missionary for 17,000 people.
> In Arabia, one missionary for 170,000 people
> In South America, one missionary for 47,000 people
> In India, one missionary for 70,000 people.

But this same person told us that in America there is a preacher for every 500 people. We cannot help but think of the statement given by Oswald Smith some years ago; "Why should anyone hear the Gospel twice before everyone has heard it once?"

We are told that there are 2,974 languages in the world. Over seventeen hundred of them do not have the Bible at this time. I am simply trying to get you to see the need of this world and the need of this present hour in which we live. Let us not accustom ourselves to thinking that all is well and that there is nothing more that we can do. Let us, like Jesus, see a world lost in sin and give ourselves to the proclaiming of this message to the ends of the world.

## HE SAW A WORLD DESIRING SALVATION, BUT BLIND TO THE SAVIOUR

Yes, men were reaching for salvation, but missing it. The Pharisees and the Sadducees are good examples of the people of that day. They had their forms of religion. They were earnest in their devotions; and yet, they turned away from Jesus Christ and they turned away, also, from God the Father.

To these sin-blinded Pharisees Jesus addressed many words. He sought to shatter their self-complacency and to destroy their self-righteousness and to bring them face to face with themselves.

In some cases He was successful, for there were Pharisees and leaders of the people who turned unto Him and received salvation. But in the main, the people went on their ways blind to the Saviour. They were so blind that they crucified the Son of God upon the cross of Calvary.

Jesus looks down upon the world today that is blind to His power to save. Yes, there are those who are preaching the Gospel of the Son of God, but there are many who are not. There are churches on every corner where little is said about Jesus and His power to save. Religion has become a form and a fashion. It has become a respectable thing to unite with the church and to attend church at least part of the time.

Men want salvation, but they want it their way. They want it the easy way. They do not want it God's way.

God grant that you might have a revelation of the heart of Christ as He looked upon the multitudes and "*. . . was moved with compassion on them, because they fainted, and were scattered abroad, as sheep having no shepherd*" (Matthew 9:36). See men as Christ saw them! Yearn for their salvation, even as He yearned over sinful men.

Do you want God to use you? Be assured that He wants to use you if you will give yourself unto Him and His service.

To be a missionary for our Saviour here at home will mean that you must be a fool as far as the world is concerned. You must often be weak so far as the successful are concerned. There are so few who are willing to pay the price to go all the way with Jesus Christ. Listen to this:

> The easy roads are crowded and the level roads are jammed,
> The pleasant little rivers with drifting folks are crammed;

> But off yonder where it's rocky, where you get a better view;
> You will find the ranks are thinning, and the travellers are few.
> Where the going's smooth and pleasant, you will always find the throng,
> For the many — more's the pity — seem to like to drift along.
> But the steps that call for courage, and the task that's hard to do,
> In the end results in glory, for the never wavering few.

It will mean a struggle for you to follow the will of God, but in the end there will be great rejoicing as you do what He says. Abraham had to give up the pleasant place, but in the end he walked in the company of God and was called the friend of God. Lot chose the beautiful plain, but in the end he was driven from a sinful city and hid away in the caves.

See a world lost in sin! See a world that is blind to the Saviour. Now give yourself to the proclamation of this Gospel that men may know of Jesus.

## HE GAVE TO MEN THE MESSAGE OF SALVATION AND PEACE

We are continuing our discussion of the greatest missionary. How different from all men was the Son of God! The message that He came to proclaim was simple and pure. It was a message of salvation through faith in His name.

The Lord was simply repeating the words given Him by the Father; words that were made ready hundreds of years before Christ came into the world. The first promise of the coming Saviour is given in Genesis 3:15. The promise is repeated in many places in the Old Testament. We have the prophecy of the place of His birth, His message, and His life. When Jesus came, it was exactly as prophesied.

> *"For the Son of man is come to seek and to save that which was lost."*
>
> —Luke 19:10

FIRST, HE CAME ACCORDING TO GOD'S PLAN FOR HIM. God had a definite plan and this was fulfilled in the coming of our Saviour and His death upon the cross.

SECOND, HE CAME IN LOVE TO SPEAK TO MEN THE MESSAGE OF SALVATION. He came to let men know for a certainty that "God is love."

How beautifully did Jesus tell Nicodemus, *"For God so loved the world. . ."* Sometimes we gain strange thoughts about God and feel that He is One who delights in condemning and punishing, but not so. God is love! How I pray that this spirit of love may lay hold of all of our hearts. It is lacking in this day and so needed! This is a commercial time when everyone is asking, "What does it pay? How much do I get out of it?" — when, in love, we should be giving all that we have to the Lord Jesus.

Someone told us the story of John Pullen, the banker, who lived in Raleigh, North Carolina. Mr. Pullen seemed to be a living daily embodiment of love. His pockets were constantly filled with gifts for children, with books or pamphlets for adults, and with some simple thing which made easy access to the heart and mind of strangers, permitting him to speak a loving word for the blessed Master.

Mr. Pullen never seemed to be happy unless he was giving, and he gave in order that he might give the message of Jesus Christ to someone.

A preacher tells the story of going to the cemetery one day to bury a pauper. To his surprise he discovered that the person was being buried, not in a potter's field, but in a beautiful portion of the cemetery. Upon inquiry, he discovered that John Pullen owned that part of the cemetery and kept it for strangers and poor ones of God's children. His life in that city was as fragrant for Christ as a rose. He was kind and gentle and helpful and loving.

Let us say with emphasis that Jesus came in love. He came with a message of salvation and peace.

THIRD, HE CAME WITH DEFINITENESS. Jesus said, "*. . .I am come that they might have life, and that they might have it more abundantly*" (John 10:10). This was the purpose for the coming of the Saviour. He did not come to establish hospitals or schools, or to revise governmental plans, but He came to give his life to be a ransom for many, that souls might be saved.

We have a gospel for this lost world. It is the Gospel of "good news" — of salvation in Jesus Christ. It is a simple Gospel — so simple that every person can understand it. Although the message is profound and eternal, it can be appreciated and appropriated by the most unlearned.

It is a serene Gospel. It was clear when Jesus stated it. It was right from the lips of the Master. It is a shining truth that we can give to any lost soul. It can be seen by anyone who opens his spiritual eyes. It can be heard by the ears of all who will listen. It is a free Gospel, and can be obtained by the needy heart without money and without price.

It is also a satisfying Gospel. It satisfies the heart of all who come unto the Lord Jesus. This testimony arises from Christians in every part of the world. It satisfies people of all stations in life and all states of development. The Gospel of Christ gives peace and satisfaction to all souls that will accept it.

This is the message that the Lord Jesus came to give unto men. It is the message that we have for souls around us.

Bring Christ into the very center of your life. Let Him lead you into missionary endeavor, soul winning efforts, and daily concern for others. Let Christ be in the very center of your life.

Some years ago a boy enlisted as a private in the Army of our nation. In the barracks of his company he discovered on the walls many obscene pictures — course, sensuous, and revolting. As he looked, there arose in him an indignant revolt. He felt that he must not, that he could not look daily upon those vile suggestions. He could not remain silent without protest in the presence of moral indignity. But he did not know how to voice his protest, how to give his indignation wise and righteous direction. He felt that it would not be enough to remove the vileness. He must supply purity. Finally, wisdom was given to him.

When the barracks room was empty, he brought from his trunk a package of pictures given him by his mother. Among them was the head of Christ. He took the picture, and slipping silently into the room, hung it in the midst of the pictures on the wall and slipped away. But he was not the only one who came silently into the room that night. Within forty-eight hours every other picture had mysteriously disappeared. Only the head of the matchless One remained upon the wall.

Somehow the pure, chaste, cleanliness of that Face had become a searchlight turned on the coarseness, the evil suggestiveness of those other pictures, and they had been taken away.

What are we saying? Simply this — put Christ in the very center of your life. When you do so, the minor and extraneous things of life are in His hands. Make Him the King of kings and Lord of lords. Follow Him into active service of soul winning and missionary endeavors.

Let us repeat it — Jesus said, "*. . .I am come that they*

*might have life, and that they might have it more abundantly.*" This was the purpose of the coming of our Saviour into this world, and our purpose is to make Him known to people everywhere.

# 37
# The End of the Missionary is Near?

*"And he said unto them, Go ye into all the world, and preach the gospel to every creature."*
— Mark 16:15

In the magazine, *Reap*, I found the picture of a bearded man carrying a banner on which were the words, "The End of the Missionary is Near?"

Along with this picture there was a word from Arthur Glasser, formerly home director of the Overseas Missionary Fellowship. Mr. Glasser said, "The role of the missionary, though never popular, will be accorded less public approval than ever in the world of the seventies."

Mr. Glasser mentions three "straws in the wind" which back his conclusion. FIRST, AN OFFICIAL DIRECTIVE THE GOVERNMENT OF MALAYSIA LIMITS MISSIONARY RESIDENCE TO TEN YEARS OUT OF FEAR OF "CULTURAL IMPERIALISM AND ECCLESIASTICAL COLONIALISM." SECOND, INDIAN CHRISTIANS ARE NOT ADVISING THOSE WHO COME TO THEIR COUNTRY TO "RETAIN THEIR SENSE OF MISSION WITHOUT BECOMING IN ANY SENSE MISSIONARIES." THIRD, THE VOCAL MONSIGNOR IVAN ILLICH OF MEXICO IS INSISTING THAT ALL "NORTH AMERICAN VOLUNTEER ARMIES" BE SHIPPED HOME FROM LATIN AMERICA — PARTICULARLY MISSIONARIES!

A Southern Baptist missionary of twenty years service in

Japan suggests "the day of the missionary in past." The missionary said that he had been trying to determine why there are only 800,000 Christians in Japan's population of 103 million. This Southern Baptist missionary, by name, Rev. Worth Grant, gave his reasons why he felt there were so few Christians in all of Japan.

Briefly stated, he tried to blame it on the foreignness of our religion and the suspicion that the Japanese have of taking money from others. He also suggested that there is doubtless a psychological scar left by religious wars which developed between the early zealous Roman Catholic missionaries and Buddhists.

In answer to the question — "The end of the missionary is near?" — may I suggest the following:

**THE BIBLE IS UNCHANGED**

> *"Heaven and earth shall pass away, but my words shall not pass away."*
>
> — Matthew 24:35
>
> *"And this word, yet once more, signifieth the removing of those things that are shaken, as of things that are made, that those things which cannot be shaken may remain."*
>
> — Hebrews 12:27
>
> *"But the word of the Lord endureth for ever. And this is the word which by the gospel is preached unto you."*
>
> — I Peter 1:25

When I say that the Bible is unchanged, then I must confess that there are many things changing in this hour.

FIRST, THE EARTH IS TURMOIL AND CHANGE. We have seen earthquakes in which scores have been killed and millions of dollars worth of buildings have been destroyed.

I can recall reading of a tragic flood in Pakistan in which almost a million lost their lives.

SECOND, NATIONS CHANGE. We have noticed great changes in our nation in the last few years. We have noticed the change in the races. We have noticed the change in moral standards. We have notices the increase in vulgarity. People are constantly changing.

FOURTH, FINANCIAL FOUNDATIONS MAY BE SHAKEN. Many of us can recall the prosperity of the twenties. We remember the depression of the thirties. We recall the change in financial matters in the last fifteen or twenty years. But even today, financial matters change day by day. Trusted business institutions, regarded as unshakeable, come down with a thud of terrible suddenness and a crash of destruction. We need to see that we are living in a time of change, and that all that we count so important may vanish in a moment.

I repeat: Life's very foundations may be shaken. A man, woman, or child in the very blush of health today may be a corpse tomorrow.

The magnificence of man's ingenuity in building and designing can come to nothing in a few seconds of time.

But, my friends, the Bible is unchanged!

> *"The grass withereth, the flower fadeth: but the word of our God shall stand for ever."*
>
> – Isaiah 40:8

The plan of God for this world and for man is unchanged. The Bible gives us this plan.

One of these days, Christ is coming — it may be at any moment. We have His promise "*. . .I will come again. . .*"

One of these days, we shall stand at the judgment seat of Christ. We shall give account of ourselves as we stand before the Lord.

One of these days, the great tribulation will touch this earth. It will be seven years in its full duration. Three and one-half years will be a time of intense suffering.

One of these days, we shall come with our Saviour out of the skies down upon this earth to reign with Him. The Bible says, *"Do ye not know that the saints shall judge the world. . ."* (I Corinthians 6:2)?

Make sure that you are basing your life upon the unchanging Word of God.

Understand what the Bible says about sin. Plainly the Word says, *"For the wages of sin is death. . ."* (Romans 6:23). *". . .sin, when it is finished, bringeth forth death"* (James 1:15).

Modern man cannot change God's Word regarding sin.

The Bible is unchanged about the matter of salvation. Clearly and plainly the message is given unto us. Salvation is through faith in Jesus Christ.

We must rest upon His truth, not upon the promises of man. We must anchor our souls to the eternal God and His Word.

## OUR COMMISSION IS UNCHANGED

We have been commanded by our Lord to *". . .Go ye into all the world, and preach the gospel. . ."* (Mark 16:15).

Jesus said before His ascension, *". . .ye shall be witnesses unto me. . ."*

The great commission was given by the Saviour and is unchanged. The great commission was a continuation of the duties which Christ, by His example, had been showing to His apostles. He commanded them to teach and preach until the end of the gospel age.

By the commission, He has given the marching orders for every true church in every century in every land.

It was not given only to the few individuals who heard it first, for they were soon to pass away. It was given to the church and to the churches, the agency Christ appointed to continue His work. The task given by the Saviour was too big for the small group who heard Him speak. It is clearly for all churches to obey this command until the end of the age.

Here is an imperative command of our Lord!

It is universal in its scope.

It involves every Christian.

FIRST, OUR COMMISSION IS TO GO TO A LOST WORLD. He said, "*. . .Go ye into all the world, and preach the gospel to every creature*" (Mark 16:15). This commission has not been abrogated.

It is an easy thing for frail mankind to say, "There is no use in going. They will not hear us." It is an easy thing for men to say, "The end of the age is near; therefore, we will pull in our missionaries and stop our going." It is an easy thing for men to say, "The communists are taking over. What can we do?"

We have a commission to take the Gospel to a lost and dying world. As a church, we must obey this. As individuals, we must not fail.

SECOND, OUR COMMISSION IS TO POINT PEOPLE TO THE LAMB OF GOD. John said, "*. . .Behold the Lamb of God, which taketh away the sin of the world*" (John 1:29)! We are to preach the Gospel of the Lord Jesus Christ.

This is our primary business. This is our essential work. We must point people to Christ.

But in this day, many things are happening.

FIRST, WE ARE TOO COMPLACENT. We are like the people of the church of Laodicea. The Spirit said to them:

> *"I know thy works, that thou art neither cold nor hot: I would thou wert cold or hot."* —Revelation 3:15

The lost world is surrounding us, but we are complacent. We are not disturbed; we are not moving. We care so little.

The devil has us deceived. Dr. Zeno Wall of Shelby, North Carolina, told the story about the young businessman who had never trusted Christ for salvation. He came to his deathbed. Dr. Wall said the young man was stricken down and was hurried away to the hospital for an emergency operation. Something went wrong, and he began to swell and suffer. In two days, he was unconscious; and in this condition he began to sing the vulgar songs he had sung around his place of business and to use vile oaths. On either side of him sat his two sisters, who were Christian Scientists — and one was patting him on the hand and saying, "You are not suffering, Brother; you just think you are." On the other side, the other sister was doing the same and saying about the same words — but he died. When he had breathed his last breath, one of them said to Dr. Zeno Wall, "My brother has gone downstairs." But oh, the tragedy of being deceived by the devil and dying without Jesus Christ! The complacency of the sisters!

Let us put away our complacency and begin to deal in dead earnest with those who are lost. Death is certain if our Lord tarries. Life is uncertain. We know not when any life will come to the termination point; therefore, we must press the matter of salvation now. Put away your complacency.

SECOND, WE ARE SELFISH. We are guilty of looking to ourselves. *"For all seek their own, not the things which are Jesus Christ's"* (Philippians 2:21). Every man is seeking to make a mark for himself in the world. He is striving to be somebody in a financial way.

THIRD, WE ARE SINFUL. We are following the flesh. Every newspaper, every magazine, every T.V. show has its stories of wicked sins. The dirt and the filth of this day are beyond comprehension.

The great need is for all of our churches to turn back to God! After a turning back to God, there must be a turning out to the lost world.

The commission is unchanged. It will remain the same throughout this age. The end of the missionary is not near. His work will continue to the end of the age, until Jesus comes.

## GOD'S POWER TO SAVE IS UNCHANGED

> *"All that the Father giveth me shall come to me; and him that cometh to me I will in no wise cast out."*
>
> —John 6:37

> *"Wherefore he is able also to save them to the uttermost that come unto God by him, seeing he ever liveth to make intercession for them."*
>
> —Hebrews 7:25

> *"Jesus Christ the same yesterday, and today, and forever."*
>
> —Hebrews 13:8

As we read of the stories of the Lord Jesus and His saving power when He walked upon this earth, so we are assured that He is the same today. As He saved men when He was here, so He saves men in this hour.

GOD'S CONCERN FOR SINNERS IS THE SAME.

GOD'S POWER TO SAVE IS UNCHANGED.

Now, this thought should encourage every one of us. I have so many people say to me regarding a certain individual, "I don't think he will ever be saved." My friend, your business is to give him the Gospel and to tell him of Jesus and His power to save, in order that we might bring our lost ones to God,

Who can save to the uttermost. May I suggest three things.

FIRST, PRAY EARNESTLY FOR OTHERS. There is power in prayer. We must pray that God will give us courage to speak. We must pray for God to work in the hearts of men.

I think sometimes that our prayers are ineffective because we are holding back instead of releasing all things into the hands of God. If a wife is praying for her husband to be saved, then she should place that one in the hands of God. It may take an accident to awaken him. It may take an illness which will bring him near to death's door to open his heart and to make him see his need of Christ. It may take the death of a child to get his eyes opened and to bring him to the Saviour. But you should be ready for all things and to say, "Lord, I want thy will to be done."

Prayer is the key! God answers prayers, not because of their length, not because of their eloquence; He answers prayers because of our faith. Someone said, "Prayer is a key which, being turned by the hand of faith, unlocks God's treasuries."

A revival was in progress in a Mountain Cove church. One night at her home, an anxious, burdened mother prayed this prayer: "Oh, Lord, please save my straying, reckless, wicked, lost boy." Then she said, "Oh, Lord, if You had a bad boy like mine is, and You should ask me to help You with him, I would do it. And Lord, You know I would." The next day when the invitation hymn was given, that son walked down the aisle confessing Christ as his Saviour.

Spurgeon said on one occasion, "Oh God, Thou hast given us a mighty weapon, and we have permitted it to rust. Would it not be a vile crime if a man had an eye given him which he would not open, or a hand that he would not lift up, or a foot that grew stiff because he would not use it?" Ah, yes, it would be a crime.

My friends, we must remind ourselves that prayer has been given us to be used. Let us not forget what James says. "*. . .ye have not, because ye ask not*" (James 4:2). Let us give ourselves to earnest prayer for others.

SECOND, LIVE DEVOTEDLY FOR CHRIST. I cannot remind you too much of what Paul said, "*. . .Destroy not him with thy meat, for whom Christ died*" (Romans 14:15). To put this in our language, it simply means that we must not live in such a way that we cause someone to turn away from Christ.

How many times we have heard the lost sinner say, "If that man is a Christian, I don't want any of it." Now, the man might be a Christian; but because of his careless living he may cause someone to turn away from Christ.

Live so that others can see Christ in you!

You have heard me give the story of the woman who was known far and wide for her faith in God. She lived such a consecrated life that people knew about her in many parts of the country. Across the state lived a young woman who read about this fine Christian and wanted to become acquainted with her. She journeyed across the state to meet and find the secret of her great service. They were introduced and the young woman exclaimed, "You are the woman with such great faith in God, are you not?"

"No," replied the calm, poised, modest lady. "I am not a woman with great faith in God — I am a woman with a little faith in a great God."

The young woman said, "I would give the world for your power."

The older Christian answered, "That is exactly what it cost me."

She was simply saying that she had given up everything to

live devotedly for Christ that others might see Jesus in her.

Finally, witness courageously by the power of God. Jesus said, "*. . .All power is given unto me in heaven and in earth. Go ye therefore. . .*" (Matthew 28:18,19).

I believe that here is one of the places where most of us fail. Many of us try to live for Christ; but we fail to witness courageously for the Saviour.

The little old-fashioned woman looked at me and said, 'Wilbur, you'd better stand.' And when I did not respond, she put her hand under my elbow and held me to stand."

Dr. Chapman said, "I had a letter from that little woman the other day, and she said, 'I'm glad I put my fingers under your elbow and lifted.' Is it nothing to you, father and mother, that you have a boy in your home that needs salvation? Is it nothing to you that your boy might be used to shake the world for Christ?"

We invite you to come to the Saviour. If you have never accepted Him, come now. The Bible is the same. Our commission is unchanged. And God's power is able to save to the uttermost.

# 38
# Missionary Journey of Paul — $1299.00

*"And when they had fasted and prayed, and laid their hands on them, they sent them away."*
— Acts 13:3

For $1299.00 you can take a sixteen day jet cruise and a tour of the "Missionary Journey of Paul." The ad tells us that tours will be leaving February 15, March 1, and March 15. In the ad we are told that we will be traveling by jet plane to many of the places touched by the Apostle Paul on his "Missionary Journey."

For $1299.00 you can stand in the approximate places where Paul stood. You can visit the towns where Paul organized New Testament churches.

For $1299.00 you can "imagine" the concern which filled the heart of Paul, as he preached the Gospel — yes, you can imagine this, but you cannot know the fullness of his heart and of his experience.

Which missionary journey of Paul is referred to by the newspaper ad? I do not know! There were three of them. However, it is doubtful if the Apostle Paul ever thought for a second that some two thousand years later, jet planes, traveling five hundred and six hundred miles per hour, would be carrying people to places where he preached the Gospel.

As we think of this ad, advertising the missionary journey of

Paul for $1299.00, there are three facts that I would like to press upon your minds.

## THE MASTER PERSON OF PAUL'S LIFE

Who was the master person of Paul's life? The answer is: Christ. From the Damascus road experience, for the rest of his days, the Lord Jesus occupied the first place in the life of the apostle.

What superb statements made by Paul, regarding the Lord Jesus. Think of some of them.

> *"For I determined not to know any thing among you, save Jesus Christ, and him crucified."*
>
> — I Corinthians 2:2

> *"Therefore if any man be in Christ, he is a new creature: old things are passed away; behold, all things are become new."*
>
> — II Corinthians 5:17

> *"For ye know the grace of our Lord Jesus Christ, that, though he was rich, yet for your sakes he became poor, that ye through his poverty might be rich.,"*
>
> — Galatians 6:14

> *"I am crucified with Christ: nevertheless I live; yet not I, but Christ liveth in me: and the life which I now live in the flesh I live by the faith of the Son of God, who loved me, and gave himself for me."*
>
> — Galatians 2:20

> *"Let this mind be in you, which was also in Christ Jesus:*
>
> *"Who, being in the form of God, thought it not robbery to be equal with God:*
>
> *"But made himself of no reputation, and took upon him the form of a servant, and was made in the like-*

> ness of men:
>
> "And being found in fashion as a man, he humbled himself, and became obedient unto death, even the death of the cross." — Philippians 2:5-8

I need not enlarge upon these statements made by the apostle. The center, the circumference, yes, all of life for Paul centered in Jesus Christ — the master Person.

Think of Paul's salvation, the miraculous experience recorded for us in Acts 9. The Lord Jesus spoke to Paul from heaven, and Paul surrendered to the Lord for salvation and for service. Miraculous? Yes, but all of salvation is miraculous. All of salvation is by the Spirit of God.

Think of Paul's summons. He was called to preach. The Lord said to Ananias about Paul, "*. . . Go thy way: for he is a chosen vessel unto me, to bear my name before the Gentiles, and kings, and the children of Israel: For I will shew him how great things he must suffer for my name's sake*" (Acts 9:15,16).

Think of Paul's salary. This is a very strange thought to present to you, and yet it needs to be considered by many people. The Apostle Paul gave himself unto the Lord for service. He did not question his support. He simply obeyed the call of God.

We have got a strange world today, and this strangeness invades every part of our living. The dollar sign is put on every enterprise. We are trained to think in terms of money values. The newspapers made comments about Howard Hughes, multimillionaire. Was he alive or dead? No one seemed to know.

I was reading the other day about Hetty Green, who left a fortune to her crippled son — a fortune of $50 million. He spent much money on steaks, yachts, jewels, stamps, and many other things trying to be happy. When he died he left $40 million.

I often think about our fine young people in Tennessee Temple University and their battles to continue their educational programs. Many come to us without money and have to work daily in order to sustain life.

I was reading about the son of a wealthy tobacco manufacturer. He was sent to Princeton and was given an income of $278,000 per year. The Court thought that was a little bit excessive, so they cut him down to $2,400.00 a month — about $80.00 per day.

I make mention of these things just to emphasize the fact of the Apostle Paul. This man was perhaps the greatest man who every walked upon the earth, outside of our Lord Jesus, and yet the matter of money was completely divorced from his life. he was concerned for others. He tried to raise money for the poor, but he cared nothing for himself.

Think of Paul's sufferings. He wrote to the church in Corinth and said:

> *"Of the Jews five times received I forty stripes save one.*
>
> *"Thrice was I beaten with rods, once was I stoned, thrice I suffered shipwreck, a night and a day I have been in the deep."*
>
> — II Corinthians 11:24,25

Think of Paul's satisfaction. In the last letters sent to Timothy, he said, *"Notwithstanding the Lord stood with me, and strenghthened me. . ."* (II Timothy 4:17). His satisfaction came through his knowledge of the Lord and Saviour, Jesus Christ. Christ was the master Person in Paul's life.

This week, I read again the poem entitled "The Man With the Hoe." This poem was written by Edwin Markham.

Through this poem Markham earned $250,000. He received his inspiration for the poem after seeing Millet's world-famous painting of a brutalized toiler. The poem begins:

"Bowed by the weight of centuries, he leans
Upon his hoe and gazes on the ground.
The emptiness of ages is in his face,
And on his back the burden of the world."

The poem has but little light and little joy for the average reader. Markham once said, "I am neither an economist nor a politician. In my writings I have only attempted to depict life as it appears to me." Yes, he pictured life with all of its drudgery and oppression, with its labor and sorrow. Much of life is that way. But, my friends, there is something better for us when we put ourselves in the hands of the Lord Jesus Christ, the Son of God. Today I beseech you: Make Him the master Person of your life.

**THE MASTER PASSION OF PAUL'S LIFE**

What was this master passion? It was to spread the Gospel.

It was to obey the great commission.

It was to place the Gospel feast before all men — Jew and Gentile.

This master passion of the Apostle Paul must be the master passion of every saved individual. Oh, how far we have wandered from this concept. Christian friend, we are commanded by the blessed Lord to share what we have. If we have salvation, then we are to hasten to give it to someone else. We cannot make them to be saved, but we can share with them the Gospel of our Lord Jesus.

Again, this must be the master passion of every church. All else is secondary. The buildings, equipment, organization, numbers, Sunday Schools, Training Unions — these are secondary objects. The first business is to get the Gospel before people. Men must hear! Why must they hear? The answer is given in this verse:

*". . .faith cometh by hearing, and hearing by the word of God."*

—Romans 10:17

Now, this was the master passion of Paul. He was saved, and he was called — he did not wander from the main business.

HE SOUGHT FOR THE SOULS OF MEN. He was concerned about Jews and Gentiles. His heartbeat was the great passion that he might bring them to the Saviour. He desired to see men born again. This seeking for souls is surely illustrated in that which happened in Philippi. First, we have the salvation of Lydia, and second, the salvation of a jailor. These simple stories illustrate completely the dedication of life on the part of Paul for the salvation of men and women.

SECOND, HE ESTABLISHED CHURCHES. In Corinth, in Ephesus, in Philippi, and other places, he organized local, New Testament churches. He centered his ministry in the local church — and so should we! This is God's ordained way to get the job done in this age.

I do not oppose other organizations. There are many worthwhile societies of various kinds in the world. But the business of the Gospel is to be carried on by churches established upon the Word of God, dedicated to the task of spreading the Gospel of Jesus Christ.

THIRD, HE SOUGHT THE DIVINE COMMENDATION. It was the master passion of Paul's life to spread the Gospel; and by so doing, he was seeking the "well done" of the Saviour.

As he wrote his last words to Timothy, he said,

> *"For I am now ready to be offered, and the time of my departure is at hand.*

> *"I have fought a good fight, I have finished my course, I have kept the faith."*
>
> — II Timothy 4:6,7

Paul believed that he had served God in a satisfactory manner, and he was not afraid to state this.

I repeat: the master passion of Paul's life was to spread the Gospel — to obey the great commission — to place the Gospel feast before all men, Jew and Gentile.

## THE MASTER PURPOSE OF PAUL'S LIFE

What was the master purpose? — To be found faithful.

> *"And I thank Christ Jesus our Lord, who hath enabled me, for that he counted me faithful, putting me into the ministry."*
>
> — I Timothy 1:12

HE DESIRED TO BE FAITHFUL TO HIS LORD IN THE TIME OF SUFFERING. And he was. As you read the full accounts given in II Corinthians 11 and 12, you will find this borne out.

It is our business to be faithful to the Lord, in all times, whether sick or well, whether in the sunshine or in the storm — we are to be faithful!

One stormy day, a Coast Guard ship was ordered to the rescue of a liner wrecked off the coast of New England. An old tried seaman was in charge, but the members of the crew were for the most part young, untested men. When one of the men comprehended the situation, he turned, white-faced, to the captain and said, "Sir, the wind is offshore; the tide is running out. We can go out, but against this wind and tide we cannot come back."

The grim old captain faced the young man and said, "Launch the boat; we go out."

"But, Sir," protested the young man.

"We don't have to come back," replied the captain.

We will all have suffering in this present world. No one is immune from the weaknesses, the sicknesses, the diseases, the affliction that touch these human bodies. It is all right to talk about your sufferings, just so you do not allow yourself to be stopped by them. It may be all right to complain once in a while, but be sure that you keep moving along despite every difficulty.

The old Negro spiritual has these words:

> "Nobody knows the trouble I've seen —
> Nobody knows, but Jesus.
> Nobody knows the trouble I've seen —
> Glory, Hallelujah!"

We have to be willing to suffer and to shout, "Glory, Hallelujah!"

A missionary tells about visiting a leper asylum in the Orient. The man in charge of this place — a Christian worker — had caught the dreaded leprosy himself. All the fingers of one hand had been eaten off by this horrible disease except the index finger. When visitors would come to the leper hospital, he would pick up his violin and play beautiful, triumphant music. He was playing with one finger, but he played beautifully; and this gives us a picture of the meaning of faithfulness in spite of suffering.

SECOND, PAUL DESIRED TO BE FAITHFUL TO HIS LORD IN THE FACE OF OPPOSITION. And he was. He was driven from cities. He was ridiculed by his own people. he was stoned and left for dead.

Very strangely, you cannot name an outstanding Christian of the past or the present who has not suffered opposition. Paul suffered; but he had the answer. He had the same answer which Shadrach, Meshach and Abednego had when they refused to worship Nebuchadnezzar's golden image. They said,

> *"If it be so, our God whom we serve is able to deliver us from the burning fiery furnace, and he will deliver us out of thine hand, O king.*
>
> *"But if not, be it known unto thee, O king, that we will not serve thy gods, nor worship the golden image which thou hast set up."*
>
> — Daniel 3:17,18

THIRD, FAITHFUL TO HIS LORD IN HOURS OF LONELINESS. You have only to read the record of the Apostle Paul to know that he was often lonely. He served God in destitute places, but he stood faithful.

Someone pointed out that God seems to have a special blessing for the lonely ones. When the common shepherds were tending their flocks near Bethlehem, they were given the announcement of the birth of our Lord. These shepherds lived a lonely, forgotten life; and yet to them came the best news that mankind has ever heard.

Lonely? Yes, but, praise God, the Lord is with us. A pastor up in Massachusetts tells about his mother and about her habit of beginning every day by reciting the first verse of the 23rd Psalm:

*"The LORD is my shepherd; I shall not want."*— Psalm 23:1

He said she did this until she was eighty years of age, and this birthday she changed and began reciting the last verse of the Psalm:

> *"Surely goodness and mercy shall follow me all the days of my life: and I will dwell in the house of the LORD for ever."*
>
> — Psalm 23:6

To this little Christian, there is peace and a poise that came by quiet faith in God. That story tells me to be faithful to my Lord in the hours of loneliness.

What should be the main purpose of your life? To be found faithful. Many people are not talented; some cannot give great sums of money; but everyone can be faithful. Get hold of this thought! It will revolutionize your life! Get Paul's master purpose in your heart — *". . .be thou faithful unto death, and I will give thee a crown of life"* (Revelation 2:10).

I think that I have said enough to drive home to your hearts: FIRST, THE MASTER PERSON OF PAUL'S LIFE; SECOND, THE MASTER PASSION OF PAUL'S LIFE: AND THIRD, THE MASTER PURPOSE OF PAUL'S LIFE.

But you see, all of this centers in one thing — in one truth — knowing Christ as Saviour! Do you know Him? Have you received Him as your Saviour?

There is nothing so important in this world as knowing Christ as Saviour.

Every day I have been driving by the old location of Central High School in Chattanooga. The bricks are being cleared away. A few months ago, I made a tour through the empty building. A few of us checked every room, even to the basement, into the furnace room — we looked at all of it.

As I see the building now, I think of a true story that I heard regarding two boys. One was a little fellow about eight years of age, by the name of Joe.

One day, Joe and his brother decided to explore an abandoned building. It was a large structure. The two of them left home and came to the deserted building. It was an old building, strongly built of steel and cement. The boys found the door going into the furnace room. It had been boarded up. They managed to pull aside one of the boards and slip inside.

When Joe and his brother got inside of the building, they were feeling their way along when suddenly little Joe slipped on the muddy underground surface of the bank and slid into the dark water before the horrified eyes of his brother. At first, his brother tried to save him; but finally he had to scream for help. People passing by on the sidewalk heard the screams and rushed to the scene. After some time, they recovered the limp but unconscious form from the cold, dark water. The boy was dead.

I use that story to impress upon you the need for salvation today! The two boys walking down the street did not think for a moment of the danger that awaited them just a few minutes away.

Every person needs Christ, and you need Him now. He is ready to save you.

> *"This is a faithful saying, and worthy of all acceptation, that Christ Jesus came into the world to save sinners; of whom I am chief."*
>
> — I Timothy 1:15

# 39
# The Latch on the Last Door

*"Then said Jesus unto his disciples, If any man will come after me, let him deny himself, and take up his cross, and follow me."*

— Matthew 16:24

Come back to verse 24: *"Then Jesus said unto his disciples, if any man will come after me, let him deny himself, and take up his cross, and follow me."*

They say that when Artur Rubenstein was visiting in the city of New York, a friend said to him, "Would you like to attend church?" (it was on the Lord's day).

He made this answer, "Yes, if you can take me to a preacher who will tempt me to do the impossible."

In this message, I am not going to tempt you to do that which is impossible, but that which is difficult. What I am going to say can be accomplished, can be done by every person. It is not an impossibility. It is in the realm of the possible, but difficult.

I'm sure that many of you recall the story which have often given about the British Bible teacher who said he was confronted one day by the Lord. He said the Lord said to him: "Now, I want you to give Me every key to your life."

He said he gave the keys to the Lord one by one. He kept on giving them until after a while he had given Him every key but one. He held that one back.

The Lord asked for the final key of his life. He said, "No, Lord, I can't give it to You. This is one thing that I reserve for myself. It represents something that I like very much. It's one thing personal that I want to retain for myself."

"Then, if you cannot give Me all of the keys, I cannot take any of them. I must have all of the keys."

There was a struggle, so this Bible teacher testified, and he felt he could not give up that one thing.

Now, if I were to mention that one thing, some of you would begin identifying with it, but I am not going to do it.

There was one single thing in his life that he wanted to hold on to. He said everything else he surrendered. He surrendered the matter of money. He surrendered the matter of position, gave it all up. He said, "One single thing I want to hold on to is this." There was a mighty struggle.

He said, "Finally, I cannot do anything else but hand the last key to the Lord." Everything was surrendered to God. The last key was handed over.

The Bible teacher gives this testimony: "After that time of full surrender of all that I had, from that moment on, I enjoyed the greatest joy in my heart. The peace of God was in my heart, as well as great usefulness in the service of Christ. But, everything had to be surrendered."

Here's our problem: we invite the Lord to come into our hearts. We say, "Lord, come in." It is like inviting Him to come into our kitchen, into the living room, into the dining room, maybe all of the rooms of our house, but one, and we hold back one place.

With most of us, this is our problem. We are holding off in one single thing of life. You may not drink, you may not carouse, you may not go to wild shows, you may not do all of this, but one single thing you are holding back.

The one problem you've got; the latch to the last door. You say, "Oh Lord, every bit of my life I give to Thee. I surrender everything into Your hands, into Your keeping." Lift the latch and say, "Lord, come in. This is Yours. Everything is Yours."

Let me illustrate by way of introduction. Simon Peter was a saved man, he was a called man, he was a man blessed of God in so many ways, but his life was unsurrendered. Because of that lack of surrender for a while, he made some strange statements. He made some boasts for which Jesus had to correct him.

There was a boistering uncertainty about Simon Peter until that day of surrender, until Pentecost, until the Spirit of God took control of him.

When everything was committed, Simon Peter became a mighty man of God. His name is known throughout the world and throughout the ages.

There's another name. John Mark was a very fine young man, a saved man. He went with Barnabas and Saul on the first missionary journey. They came to Pamphylia in Asia Minor and in that place John Mark said, "I'm going home. I'm quitting. I'm going back." He did go back.

Because of that, the next time that Barnabas and Paul started to go out, Paul said, "I don't want this young fellow. He's a quitter. There's something about him that is wrong, and if you don't mind, just let him stay at home." Because of that, Barnabas and Paul separated. Barnabas went one way and took John Mark with him. Paul went the other way.

However, this young fellow, John Mark, got hold of himself. There must have been one thing that caused fearfulness. There must have been something in his life that hindered him. He was saved. He loved the Lord, he went with these missionaries on the first trip. And yet, this one thing was holding him back.

Finally, this was surrendered and John Mark became an outstanding man, and was commended by the Apostle Paul, and became the author, on the human side, of the Gospel of Mark.

We can go ahead. We can talk about Nicodemus and Joseph of Arimathaea. These men are saved. Nicodemus came by night and was saved. Joseph was saved also. They somehow hid their life. They were afraid. There was a fearfulness about their position. they were saved, altogether saved, and doubtless were good men in many ways. However, there was one single drawer that was still latched against the Lord. There was one room of their houses that was not open to the Saviour.

These men allowed Jesus to die on the cross, and then they asked for his body to put it away. But, before that time, they would not identify themselves with the people of God.

I can mention the name of Demas. I have given it so often here until it is a common name with us. I believe Demas was a saved man; and yet, of this man the Bible says, ". . .*Demas hath forsaken me, having loved this present world. . .*" (II Timothy 4:10). There was a room that wasn't open to the Lord Jesus. There was a latch that was still fastened and he did not turn it over to the Lord.

Demas has many followers. Some of you are just as sweet as you can be and just as saved as you can be, but in spite of everything, you are hanging on to one thing. Because of that, you are not following Christ fully, you are not surrendered to Him, you haven't opened up every door to Him. There is something that you are holding back at this time.

The call of Jesus: ". . .*If any man will come after me, let him deny himself, and take up his cross and foillow me.*" I want you to break this down briefly, if you will.

## THE BARRIERS TO COMPLETE SURRENDER

*"And he said to them all, If any man will come after me, let him deny himself, and take up his cross daily, and follow me"* (Luke 9:23). This message appears through all of the Gospels. The flesh rebels against taking up the cross. Note that the cross is not some physical infirmity of mental anguish. Some people talk about having a cross. They say, "I have such a heavy burden to bear, such a heavy cross."

No, no, that is not what he is talking about. The cross is a pathway, deliberately chosen by the one who is going to walk in the steps of the Lord Jesus Christ.

The cross symbolizes the shame, persecution, and the abuse which the world heaped upon the Son of God Himself, and that which will come upon you and me, if we walk with Jesus.

We accept the position of walking after Him, and following Him. When we do so, we of course, get many things that come upon us because of the sinful, evil, wicked world.

THE SELF-LIFE WANTS THE EASY WAY. Here is where many people stop. They don't mind being saved, they want to be saved, but they don't like to make too big a difference in the office where they work. They don't want to make too big a show in the school where they attend, whatever school it may be: high school, elementary school, college or university.

The self-life wants the easy way, the way that rather falls in with society so there is no great embarrassment to you because of your faith in Christ. The lazy way, the way of least resistance, the way of the crowd — that is what the flesh wants. That is what you have to fight.

You see, that is what John Mark was having trouble with. That is the reason he went back home. He was following the flesh.

That's the reason Demas turned away. He was following the flesh.

It may be that these were good men in every respect, but in one way there was one latch on one door that was still locked against the Lord and they would not open that. The self-life wants the easy way.

We had a young man come to see us two or three years ago. He talked to me, and then he talked to Dr. Faulkner. I'm not sure which one of us was first, but he came to see us. Here is what he said: "I want all of the secrets of the building of a great church! How do you get the crowds in Sunday School? How do you get the money for the building? I want to get all of this right together. I'm going to a certain city. I plan to spend some time. I think that by the first year, maybe the second year, I may have as many as 10,000 in Sunday School. He kept on going. I don't recall it all.

That lad was not thinking. He was fine. He was educated, he was talented, he had a nice personality. Yet, in his mind he was trying to find some easy way. There is no easy way. The self-life is always looking for something else, but it is not there.

THE SELF-LIFE WANTS TO HOLD ON TO SOME SIN. It may be a little sin, as we think of sin. It may be a sin that doesn't seem to harm your personality and hinder your influence in the world, but there is some sin.

We have got to face our sin. We have got to be brutal in facing the sin that we have and in dealing with that sin. Confess the sin to God. Claim the forgiveness that He promises in I John 1:9: "*If we confess our sins, he is faithful and just to forgive us our sins, and to cleanse us from all unrighteousness.*" Confess it and forsake it.

You are on the heavenward way when you accept Jesus,

but the way is not always easy. Young people, mothers and dads, it is not easy for any of us.

I have celebrated many birthdays in this life. I am glad, and God has been so good. I praise God for His goodness. But my dear friend, there is no resting in the battle at all. I've still got a battle! I've still got it! Satan is still working. Pride will come in, selfishness will enter into the heart, and the critical spirit will be an enemy of yours.

You have got to be on the alert always to see things as they are. The world, the flesh and the devil will seek to derail you from the pathway of the victorious life, turn aside and hinder your complete surrender.

I was preaching sometime ago in a certain church. They called on a man to lead in prayer. This fellow was eloquent, and not only so, but he prayed with power. I listened to him and I said, "My, that is a great man. Imagine having a man in the church to just stand up and pray. He prayed like an evangelist, like a preacher, like someone who had been at it for a long time. He got hold of me. I was blessed in my heart as I listened to him.

At the end of the service, he asked me if he could speak to me. I said, "Well, yes, sir." I was really respectful because the man was beautifully dressed, handsomely dressed, expensively dressed, nice in his appearance, beautiful in his voice, everything lovely about him!

To my shocking surprise, when he took me aside he said, "I want your prayers. I have got one sin, one single sin that is hindering my whole life."

Do you know what he did? He confessed that sin to me. A dirty, mean, dastardly sin. I could not believe it. I thought of the man. I thought of his prayer. I thought of his appearance —I thought of all of it.

Oh, the wickedness of self, the flesh; the viciousness of self to pull a man away from his God. Here is a man, though in many ways with everything you could ask for, confessing that a certain sin was upsetting his life.

I want you to see the barrier to complete surrender. Lift the latch to the last door.

There may be something in your life — think what it is! It may be selfishness, it may be lust, it may be evil speaking, it may be any one of a thousand things the devil works on. You are a child of God, but you have failed to come and to lay everything down, to deny self and take up your cross and follow Him. Walk with Him and talk with Him.

## THE BOUNDARIES OF COMPLETE SURRENDER

*". . .If any man will come after me, let him deny himself, and take up his cross, and follow me"* (Matthew 16:24). Here are the boundaries: *". . .and follow me, come after me, deny himself, take up his cross, follow Me."*

Listen to these words of the Saviour:

> *"Enter ye in at the strait gate: for wide is the gate, and broad is the way, that leadeth to destruction, and many there be which go in thereat:*
>
> *"Because strait is the gate, and narrow is the way, which leadeth unto life, and few there be that find it."*
>
> — Matthew 7:13,14

There is a way, a definite way, and that is the way after Christ — following after Him, receiving Him as Saviour, walking after Him. These are the boundaries. These are the lines that are set up for you. We are to follow Christ in every way!

You see, I use rather simple procedures. If you are saved, my dear friend, if you are a child of God, if you have been born again, then you should say, "I shall step in the way of Jesus. I will walk after Him."

FIRST, IT MEANS THAT YOU ARE TO BE BAPTIZED. Openly confess your faith and say, "I am saved." Then, follow Jesus in believer's baptism.

You see, that follows in line, that is something you can do, that is something that you can respond to at once. You should not delay this. You should not argue with God.

You don't have to read your Bible on that, just take what the Word of God says, no need for a long study course on baptism. If you are saved, you ought to follow the Lord, obey Him in believer's baptism. That's just a simple thing of following Him.

SECOND, YOU OUGHT TO FOLLOW HIM IN IDENTIFYING YOURSELF WITH THE PEOPLE OF GOD. You say, "I now am saved. I want to be baptized. I want to be identified with the people of God. I shall now at once identify myself with God's people."

There will be a separation from the world. It will be a turning aside from some of the old crowd. You will have to walk with God day by day. You will identify yourself with the people of God.

THIRD, IT MEANS YOU ARE GOING TO FOLLOW HIM IN SERVICE. You will walk after Him and do what He says. You will be concerned about winning souls, getting others saved, getting others to know Jesus as you know Him. You will walk after Him.

FOURTH, IT MEANS TO FOLLOW HIM IN HOLY LIVING. This may seem a little narrow to some people.

You see, I am trying to point out the boundaries. Dear friend, if you don't like this, it's all right, you just have to take it. The boundaries are set.

The boundaries of this matter of surrender are set by your walking after Jesus. If you don't want to walk after Him, that is your business. If you prefer something else, take it! I can only say that you are a fool, because the only happy life in this world that I know anything about (and I've talked to thousands) is walking after Jesus.

Jesus said, "*. . .come and follow me. . .*" Now, if you don't like that, you don't like the boundaries.

You say, "Well, I can't take it." If you are not going to follow Him in holy living, the thing He is saying to us is right here in the Word of God.

Turn your back on the world. Get rid of sin. Turn your life over to God and walk after Him. Deny yourself, turn away from these things and follow after Jesus! Turn from the flesh and follow after Him in holy living.

You see, there is danger in a service like this. You listen to what I'm saying and then you turn away from it. You say, "Well, it sounds good to me," but you toss it overboard.

This is a strange, disposable day. Have you ever thought of that? This is what we can call a "throw away society." Kleenex — throw them away; diapers — throw them away; paper towels — throw them away; TV dinners — throw them away.

Some people have developed a throw away mentality. If they don't like something, they throw it away! "Well, I don't need that so I cast it overboard!"

You say, "Preacher, you can do that if you want to, but I don't want it." I am just trying to show you something. I'm trying to show you the boundaries for complete surrender. The boundaries are laid down by our blessed Lord. Walk after Him. Simply walk after Him in big matters, small matters, and in all matters. Seek to be Christ-like.

If I'm lifting it up too high, I can't help that. I'm lifting it up for myself because I know this is right. If I fail, I fail knowing what is right. We have got to walk after Him. Here are the boundaries that are laid down for us.

## THE BLESSINGS OF COMPLETE SURRENDER

FIRST, WE HAVE THE BARRIERS. SECOND, THE BOUNDARIES, AND THIRD, THE BLESSINGS.

"All to Jesus I surrender." Remember singing that? "all to Him I freely give. I will ever love and trust Him. In His presence daily live."

Listen to it again: "all to Jesus I surrender, humbly at His feet I bow. Worldly pleasures all forsaken, take me Jesus, take me now." The blessings of complete surrender—we sing that sometimes without really thinking about it.

THE BLESSING OF SURRENDER IS THE BLESSING OF STEADFASTNESS. When one is surrendered to our blessed Lord, completely and entirely sold out to Him in all ways—Sunday morning, Sunday night, Wednesday night, Thursday night, Friday night, every night, every day—blessed things happen in the life. There is a blessing of complete surrrender.

Some folks never make it. We've got some sweet people in the church here. But you see, you couldn't drag them out to a Sunday night service with a chain. They don't come, no, they care not for it. They know what they ought to do, but they don't want to do it. They offer every excuse in the world.

There are some folk who are sweet and kind, but they won't tithe. They won't obey the Lord. They don't want to follow Him, they would rather follow themselves. They refuse to be tithers and have a part in the great missionary program and do the job for God. They turn away!

The blessing of surrender is the blessing of steadfastness, doing the work and standing true in doing it.

We said "good-bye," some time ago to one of our fine, faithful ladies of our church, Mrs. Wayman Farrar. In many ways, she was one of the most faithful—gracious and sweet and faithful in everything.

The last act of her life was coming to visitation on Thursday night, one of the last things she ever did.

Prayer meeting Wednesday night, visitation Thursday night — she kept up with it all the way through. I know what I am talking about.

She didn't ask for any recognition. She didn't do anything but teach a Sunday School class, go out to visit, knock on doors, and win souls to the Lord. She kept on going. There was something about her that was steadfast.

She didn't make any boast about being sick, wouldn't even tell her family in all of the sicknesses or illnesses that she might have, just went on her way, just kept on going.

That is the thing that I want you to see. That was a blessing to every one of us, and I recall it, and you recall it. We have had others, of course, who have had the same characteristics. The blessing of surrender is steadfastness.

THE BLESSING OF SURRENDER IS PEACE OF HEART. He wants you to have peace of heart. The blessing of surrender is that you will have that peace of heart. You had better come and say, "Lord, here I am."

I love music. I sit and listen to the beautiful music of our church — the trio, the quartet, and others sing — and I cry. I cry because I think of the fact that I might someday be where I wouldn't hear the beautiful music I hear here. Then, I remember that in heaven it will be this beautiful, and far more beautiful in the presence of our Lord.

I fought battles when I was just a young preacher. I had a battle. I fought a battle. I thought I couldn't make it. I was saved, I was called to preach; and yet, the battle was still there. I was singing on WSM in Nashville, Tennessee — paid for my services. I sang on WMC in Memphis, Tennessee, for one year every night — paid to do it. I kept it up.

I had been with all kinds of organizations. That was back in the days of my early twenties. I kept fighting a battle until one day I had to make a decision: "If I'm going to follow my Lord, do what He says, I've got to say 'good-bye' to that." I turned away from it and I have never been sorry.

I love music. Praise God for the music! Praise God for the beautiful gospel music, but I said, "This is it."

I fought a battle with evangelism. What a battle I had. If ever anyone in this world wanted to be an evangelist, I was it. I used to hold revival meetings when I was a country preacher. I was so happy when the Birmingham Baptist Association (Southern Baptist Convention) hired me to be the evangelist for the Association. In Birmingham alone I held 55 revival meetings, in one city. Two week revivals, some three week revivals, and I rejoiced in all of that.

Then God said, "No, there is something else that I want you to do. I've got a job for you." He sent me to Fairfield, Alabama, for five years, and then sent me here in 1942. It was a struggle. My, my, I still liked it! I still liked to hold revivals! I began holding revivals, I kept on in different places and God blessed in all of them.

At the Green Street Church in Highpoint, we had 242 saved the first meeting I had there.

The church in Alabama, where Brother Homer Britton worked with me as a singer, we had many hundreds saved in a meeting. Oh, what a meeting! I said, "This is it. I'm going to pastor the church and hold revival meetings."

I was preaching in the Central Baptist Church in Augusta, Georgia, holding a revival there and enjoying it. There came a message of the death of Bob Shedd. Bob Shedd was Chairman of our Board of Deacons. They said the funeral service would be Sunday afternoon. I went to the airport to hire some fellows to fly me up here for the funeral services. They flew me here to the city.

I sat in the back of the plane and I prayed. I said, "Oh, Lord, there is something wrong with me. My church is in Chattanooga. My work is there and I am off holding meetings. I like it. This is what I like to do, but it is not right. I have to fly back home for a funeral service. Now I'll fly back to the church tonight in Augusta."

As I sat in that plane and the men were flying the plane, I said, "Oh Lord, this is my last meeting. This is the last one!" I cancelled everything that I had. I have never had one since. Not a lengthy revival, just one or two nights in a place. That is all I can do. I want to be here, I want to be ready any time!

This has given me peace. You say, "You have given up something." I know, but my dear friends, this surrender meant peace of heart! I have had no more battles inside at all! I surrendered it all!

You have got to say "Yes" to the Lord. Sometimes it may not be easy, but that surrender must come and then the blessing of God will come upon you.

THE BLESSING OF SURRENDER IS THE TASK OF WITNESSING FOR HIM. Witnessing, telling folk about the Saviour day by day. I had the joy of witnessing to and baptizing many who came into our church.

Oh, the blessing of the Spirit's fullness. Say, "Oh God, this I know: the Holy Spirit fills. He'll fill me! He'll empower me and use me! I surrender myself to Him completely."

Christian, listen to me. Surrender everything, "*. . .if any man will come after me, let him deny himself. . .turn away from self. . .let him take up his cross*" (Matthew 16:24) The cross of following Jesus, not some affliction of your body, not some difficulty, but walking after Him, taking the abuse, scorn and scoffing of the crowd. That's the cross.

He said, "*. . .follow me. . .*" That's the thing that will bring the joy.

Talented young people—listen to me—mothers and daddies, rich people, poor people, whoever you are, let Christ take over. You will find the blessing of complete surrender.

Lift the latch on the last door and say, "Lord, come in!" When you do that, some mighty things are going to happen. I will tell you, it will touch your pocketbook, it will touch your life, it will touch your talents, it will touch all of you, your personality. Everything will be changed when you simply say, "Lord, take over my life."

Lift the latch. What is the thing that is hurting? What is the thing you have been hanging on to? Selfishness, pride, love for ease, seeking something for yourself all the time. You always have to fight it!

When I came here to this church, the first week I was here in the office, a man walked in. He said, "Brother Roberson, I guess you know who I am, don't you?"

"No sir, I don't."

"I'm the printer. I'm a member of this church. I expect to have all of your printing. If I don't get it all, I'll join another church!" Words just like that.

"Brother, if you feel like that, you won't get it all," and he didn't.

He left us and joined another church. I can tell you which one. Thirty-three years ago, almost, at this time. He said, "If I can't have it all, all of your printing. . ."

You say, "Brother Roberson, why didn't you go ahead?" I thought the man had sense enough to open his eyes and see something. Selfishness is a thing that kills most of us! Here is the thing that ruins the testimony of your life — when you follow after yourself.

Lift the latch on the last door, whatever it may be for you. Lift that latch and say, "Lord, come in. I am tired of self. I am tired of selfishness. I am tired of my way. I'll lift the latch." Do it right now.

I shouldn't say it again, but I am going to say it again because I think it tells the story so well.

In Louisville, Kentucky, when I was a boy, two kinfolks lived down the street from us, Aunt Cora and Uncle Walter. We lived about a block away from them.

If anybody in this world ever heard of poverty, we had it all. I am not joking. I've said this so many times. We ate off a box for a table. We had boxes for the chairs. We had one bed. I slept on the floor, as a boy, on a pallet. We were poverty-stricken.

My dad worked on the street railway, made 25 cents an hour when he worked, and that's all. We paid the rent, wasn't very much, and had to have what we could get. I was going to Henry Clay School.

I'm not exaggerating, our poverty was outstanding and unique. We were so deep down without anything. I would go up the street to see Uncle Walter and Aunt Cora maybe once or twice a week. I would go to see them sometime and they would invite me to have dinner with them. I would sit down and eat with them. What we had on our table was a banquet, compared to what they had. I thought to myself, when I got away, as a young boy in elementary school, "This is awful. Those poor folks are about to die."

Aunt Cora never had a new dress. She wore things that people gave her. Aunt Cora had never seen a doctor in all the days of her life. They didn't have any money, couldn't do it.

They were poverty-stricken.

They lived in a four-room house that was a shotgun thing built down in the old part of Louisville on Madison Street. Madison is gone now, all but a shotgun house. One, two, three, four tiny rooms. That is where they lived. They had no conveniences at all. We lived down the street a half-block away.

There came a day when Uncle Walter came down to the house, saw my dad and said, "Charlie, I want you to go with me and help me get a new truck. I am going to move. I am quitting my job, I am going back to Indiana."

My dad said, "Walter, I can't do it, I'm busy. I've got work to do. I can't get away. Let my boy go!" He meant that I should go.

I walked up the street, a block away, and I helped Uncle Walter as he carried out the few little old chairs he had, and one bed, and some little articles from the house, and put them in the back of an old T-Model Ford truck (that has been years ago).

When I got it all loaded on (it wasn't very much, because it was only half full) he said, "Come with me." We walked around the side of the shotgun house.

Now you would have to see the picture, the four room house, nothing like it, never thought of garages back in those days. The lots are about 30 feet wide, not more than 30 feet wide in that part of the city.

We walked to the side of the house, he got around to the back and opened the doors to the cellar. He opened up the doors and walked down inside. The boards going down were little one-by-four boards stuck in the side of the dirt. Down in the cellar was dirt, no concrete, never thought of that, just a dirt floor. Up on the side were shelves where they put the canned goods for the winter time. The cellar was empty.

Uncle Walter grabbed a piece of a shovel and began digging on the ground, throwing the dirt aside. I could see him. The dirt was scattered around me. Finally, he threw the shovel away and got on his knees and pulled up a big old brown canvas sack and shoved it in my arms and said, "Hold that." Then, he pulled up another container, shoved that in my arms, until my arms were full.

He said, "Just a minute." We went down into the hole and he got a few more things out in his own arms. Then he said, "That's all, let's go."

He came up the steps, got outside, and said, "Let's go in here." We stepped into the kitchen of the four-room house. He had left a piece of the table there. He said, "Drop it on the table." I dropped it on the table.

I can see him when he stood back from the table and took his knife and sliced open that canvas bag. When he did, out of the bag poured money as I have never seen it before in my life. Maybe not seen it since, I do not know. He cut it and money poured out. Five dollar gold pieces, you know the kind. Then old-fashioned bills, just lots of them. He opened up the other containers and dumped them out, until when he finished there was a mound of money.

I watched Uncle Walter as he dumped the money out. I saw him stand back and say this, "It's all mine. It's all mine."

All of a sudden, as a boy, in elementary school, Henry Clay School, I thought to myself, that is strange, all that money there in a hole, in the dirt, in the cellar. They had no food on the table. Aunt Cora never had a new dress. She had never been to a doctor in her life. I had heard people comment about that.

I said, "Here is all of this money in the hole."

He said, "Help me." He got a big old canvas sack, big old gunny sack, and put it at the end of the table. I began rolling the money in the sack. He got it all inside and tied the top of it, and threw it over his shoulder. He said, "Well, good-bye son, I'll be going." He walked out of there, went to the truck and drove off.

My dad said, "We will not bother them again." We loved Aunt Cora, she was sweet. We didn't care much for Uncle Walter.

I didn't know what to say. I had told him what had happened.

Days went along. Months went by. One day there came the message that Aunt Cora was dead. My dad said, "We will have to go to the funeral. She was sweet. We will have to go."

We had an old T-Model Ford car, a touring car. It cost $588. We got in the car and we drove over the 26th Street Bridge (one bridge over the Ohio River then), down to English, Indiana.

When we got to English, my dad said, "Now it is about six miles away from Taswell." That is where they lived. I have been to all of these places hundreds of times.

We drove to Taswell. When we got to Taswell he said, "Let's find the church." It just had one church. It was on the side of the hill, an old country church with only one room. My dad drove up there and stopped the car. We went inside. A few folk were there, so we waited.

After some time, a door opened in the back and the casket was brought in. Some men rolled it down to the front.

When they put the casket in place they opened it up. I looked over from my place and saw the face of Aunt Cora. She had been a friend of mine as a boy. I saw the face and I was saddened by the fact that she was dead and I knew what death was. I could understand that. I wasn't a Christian boy then, but I can remember understanding the whole thing.

A few people came in. After a while, down the aisle came Uncle Walter. Uncle Walter had with him a bunch of his friends, some of his cronies, in relation to him being a miser and robbing everybody he could and holding it all to himself. He loved to gamble, and he could win. They sat on the front pew.

After a while the back door of the old church building opened up and the preacher walked in. He had a big Bible in his hand. He opened up to a few pages and began to read. He read, without a song or anything else at the beginning of the service. Nothing there at all, not even a piano or organ, just the little crowd of people.

As he read from the Word of God, Uncle Walter suddenly jumped for the casket and draped his body over the face of his wife. I can still hear him, all through these years. I can hear his voice as he cried, "Honey, come back, come back, come back. Darling, I didn't mean it. I'll give you anything you want. You can have a doctor, you can have a new dress. You can have anything you want. Come back, come back."

I saw his cronies come from the front bench, grab him by the seat and pull him back to the front bench.

You see my dear friends, he could cry all he wanted to, it wouldn't do any good. She was dead.

Are you listening to me? That little story ought to stay with you. That story ought to help you say, "Oh God, help me to do what You want me to do."

Right now you say, ' I surrender all." Everything to Him! Everything! Young man, young woman, mother and dad, surrender all to Him!

Sinner, if you have never been saved, get saved now!

Come to Jesus now!

If you are a child of God and you need to get some things straightened out, do it now.